THE JEHOVAH'S WITNESSES AND THE NAZIS

Persecution, Deportation, and Murder,
1933–1945

Michel Reynaud
and Sylvie Graffard

Translated by James A. Moorehouse
Introduction by Michael Berenbaum

First Cooper Square Press edition 2001

This Cooper Square Press hardcover edition of *The Jehovah's Witnesses and the Nazis* is an original English-language translation of the edition first published under the title *Les Bibelforscher et le nazisme* in Paris, France in 1990, and here supplemented with new photographs and an introduction by Michael Berenbaum. It is reprinted by arrangement with the authors. The photographs are reproduced by arrangement with Archive Photos and the United States Holocaust Memorial Museum.

Published by Cooper Square Press
An Imprint of the Rowman & Littlefield Publishing Group
150 Fifth Avenue, Suite 911
New York, New York 10011

Distributed by National Book Network

Library of Congress Cataloging-in-Publication Data

Graffard, Sylvie.
[Bibelforscher et le nazisme, 1933-1945. English]
The Jehovah's Witnesses and the Nazis : persecution, deportation, and murder, 1933–1945 / Michel Reynaud and Sylvie Graffard ; translation by James A. Moorehouse ; introduction by Michael Berenbaum.—1st Cooper Square Press. ed.
p. cm.
Original French ed. By Sylvie Graffard and Léo Tristan; publishe by Editions Tirésias Michel Reynaud; translation supplemented with new photographs and new introd.
Includes bibliographical references and index.
ISBN 0-8154-1076-X (alk. Paper)
1. Jehovah's Witnesses—Nazi persecution. 2. National socialism. 3. Germany—Politics and government—1933-1945. 4. Germany—Religion—1933–1945. I. Reynaud, Michel, 1951- . II. Title.
BX8525.8.G3 G713 2001
289.9'2'0943094̄3—dc21 00-065826

∞™ The paper used in this publication meets the minimum requirements of American National Standard for Information Sciences—Permanence of Paper for Printed Library Materials, ANSI/NISO Z39.48–1992.
Manufactured in the United States of America.

CONTENTS

Konzentrationslager ——————
Abteilung II

Erklärung.

Ich, - der - die — ——————————————

geboren am: ——————————— in: ———————————

gebe hiermit folgende Erklärung ab:

1. Ich habe erkannt, dass die Internationale Bibelforschervereinigung eine Irrlehre verbreitet und unter dem Deckmantel religiöser Betätigung lediglich staatsfeindliche Ziele verfolgt.
2. Ich habe mich deshalb voll und ganz von dieser Organisation abgewandt, und mich auch innerlich von dieser Sekte freigemacht.
3. Ich versichere hiermit, dass ich mich nie wieder für die Internationale Bibelforschervereinigung betätigen werde. Personen, die für die Irrlehre der Bibelforscher an mich werbend herantreten oder in anderer Weise ihre Einstellung als Bibelforscher bekunden, werde ich unverzüglich zur Anzeige bringen. Sollten mir Bibelforscherschriften zugesandt werden, so werde ich diese umgehend bei der nächsten Polizeidienststelle abgeben.
4. Ich will künftig die Gesetze des Staates achten, insbesondere im Falle eines Krieges mein Vaterland mit der Waffe in der Hand verteidigen und mich voll und ganz in die Volksgemeinschaft eingliedern.
5. Mir ist eröffnet worden, dass ich mit meiner erneuten Inschutzhaftnahme zu rechnen habe, wenn ich meiner heute abgegebenen Erklärung zuwiderhandle.

——————————, den ——————————

——————————
Unterschrift.

KL/47-4. 43 5000

"The Declaration Renouncing Beliefs." The statement that a Jehovah's Witness could sign that would free him or her from incarceration. Witnesses were the only minority persecuted by the Nazis who had the option to renounce their beliefs and obtain freedom. It was an option very few took.

Das Goldene Zietalter. a publication that provoked the creation of a special Gestapo unit charged with the fight against the Jehovah's Witnesses.

The formal accusation against Gertrude Plotzinger, who survived to be interviewed by the authors.

Der Oberstaatsanwalt
als Leiter der Anklagebehörde
bei dem Sondergericht.
Sg 16 Js 1100/37
Sg 16 KMs 239/37

Breslau, den 30. Dezember 1937

An den
Herrn Vorsitzenden des Sondergerichts
für den Oberlandesgerichtsbezirk Breslau,
in Breslau.

F.

Haftsache!

Anklage.

Die Ehefrau Gertrud Pötzinger geb. Mende, aus München, Straudolphstr.16, in dieser Sache seit dem 24. September 1937 in Untersuchungsgefängnis in Breslau in Untersuchungshaft, geb. am 1.1.1912 in Hirschberg i.Schles. Reichsdeutsche, unbestraft

wird angeklagt

im Jahre 1937 in Schlesien
fortgesetzt

I. einer von der Obersten Landesbehörde zur Durchführung der Verordnung des Reichspräsidenten zum Schutze von Volk und Staat vom 28.2.1933 erlassenen Anordnung nämlich der Anordnung des Preußischen Ministers des Innern vom 24.6.1933 zuwidergehandelt zu haben,

und durch dieselbe Handlung

II. vorsätzlich unwahre Behauptungen tatsächlicher Art verbreitet zu haben, die geeignet sind, das Wohl des Reichs und das Ansehen der Reichsregierung schwer zu schädigen.

– Vergehen, strafbar nach § 4 der V.O. vom 28.2.1933 (RGBl.I.S.83) in Verbindung mit der Anordnung des Preußischen Ministers des Innern vom 24.6.1933, § 1 BtG, § 73 StGB.

Beweismittel:

I. Geständnis der Angeschuldigten.

Wesentliches Ermittlungsergebnis.

Die Angeschuldigte ist Anhängerin der Internationalen Bibelforscher-Vereinigung, auch "Zeugen Jehovas" genannt, die durch die Anordnung des Preußischen Ministers des Innern vom 24.6.1933 rechtsgültig aufgelöst und verboten worden ist. Das Verbot war ihr bekannt.

Von 1932 bis Mai 1936 hielt sich die Angeschuldigte im Auslande auf. Sie war in dieser Zeit in der Tschechoslowakei

Acte d'accusation de Gertrud Pötzinger

An example of the crude Nazi propaganda campaign waged against the Jehovah's Witnesses.

Inmate mug shots taken of Jehovah's Witnesses. [*Archiwum Panstwowego Muzeum w Oswiecimiu*, courtesy of the United States Holocaust Memorial Museum Photo Archives]

[*Archiwum Panstwowego Muzeum w Oswiecimiu*, courtesy of the United States Holocaust Memorial Museum Photo Archives]

Inmate mug shots taken of Jehovah's Witnesses. [*Archiwum Panstwowego Muzeum w Oswiecimiu*, courtesy of the United States Holocaust Memorial Museum Photo Archives]

[*Archiwum Panstwowego Muzeum w Oswiecimiu*, courtesy of the United States Holocaust Memorial Museum Photo Archives]

Heinrich Himmler (1900–1945), the chief of the SS and the Gestapo and an avowed enemy of the Jehovah's Witnesses, who nonetheless admired their integrity and commitment to their beliefs. [Hilton Getty Picture Library/Archive Photos]

Adolph Hitler (1889–1945), the Austrian-born Fascist dictator responsible for the Holocaust. He saw the Witnesses as ideological foes who had to be destroyed. [Hilton Getty Picture Library/Archive Photos]

Berlin-Plotzensee prison, where Witness Franz Mattischeks was guillotined for his beliefs. The former penitentiary now houses a youth reformatory. [Hulton Getty Picture Library/Archive Photos]

Heinrich Dickmann saw a blackboard in a Dinslaken rolling mill factory courtyard with a pig drawn on it and with the word "Jehovah" chalked in. Fired for his refusal to give the Nazi salute, he was jailed as an alleged saboteur under *Schutzhaft* for ten days as an enemy of the state. [United States Holocaust Memorial Museum Photo Archives]

The Kusserow family. Magdelena, Paul-Gerhard, and Elisabeth Kusserow in the yard of the family home in Bad Lippspringe. [Waltraud and Annemarie Kusserow, courtesy of the United States Holocaust Memorial Museum]

The entire Kusserow family.

The Kusserow brothers, Wolfgang, Wilhelm, and Karl-Heinz, in the countryside near the family home in Bad Lippspringe. [United States Holocaust Memorial Museum Photo Archives]

Erich Frost, a devoted Witness who provided comfort to his fellow prisoners, once remarked, "Harsh is life on God's Soldiers. They do not seek the approval of the prideful."

Adolf Arnold. arrested and later subjected to medical experiments.

This is a fragment of the Bible baked into cookies and smuggled into Dachau by Adolph Arnold's sister. [Simone Liebster. courtesy of the United States Holocaust Memorial Museum Photo Archives]

The railway tracks leading into the entrance of Auschwitz. [Archive Photos]

The main entrance to Dachau concentration camp. [Hulton Getty Picture Library/Archive Photos]

Group photograph of liberated Jehovah's Witnesses in their prison camp uniforms at the Niederhagen bei Wewelsburg concentration camp in May 1945. [United States Holocaust Memorial Museum Photo Archives]

Another group of liberated Jehovah's Witnesses at the Niederhagen bei Wewelsburg concentration camp in May 1945. [United States Holocaust Memorial Museum Photo Archives]

INTRODUCTION

Michael Berenbaum

The Holocaust is the common and appropriate name for the genocidal efforts of the Nazis to annihilate the Jewish people. From 1933 through the last hours of the Third Reich in 1945, Jews were the major target of Nazi racism and ideology and bore the full brunt of Nazi hatred: They were defined in racial and ideological terms, their assets and property were expropriated, and they were forced to emigrate—yet there were few places where they were offered a haven, fewer still where they were welcomed. After the German invasion of Poland in September 1939, Jews were forced into ghettos, and from 1941 on, they were systematically murdered. The goal was the "Final Solution to the Jewish Problem," the murder of all Jews—men, women, and children.

During the years 1933–1939, some groups were victimized for what they did, others for what they refused to do, and still others for what they were. For example, political dissidents—communists, socialists, and liberals alike—and trade unionists were persecuted because of their politics. Dissenting clergy were arrested when they spoke out against the regime. German male homosexuals were incarcerated and their institutions destroyed because of their sexual practices.

Roma and *Sinti* (Gypsies), traditional outsiders, were distrusted and despised. Regarded as a menace, they were deported and incarcerated. Still later, many were killed. Along with the Jews, they were the only other group killed in their entirety: Men, women, and children were gassed together at Birkenbau, the death camp of Auschwitz.

Mentally retarded, physically handicapped, or emotionally dis-

turbed *Germans* were not considered by the Nazis to be suitabl
raw material for breeding the "master race." They, too, suffered a
the hands of the Nazis. By September 1939, a state-sponsore
murder program was in place. Six killing centers were established
Gas chambers and crematoria were developed to kill these Ger
mans, and physicians who began their career in the T-4 operation
later staffed the death camps of *Aktions Reinhard,* where mor
than 1.5 millions Jews were killed in 1942–1943.

In the Nazi mind-set, the world was divided into a series c
lesser races by color, ethnicity, culture, or national identity. Black
Slavs, and others deemed of lesser worth were a special target c
Nazi animosity.

Still, even in this world, the fate of the Jehovah's Witnesses wa
distinct.

Jehovah's Witnesses were isolated and harangued from 1933 o
Suspicion and harassment turned into bitter persecution as th
Witnesses refused to surrender. They refused to enlist in the arm
to undertake air raid drills, and to stop meeting or proselytizin
"Heil Hitler" never passed their lips. The Nazis believed the Wi
nesses to have American connections and international aspiration
They read a political message into the Witnesses' description c
chaos, anarchy, and revolution that would precede the coming c
the millennium. Prophecies about the return of Jews to the Ho
Land prior to Armageddon classified the Witnesses in Nazi eyes a
Zionists.

Twenty thousand among sixty-five million Germans, the Wi
nesses entered the battle against the Nazis as soldiers of Jehova
in the spiritual war between good and evil. They taught that Jeho
vah's forces would defeat Satan. Nazi ideology could not tolerat
such "false gods."

Persecution began immediately in 1933 and continued unt
1945. After 1937, Witnesses were sent to concentration camp
Outside the camps, Witnesses lost children, jobs, pensions, and a
civil rights.

Throughout their struggle, Witnesses continued to mee
preach, and distribute literature. Posters and tracts were even de
livered to the party headquarters. Five thousand Witnesses we

sent to concentration camps where they alone were "voluntary prisoners." The moment they recanted their views, they could be freed. So faithful were they to the tradition of nonviolence that even in the camps, Witnesses could serve as barbers and shave their oppressors, holding a razor blade to their throat. Such behavior is astounding, to be admired for its fidelity to commitment, even where one disagrees with such a tradition.

It is because of the integrity of the Witnesses' behavior, their fidelity to their own tradition and belief, that they have a special place in my heart.

We at the Survivors of the Shoah Visual History Foundation have made every effort to record their stories and to capture their testimony. We have interviewed more than 50,000 survivors and eyewitnesses in thirty-one languages and in fifty-seven countries. We have compiled a historical record of more than 100,000 hours, one that would take you more than thirteen years to view. Regretfully, so few of the records are from Witnesses, for the hour is late, and the surviving Witnesses are diminished in numbers, though not in spirit. In the history of those dark years, too little is known of the particular persecution of the Witnesses. Therefore, this book is deeply welcome and its task so very important.

Michael Berenbaum is an eminent Holocaust historian and the president of the Survivors of the Shoah Visual History Foundation.

FROM A LETTER FROM THOMAS MANN

Kusnacht-Zurich
August 2, 1938

Honorable Mr. Harbeck,

Thanking you for your gift book, *Crusade against Christianity*, is a mere gesture of politeness. I owe you more; I owe you a debt of gratitude. I read, with considerable emotion, your book filled with appalling documentation and cannot describe the combination of contempt and horror which overcame me as I leafed through these accounts of unrivaled human depravity and nameless cruelty. Language fails in describing the abject mentality revealed in these pages and the recounting of horrible sufferings of innocent victims so strongly attached to their faith. We are speechless when confronted with the indescribable; but, would not our conscience reproach our silence? Would not our conscience accuse us of encouraging moral apathy in this world and, thereby, tacitly approving the cowardly principle of non-intervention—or would it be shaken, if only for a moment—by the lengthy series of facts you present? We can scarcely hope for that outcome. But, in any event you have done your duty by offering this book to the public and it seems to me that there can be no more urgent appeal to the world's conscience.

Yours very devotedly,
Thomas Mann

Thomas Mann (1875–1955 was a german novelist, author of Death in Venice *and* Magic Mountain, *winner of the 1929 Nobel Prize for Literature, and an outspoken critic of the Third Reich who chose self-imposed exile from his homeland in 1933 and was deprived of German citizenship in 1936.*

FROM A LETTER FROM GERMAINE TILLION

Paris
September 2, 1998

In 1989, Mr. Michel Reynaud, Editor of Editions Tiresias, contacted me for information concerning the *Bibelforscherinnen* whom I described early on in my work *Ravensbrück* (published in 1947) and its subsequent editions. Therefore, I met with Mr. Reynaud as an historian of the period myself and as a deportee. I congratulated them on their project because it is true that until then no book had been devoted to the Jehovah's Witnesses, and I noted the important and historical contribution made when their work was first published in 1990.

I can say that *The Jehovah's Witnesses and the Nazis* is exceptionally interesting and recalls the various stages of repressive legislation in Germany. It is rare to see the concept of *Schutzhaft* described with such precision. Chapters are brief, therefore easily readable, and the references at the end of each chapter are many and meticulously researched. Individual accounts can be readily grasped. It is true that many people, even those who have some knowledge of concentration camps, were unaware of the presence of Jehovah's Witnesses and their martyrdom in German prison camps, and even less so eight years ago before the book was first published.

I might add, as a deportee at Ravensbrück, a special unit of Jehovah's Witnesses (as historically documented by Editions Tiresias) was located in the camp, and that the *Blockwa* (who had responsibility for the unit) was Mme. Margerete Buber-Neumann, whom I personally met several times. I also associated frequently with Mme. Anise Postel-Vinay (maiden name Girard). A chapter in the book reconstructs the period, and Milena and Mme. Genevieve de Gaulle, who had direct contact with the Witnessess, were themselves witnesses who have offered their own insights.

I remind the reader that this is the *first* work specifically devoted to the persecution of Jehovah's Witnesses in Europe, and it is an honor that a French editor has corrected this historical oversight. It should be noted that the work deals with the period from 1933 to 1945. Published for the first time in 1990, the editor has confirmed the book is now in its sixth edition and is available in several languages.

Germaine Tillion
Commandeur and Grand Croix of the Legion of Honor
Croix de Guerre with Palm
Grand Croix of the Order of Merit
Honorary Director of Studies, School of Advanced Social Sciences

Germaine Tillion is a historian, French Resistance worker, deportee, and author of Ravensbrück, *among other books.*

NOTE TO READERS

The authors have absolutely no affiliation with the Jehovah's Witness movement. Personal accounts have been reproduced verbatim, as closely as possible, in translation. Should individual accounts contain errors (of a theological, religious, or historical character), they are the sole responsibility of the source(s). To facilitate ease of reading, all footnotes and references are listed at the end of each chapter. A glossary is appended at the end of the book. All quotations are taken from the French references.

SYMBOLS OF PERSECUTION

Each inmate wore a colored triangle (generally pointing downward) sewn (or painted) on his or her uniform. Color codes denoted various categories.

Political prisoners wore a red triangle with a letter denoting their nationality (except for Germans).

Jewish political prisoners wore a red triangle pointing upward with a superimposed yellow triangle pointing downward.

Ordinary Jewish inmates were assigned a yellow star (formed by inverted triangles).

The Jehovah's Witnesses (known to the Germans as *Bibelforscher*) wore a violet triangle.
According to sources, some *Bibelforscher* were made to wear a violet triangle and a superimposed yellow one.

Common criminals wore green triangles and "antisocials" black ones.

Miscegenists were assigned a black triangle overlaid with a yellow one.

Homosexuals were assigned pink triangles.

Gypsies were assigned brown triangles.

Stateless persons and émigrés (Spanish Republicans) were assigned blue triangles.

The SAW (*Sonderaktion* Wehrmacht—individuals purged from the German army) wore a red triangle pointing upward.

CHRONOLOGY

1884: Founding of American Watch Tower and Bible and Tract Society.

1903: First affiliate of the Watch Tower and Bible and Tract Society is introduced in Germany.

1921: The Watch Tower Bible and Tract Society is recognized as a legal association in Germany.

1933: On von Schliecher's resignation, President Paul von Hindenberg names Adolf Hitler Reich chancellor and Franz von Papen vice president.

FEBRUARY 1: Promulgation of decree law by the president of the republic dissolving the Reichstag.

FEBRUARY 27: There is a fire at the Reichstag.

February 28: Promulgation of decree law by the president of the republic for the protection of the people and the state results in the mass arrests of approximately 10,000 opponents.

MARCH 21: Potsdam Day, during which the Nazis organize a giant spectacle at the Potsdam Church and issued a decree absolving all criminal acts "committed during the struggle for the national reawakening of the German people," a law promulgated on "prevention of harmful gossip against the Government," and a decree establishing special tribunals.

MARCH 28: Declaration of the Conference of Bishops at Fulda calling on Catholics to collaborate with the new Reich.

APRIL 10: Banning of the Jehovah's Witness movement in Mecklenburg-Schwerin.

APRIL 13: Banning of the Jehovah's Witness movement in Bavaria.

APRIL 18: Banning of the Jehovah's Witness movement in Saxony.

APRIL 26: Gestapo established by Goering in Prussia. Restrictions placed on movement of Jehovah's Witnesses in Thuringia.

APRIL 28: Radio announcement that the Watch Tower Society may reoccupy its premises in Magdeburg.

APRIL 29: Confiscated assets of the Watch Tower Society restored.

APRIL–JULY: Banning of Jehovah's Witness activities in most German states, then across the entire nation.

JUNE 24: Banning of the Watch Tower Society in Prussia.

JUNE 25: Berlin assembly of 7,000 Jehovah's Witnesses.

JUNE 27: Orders issues that all congregations are to be searched.

JUNE 28: Reoccupation by the SS of the Watch Tower Society headquarters in Magdeburg.

JULY 20: Signature of the concordat between von Papen and Vatican Secretary-General, Cardinal Paceli (future Pope Pius XII) guaranteeing Roman Catholic religious freedom and public profession of faith in Germany. Bishops named by the Vatican to swear oaths to the Third Reich. Reich Interior Minister Frick instructs all government employees to adopt the Hitler salute.

JULY 24: Banning of the Association of *Bibelforscher* throughout Germany.

AUGUST 21, 23: Public burning of books confiscated from the Association of Bible Students.

OCTOBER 4: Decree by Prussian Interior Minister Hermann Göring stipulating that fire be opened "mercilessly" on distributors of tracts who ignore police summons.

OCTOBER 7: Partial relaxation of ban on Jehovah's Witnesses.

DECEMBER: Reinhard Heydrich orders the arrest of all "fanatics" (the *Bibelforscher*, or Jehovah's Witnesses).

1934

FEBRUARY: Decree by French President Laval declaring Watch Tower Society publications subversive.

MARCH 9: Dissolution of the *Bund für Bibel und Bekenntnis.*
JUNE 30: "Night of the Long Knives" (bloody purge of the SA).
JULY: 15,000 incarcerated in Prussia under provisions of *Schutzhaft.*
AUGUST 1: Law on German Reich chief of state. After Marshal von Hindenburg's death, Hitler becomes Führer and Reich chancellor.
SEPTEMBER 7–9: Bible Students assembly in Basel.
SEPTEMBER 13: Following protests from U.S. leadership, Reich interior minister issues decree nullifying some of the measures against Jehovah's Witnesses.
OCTOBER 7: Letter directed by Bible Students to Reich government functionaries and telegram to Chancellor Hitler.

1935

MARCH 16: Hitler decrees military conscription. Conscientious objectors and Jehovah's Witnesses shipped in growing numbers to concentration camps.
APRIL 1: Law forbidding all activity by Jehovah's Witnesses.
JULY 13: Reich interior minister decrees dissolution and confiscation of all Jehovah's Witness Association assets.
SEPTEMBER 15: Nuremberg anti-Semitic laws on the "protection of German blood" issued.

1936

APRIL 29: Ordinance dissolving the *Bibelforscher* Association.
JUNE 24: Creation in the Gestapo of special unit charged with the fight against the *Bibelforscher.*
AUGUST 21: Circular issued by Reich secret police confiscating passports of *Bibelforscher* seeking to travel to Lucerne.
SEPTEMBER 9: Lucerne Congress (Congress resolution to Hitler and the pope dispatched from Bern).
December: Munich Gestapo circular pertaining to Jehovah's Witnesses refusing to perform military service.

1937

MAY–JUNE: Gestapo circulars in a number of German regions specifying that *Bibelforscher* may be interned in concentration camps on mere suspicion.

JUNE 20: Distribution of a *Bibelforscher* tract in Germany. This "Open Letter to the People of Germany Who Believe in the Bible and Love Christ" describes atrocities inflicted against the *Bibelforscher*. The Gestapo responds with renewed repression against Jehovah's Witnesses.

AUGUST 5: Gestapo circular ordering concentration camp internment for all *Bibelforscher* and conscientious objectors in case of their acquittal by the courts or on completion of their sentences.

1938

MARCH 13 : Germany annexation of Austria.

NOVEMBER 9–10: "Crystal Night" (*Reichskristallnacht*).

1939

MARCH 30: Gestapo confiscation of *Bibelforscher* Association assets in Prague.

APRIL 27: Suppression of Communist newspapers in France.

AUGUST 8: Ordinance from Reich Chancellery stipulating that inmates under *Schutzhaft* fall under the authority of the chief of the SS and no longer under the Justice Ministry.

AUGUST 23: Nazi–Soviet Non-Aggression Pact.

SEPTEMBER 1: Invasion of Poland.

SEPTEMBER 21: Italian Ministry of Interior draws up list of subscribers to *The Watch Tower* and requests information on their activities.

OCTOBER: Jehovah's Witness organization forbidden in France.

1940

JANUARY 3: ORVA (Italian Fascist police) circular provides listing of Jehovah's Witnesses.

MARCH 30: Banning of Belgian community of Jehovah's Witness

publications by Belgian Interior Ministry for "sapping the troop's and population's morale."

MAY 29: Third Reich Commissar Seys-Inquart proclaims ban on Jehovah's Witness Association in the Netherlands.

JUNE 8: Berlin RSHA ordinance directing arrest of all members of the Jehovah's Witness Association on Third Reich territory.

OCTOBER: Gestapo search of Belgian Jehovah's Witness headquarters.

NOVEMBER 15: Warsaw ghetto sealed off.

1941

JUNE 22: Wehrmacht attacks the Soviet Union.

SEPTEMBER 3: First gassing tests of undertaken at Auschwitz on 600 Soviet prisoners and 300 sick inmates.

DECEMBER: Application of the *Nacht und Nebel* decree signed by Keitel.

1942

JANUARY: First mass gassings at Auchwitz-Birkenau.

JANUARY 8: Rutherford's death.

JANUARY 20: Wannsee Conference, during which participants "coordinated" final solution of the Jewish question.

JULY 17: Vel d'Hiv roundup; 12,884 Jews arrested and held at the Vel d'Hiver (Paris).

NOVEMBER 13: Knorr named president of the Watch Tower Society.

NOVEMBER 24: U.S. State Department notes two million Jews murdered and extermination plan in place.

DECEMBER 17: Allied declaration on war crimes: "Those responsible for these crimes shall reap the fate they deserve."

1943

APRIL 19: Uprising of the Warsaw ghetto.

AUGUST 2: Armed inmate uprising in the Treblinka extermination camp.

1944

AUGUST 1: Gypsies gassed at Auschwitz-Birkenau.

1945

JANUARY 15: WVHA inmate census enumerates 511,537 men and 202,674 in concentration camps.
JANUARY 18: Evacuation of Auschwitz camp.
APRIL 28: Liberation of the Ravensbrück concentration camp.
APRIL 29: Entry of U.S. troops into Dachau concentration camp and freeing of prisoners.
APRIL 30: Hitler's suicide in his Berlin bunker.
NOVEMBER 14: Deliberations begin at the Nuremberg War Crimes Tribunal.

1946

OCTOBER 1: Nuremberg tribunal verdict.

1

THE NAZI TAKEOVER

> Thirsting for Christian blood, Nero put Rome to the torch. When she was reduced to embers and ash, he held Christians up as the villains. A certain Herman Goering learned this story as a child.
>
> —Bertold Brecht

On January 30, 1933, following Kurt von Schleicher's resignation, Adolf Hitler was named Reich chancellor by President Hindenburg. As soon as the Nazis came to power, the *Bibelforscher* (Jehovah's Winesses) were legally hunted down under provisions of the Security Protection Laws promulgated on February 4, 1933, and enacted after the Reichstag fire by the President's February 28, 1933 Decree for Protection of the People and State. This decree stipulated, among other provisions, that "in conformity with Article 48-2 of the Reich Constitution, the following measures are ordered to protect the State against dangerous acts of communist violence:

1. Articles 114, 115, 116, 117, 123, 124 and 153 of the Reich Constitution are repealed until further notice." Consequently, restrictions exceeding even legal limits were authorized over individual liberties and freedoms of the press, assembly, and association. Mail, telephone, and telegraph privacy laws were also ignored as search warrant and property confiscation provisions were enacted.
2. In the event the Lander [states] failed to take measures necessary to restore security and public order, "the govern-

ment of the Reich can temporarily replace that state's authorities."

Soon after the February 22 formalization of various paramilitary organizations (among them the Steel Helmets, the Brown and Black Shirts, and Prussian Interior Minister and Chief of Police Hermann Göring's auxiliary police), the decree was signed by Reich President Hindenburg, Chancellor Hitler, Reich Interior Minister Wilhelm Frick, and Justice Minister Franz Gurtner.

Enforcing these ordinances, the Nazis abolished basic rights guaranteed under the Weimar Constitution. In doing so, they accorded an aura of legitimacy to police searches, censorship, as well as "protective internment" and "protective custody," which the regime's brutally repressive forces implemented against any who opposed them. Neither constitutional rights nor justice itself could be invoked against these repressive acts. Freedom and democratic rights were crushed. Arbitrary measures intensified against "recalcitrants."

On March 24, 1933, following the Reichstag elections earlier that month, the NSDAP newspaper *Volkische Beobachter*'s headline crowed, "Confronted by a New Germany—The Parliamentary System Capitulates." Joseph Goebbels himself had declared March 5 a "Day of National Awakening."

On March 21, Hitler had organized a daylong event at the Potsdam Garrison Church, celebrating the swearing in of the new Reichstag, which had been elected into office on March 5. This was the first of many national festivals organized to impress the public. "The dazzling day at Potsdam was broadly disseminated by images, the press, and radio—and was a far cry from the specter of concentration camps and the harsh discrimination against Jews represented by the darker side of National Socialist policy. But though this festival did nothing to contradict negative aspects of the regime, the darker aspects of the regime were ignored by a larger percentage of the populace. . . . The Day at Potsdam represented a grandiose psychological preparation of public opinion preceding adoption of the law of full powers or Enabling Act of 23 March." On Potsdam Day, a chilling decree was issued providing amnesty for all criminal acts committed "during the struggle for the national reawakening of the German people." In contrast to this incredible spectacle of national pride, tens of thousands Germans were incarcerated in prisons, subjected to solitary confinement and other brutalities in detention centers where the SA and SS militias and secret police agents ruled without restraint.

On their own initiative, under the guise of legality, local SS and SA units set up a number of detention centers. Inmates often languished in protective custody in these facilities and had no recourse to the legal system. These unofficial sites eventually became concentration camps. On March 8, 1933, Reich Minister of the Interior Frick signed the Decree of February 28, which officially established camps set up to deal with "enemies of the State."

On March 20, the SA officially opened the Oranienburg concentration camp. Located near Potsdam, on the grounds and in the buildings of an old brewery, it was authorized under provisions of the Erlass II C.I.59 Law.

On March 21, an official release from the Munich Prefect of Police, reprinted in the city newspaper *Neueste Nachrichten*, reported the imminent opening of the Dachau concentration camp. The announcement was made in the presence of Heinrich Himmler and SS *Gruppenführer* Reinhard Heydrich, both leaders of the Bavarian police at that time. Supervision of the camp—established to hold 5,000 prisoners—was assigned to a special unit of SS volunteers. This special cadre, known as the Death's Head Unit, was renowned for its cruelty. The official title of the Enabling Act of March 23 was *Gesetz Behebung der Not von Volk und Stadt* (Law for Removing the Distress of People and Reich).

By the end of the spring of 1933, fifty detention camps had been set up within German borders. Saxony alone held three: the Sachsenburg camp near Heinischen, the Colditz camp near Zwickau in the Osterstein fortress, and the Hohenstein fortress near Pirna. The latter camp was notorious for the torture of forcing inmates to stand under a fountain dripping water at lengthy intervals, causing infected head sores. In the marshy Emsland region, ten to fifteen camps were set up along the Ems River, chief among these being Papenburg, Esterwagen, the Oldenburg camp, and the Boyenmoor (or Borgermoor) camp on the outskirts of Osnabrück. It was at Osnabrück that the moving hymn "Song of the Marshes" was composed in May 1933. These "marsh camps" (*Moorlager*) were administered by the SA and the SS as well as by the state police. In Prussia, the Sonnenburg prison was converted into a concentration camp, as was the detention center in Brandenburg.

These first unofficial or regular concentration camps were established by the Nazis in order to protect their powers and sow fear in the hearts of the German people. They spread a system of terror among those who opposed the regime, and those suspected of opposing it. The Nazis imprisoned people without due process, placing them in protective custody and in concentration camps; they submitted them to persecutions by degrading them, depriving them of their property, and enslaving, torturing, and murdering them.

Who were these so-called undesirables? The first Germans interned in the camps were Communists, Social Democrats, labor leaders, and the Jehovah's Witnesses. Besides disposing of their political opponents, the Nazis persecuted those whom they deemed obstacles to the continuous exercise of their total control in Germany. Persecution of pacifist groups, including religious pacifist movements, was particularly cruel and ruthless.

The Witnesses were among the pacifists. This community had been founded by the American Charles Taze Russel, who began publishing *The Watch Tower*, the official journal of the Witnesses, in July 1879. He later established a publishing house and the Watch Tower Society in Pittsburgh, Pennsylvania, which later became the Watch Tower Bible and Tract Society. Those headquarters moved to Brooklyn, New York, in 1909. Russel and his seven directors headed the organization until his death on October 31, 1916. At a congress in 1931, the new name "Jehovah's Witnesses" was adopted, replacing "Bible Students," which continued to be used colloquially. The word "martyr" comes from the Greek word *martur*, which also means "witness" or "witness of God." Other possible derivations include "martyr" from the Greek *martus* or *marturos*, which also means "witness."

This religious movement, called the *Internationale Bibelforscherveringung* (IBV; International Association of Bible Students), established itself in Germany at the beginning of the twentieth century, initially in the Black Forest and Westphalia. By 1918, there were 5,545 members. Around that time, an American lawyer, Joseph F. Rutherford, succeeded Russel. By 1926, their numbers in Germany had nearly quadrupled—with 20,000 Witnesses grouped into 316 congregations. In 1933, when the Nazi's engineered their takeover, the IBV had 25,000 followers, of which 19,268 were active practitioners.

To understand what motivated the Witnesses' faith, it is important to understand what they believed. They were awaiting what they referred to as the millennium of Jehovah on Earth, during which the Kingdom of God would annihilate Satan's powers (represented by politics, churches, capital, and so on). According to Witness beliefs, only Jehovah's reign on Earth would resolve the world's problems, and man's salvation could be achieved only through strict adherence to the Bible's commandments. Each Jehovah's Witness had a duty, therefore, to spread or bear witness to the doctrine that the Apocalypse is near and that Evil must be destroyed. Moreover, the *Bibelforscher* were strict believers in the fifth precept of the Decalogue, which commands "Thou shalt not kill" (Deuteronomy 5:17). For this reason, they were pacifists and rejected military service absolutely.

As Christine Elizabeth noted in her study, "For the Nazis, the Witnesses incarnated all they despised: the movement was international, there were Jewish influences by the use of the Old Testament, and in their eschatological beliefs. The Witness was also viewed as Marxist. Of all the sects, it was the least politicized, hence the most dangerous. Politics were of no interest and were considered corrupt. But, by their attitude, the believers placed themselves in a non-compromising hostile position, appearing (to the Nazis at least) politicized. Their teachings on military services were intolerable, not so much as a practical danger but as an ideological challenge to the National Socialist Party." It was an ideological battle that set the Witnesses on a collision course with the Nazis. "The real reason for the clash between this sect and the

Nazis resides in the clash of two totalitarian systems. Each system promised a thousand-year Reich, each system expected its membership to demonstrate total support and unquestioning obedience."

During the second week of April 1933, the Witnesses launched a propaganda and preaching campaign to attract new converts. In eight days, they distributed more than two million leaflets, and by April 9 almost 25,000 followers (or 10,000 more than 1932) took part in a major commemoration, which is a symbolic celebration of Christ's sacrifice on the full moon of the spring equinox.

On April 7, 1933, the government enacted the Second Law on Centralization of the Lander with the Reich. Jehovah's Witnesses were banned by decree in several German states, including Mecklenburg-Schwerin (April 10), Bavaria (April 13), and Saxony (April 18). (It should be noted that this was an international movement with worldwide representation, a theme to which the authors will return before addressing the advance of Nazism on Europe.)

Later that April, Minister Otto, a Lutheran Church spokesman, declared in a radio address, "The German Lutheran Church of Saxony has conscientiously adapted to the new situation and pledges itself, in close cooperation with the peoples' political authorities, to convey the strength of the Old Testament of Jesus Christ to the entire nation. Today's ban of Jehovah's Witnesses and its associations in Saxony can be considered as a first manifestation of this cooperation."

On April 22, the day after Hitler's forty-fifth birthday, the Witnesses' periodicals *The Watch Tower* and *Golden Age* were seized by authorities, as were its brochures *The Kingdom* and *The Crisis*. The National Socialists broke in to and searched the group's headquarters, notably the print shop in Magdeburg, and made off with all its books, which they incinerated in an enormous bonfire. The Witnesses' headquarters was occupied and the building closed under the argument that the group had close ties to the Communists.

On April 26, the Witnesses were banned in Thuringia. The Society's American representative protested, reminding authorities that the Watch Tower Bible and Tract Society was an American entity founded under U.S. law in 1884 and thus was recognized as a legal association in Germany. A Reich decree of April 30, 1930, had classified the organization as "philanthropic and not political." Representatives ensured authorities that the group had nothing to do with Communists or the Jewish community and that its beliefs were based strictly on the Bible's teachings. Following these clarifications, it was announced on the radio that the association could reclaim its premises. On April 29, the Magdeburg press published the following: "We have learned from official sources that the assets of the Watch Tower Bible and Tract Society were confiscated because a complaint was lodged against this Association for conducting Communist propaganda . . . but the land, buildings and equipment, as well as the furniture and confiscated books, were returned to the representatives of this society." In addition, it was officially announced that *Golden Age* was authorized to reappear and that Bible Students could freely spread their doctrine in Prussia. A weeklong inspection of their papers and different offices had "failed to lead to the discovery of any communist documents incriminating said society."

Nonetheless, many Witnesses were victims of continuing extortion as they were practicing their faith. One recounted how, at the end of April 1933, a Nazi leader confiscated the leaflets he was distributing as well as his identity papers and all the money he had in his possession. This was done with the approval of the local National Socialist Party office despite the fact that no official ban on propagating such literature had yet been passed. He also recalled that a Catholic priest, on coming to the Nazi chief's office and being told of the seized literature, remarked, "Jesus was a friend of the poor, but these works explaining the Bible must not be given to the people." In early March, Göring spoke in Frankfurt, during which time he thundered that the repressive measures "are not hindered by any judicial considerations. I *do not* have to provide justice—just stamp out and *exterminate*—nothing else." In May, book burnings were staged in German university towns, as the Fascists systematically consigned books and works of socialist, Communist, humanist, and Jewish authors to the flames—everything they deemed "non-German literature." On May 15, the

International Association of Bible Students was outlawed in the grand duchy of Bade, and numerous trail proceedings were instituted before special courts. There would be a total of 167 such proceedings in the grand duchy.

On June 14, the Law of Confiscation of Assets of the Enemies of the People and the State was enacted in the official record, which relates to paragraph 1 of the Law of Confiscation of Communist Fortunes of May 26, and on June 24 the Watch Tower Society was finally completely outlawed in Prussia. The Prussian interior minister's ban stipulates (Berlin, June 24, 1933), "Under terms of Paragraph 1 of the Reich Presidential Decree of February 28, 1933 for the protection of the people and the state (R.G.B1.I.p.83) in relation to paragraph 14 P.V.G. the International Association of Bible Students, as well as all other organizations (Watch Tower Bible and Tract Society, Lunen-Magdeburg, the Sect of New Apostles, etc.) are hereby dissolved and banned on the territory of the Republic of Prussia. Their assets will be seized and confiscated. Any violation of these ordinances are punishable according to paragraph 4 of the decree of February 28th 1933." This was stated on the grounds that

> hiding behind the mask of a group of seekers meeting to conduct scientific scriptural studies, the International Association of Bible Students and its secondary organizations are verbally and by writings agitating the people against the State and ecclesiastical institutions. In affirming that both are Satan's works, they undermine the very foundations of communal life. In their numerous writings such as "Millions of Living Men Will Never Die" (page 18) "War or Peace", "Prosperity Assured," "The People's Standard," "Crimes and Calamities," "Heaven and Purgatory," "The Crisis" . . . and many others, they insult State and Church institutions and, knowingly and maliciously, distort Biblical parables.
>
> Their battle plan is characterized by influences designed to fanaticize their members; by powerful financial means and stubborn efforts of Bolshevik decay, their power increases incessantly.
>
> It is in part due to strange ceremonies that they influence and whip up those who listen to them, instantly deranging their spiritual equilibrium.

> Given the tendency of the said association's contradiction with today's State and its cultural and moral structure, the Students of the Bible see an adversary in the Christian-National State resulting from its national elevation and have reinforced their means of combat. This is proven by multiple hateful attacks by its leaders who have, once again, recently attacked National Socialism verbally and in writing.
>
> The dangerous intrigues of said Association against today's State have been reinforced by the fact that for some time former Communists and Marxists have joined their ranks hoping to find shelter and allowing them to fight the Government. The Association of Students of the Bible and its allied organizations, therefore, favored Communism and welcomes into the organization the most varied elements hostile to the State, notably Communists belonging to very active organized groups. In order to fight these Communist intrigues and for the maintenance of public order and safety, this movement is dissolved.
>
> In replacement: signed: Grauert
> Secretary of the Ministerial Chancellery

This text shows the willingness of German authorities to terminate activities of the followers of the International Association of Bible Students by arbitrarily and unfairly comparing the principles of Jehovah's Witnesses to those of the Communists. It is telling that a mere three months earlier, Göring had set up the Gestapo as a political police force for the state of Prussia's Ministry of Interior.

Despite the repression they faced, the Witnesses organized a large assembly of 7,000 members in Berlin on June 25, 1933. There, the participants drafted a statement to Reich authorities to protest the persecution they faced. This statement was forwarded to all government functionaries, and two million copies were also distributed to the public. These actions triggered a swift and brutal response from police authorities.

On June 27, all police officials received orders to search Witness offices and businesses and to confiscate all materials hostile to the state. On June 28, about thirty SA troopers occupied the Watch Tower Building in Magdeburg, closing it off and hoisting the swastika flag. A police decree prohibited all Bible readings, meetings, and prayer on the premises. The official announcement was broadcast over the radio the next day.

2

THE ENEMY IDENTIFIED

There, where books are burned, men also burn.
—Heinrich Heine

By July 1933, the NSDAP had emerged as the only approved political party in Germany. The KPD was banned in March, the SPD was banned in June, and the other parties, weakened by fear, capitulation, and collaboration, dissolved during June and July. Their organizations were banned, subverted, or absorbed. On July 14, the Law against the Reconstitution of Parties was enacted, declaring the NSDAP the only legal political party and threatening prison terms of up to three years for any attempts to form new parties or to maintain existing ones. On July 20, Reich Interior Minister Wilhelm Frick ordered all civil servants to adopt the Nazi salute as "the German salute . . . because parties in Germany have ceased to exist and the entire German Reich administration is now under the direction of Reich Chancellor Adolf Hitler."

On July 24, the Jehovah's Witnesses were banned throughout Germany. About three weeks later, the Nazis confiscated three truckloads of documents at the group's Magdeburg headquarters, and during the third week of August they organized enormous public book burnings. At Magdeburg and in the surrounding region, more than sixty-five tons of books, engravings, and Bibles were reduced to ashes.

In May, public and university libraries were burned under the aegis of the so-called *Bekampfung von Schmutz und Schund* operation. Publications were incinerated in other cities as well, and searches and arrests were undertaken in Mainz, Cologne, and Freiburg. On July 26, another law was passed, titled the Prosecution of Intrigues against the German People, further perpetrating the regime of special and arbitrary measures against "enemies of the state."

On August 5, the Criminal Investigation Department in Dresden issued a circular regulating the establishment and administration of concentration camps and published a list of "protective" internment camps established in the region: the Dresden Mathildenstrasse prison, the Osterstein castle at Zwickau, the Colditz prison, the Hohenstein castle, and the Sachsenburg camp near Franckenberg. This circular also stipulated that commandants and guards at these camps, not already police officials, were to be considered members of the auxiliary police. It also pointed out that "all persons placed in *Schutzhaft* [internment] were judged to be harmful to the ethnic German body politic and further adjudged intractible in their political opinions."

In early October, Hermann Göring published a decree ordering police to "open fire mercilessly on distributors of tracts who fail to follow police orders immediately." Some relief from these repressive measures resulted when, in early October, the U.S. government's consul lodged an official protest: The ban against Jehovah's Witnesses was partially lifted, and its printing presses were allowed to be shipped out of Germany. The newer decree had specified that "the Society's property [be] returned so that it can use it freely, except that it is forbidden to engage in any activity, print publications or hold meetings." In brief, although the Watch Tower Society regained its offices, it was forbidden to use them to proselytize or for public relations purposes.

Paul Balzereit, elected in November 1920, headed the German Bethel during the early 1930s. When the Magdeburg headquarters was authorized to reopen in early May 1933, he attempted to work out a compromise with the Nazi authorities. He published a statement proclaiming that the Witnesses maintained absolutely no links to political parties such as the SPD or KPD. (It should be noted, however, that Karl and Horst Kohl, two of the Watch Tower Society's legal advisers in Munich, were members of the NSDAP.)

Repression continued against their organization following the mass meeting in Berlin-Wilmersdorf in late June 1933, at which several motions reaffirming the Witnesses' loyalty to the "National Government" were adopted. Paul Balzereit fled into exile to Prague with other leaders of the Magdeburg Bethel. There, they edited the *Golden Age* review. Balzereit returned to Germany in March 1934. He was arrested in May 1935 and sentenced by a tribunal in December 1935 to a prison term of two and a half years. While being held at the Sachsenhausen concentration camp in December 1937, he became one of the few Witnesses to sign a statement recanting his faith. The SS further humiliated him by referring to him as "Belzebuth," another name for the Devil, and they forced him to read his recantation before 300 Witnesses in the camp. He was released a year later. Balzereit's actions were then severely criticized by the Watch Tower Society, especially his statements before the tribunal in Halle, where he had refused to witness his absolute faith in Jehovah. In 1935, Jehovah's Witness President Rutherford expelled him from the Watch Tower Society, and in 1935 Rutherford appointed Fritz Winkler to lead the Bethel in Germany. After Winkler was in place, the Bethel rejected any compromise, and they excoriated Balzereit for his part in the accommodations with the Nazis that began under his presidency.[1]

In October 1933, a few days after this decree, an ordinance on *Schutzhaft* procedures was issued by Interior Secretary of State Grauert: "In accordance with his circular of June 16 1933 II 6, 1600/16, the Prussian Minister of Interior announces the following decisions: all persons arrested by virtue of Reich Presidential Ordinance for the Protection of the People and the State of February 28, 1933 and in accordance with paragraph P06 of police internment [*Polizeihaft*] must, as a matter of principle and given the nature of their arrests, be placed in a concentration camp and held under control of police authorities. Restrictions on their personal freedom cannot be considered a short-term internment." The ordinance further legitimized placement in *Schutzhaft*, which it defined as "detention for security purposes, of unlimited duration, without recourse or appeal, with enforcement arbitrarily handed over to police officials"—the ordinance applied to the Jehovah's

Witnesses. The ordinance goes on: "All persons arrested by the SS under charges of this nature were to be detained in concentration camps and judges granted no discretionary powers over these internments."

By late July 1934, almost 15,000 people were incarcerated in Prussia under *Schutzhaft* provisions. Statistics published by the Ministry of Interior total 26,789 individuals jailed under *Schutzhaft* (of which 14,906 were in Prussia) and confined to prisons, jails, and concentrations camps.

The plebiscite of November 1933 posed the question to all Germans: "Men and women, do you approve of your Government's policies, and are you able to recognize therein the expression of your own beliefs and will and profess therein your solemn faith?" Invoking their Christian neutrality and basing themselves on the Gospel according to St. John, which plainly states, "You are no part of this world," the Witnesses refused to go to the polls and openly declared opposition to the Reichstag elections. Their vote *could* be interpreted as an act of faith in the Third Reich. It should be recalled that 95 percent of the eligible population voted, but there were nonetheless 5 percent abstentions despite reprisals and repressive violence. One man, the owner of a saddlery-upholstery shop, was called on by the assistant to the mayor of his town. As the man recalled later, "Briefly, I explained to him that, because of my knowledge of the Bible, my conscience does not permit me to take part in any election." On the evening of the voting, in which he did not take part, his store was ransacked, and on its walls were scrawled the inscription "Herein lives traitor X . . . do not enter." After this, the authorities did all they could to discourage customers from visiting his store. "Thus my business, which previously was very prosperous and esteemed, was completely ruined."

A few days after the November elections, Heinrich Dickmann, a Witness who worked in a rolling mill, saw a blackboard in the factory courtyard with a pig drawn on it labeled "Jehovah." He did not respond to the affront, as he did not want to be drawn into the campaign against the Witnesses.

Repressive measures were not limited to verbal provocation and the undermining of businesses. Physical cruelty was also inflicted on those who do not take part in the voting. A Witness reports, "On November 13, 1933 at 6:00 o'clock in the evening, the SA burst into our house and took my husband and said he would be interrogated at the Standarte (441, Kosthaus Stahlausen)." Her husband was badly bludgeoned, and when she tried to help him, she was violently beaten. Another person, a Christian who was beaten and threatened with death, relates, "On November 14th 1933 at 9:15 in the evening, three SA came to get me at home and took me to the SS station." The SA told him, "You will be shot, bastard." The SA did not even spare disabled persons. One such person was dragged from his home and subjected to brutalities that resulted in his death. The SA told his wife that they threw him onto the street, saying, "Go away traitor, we've finished with you." "We returned to our home and some SA followed us, shouting 'traitors.' Since that tragic night, the state of the unfortunate worsened rapidly, and he died a few months later."

A man named Max Schubert recalled that he and his wife were taken to a voting booth five times by the Nazis in an effort to get him to cast a ballot. He refused because he thought it pointless to vote for anyone but God. One day after work, he was taken to the offices of the National Socialists, in front of which sat a small cart drawn by two horses. Schubert was forced to sit in it between SA officers. These officers held a sign on which was inscribed "I am a scoundrel and a traitor to my homeland because I did not vote." To further provoke the populace, the SS blew horns and beat a drum while parading the unfortunate man. The town's inhabitants responded with taunts and demanded, "Where should we send him?" The *children* in the crowd replied, "To the concentration camp!"

The children of Oschatz were well aware of the existence of the concentration camps. On October 1, Dachau Commandant Theodor Eicke[2] enacted the Disciplinary and Penal Rules at the concentration camp. The regulations he imposed were subsequently applied in all concentration camps. Eicke spelled out sanctions in line with the Nazi ideology of *Toleranz bedeutet Schwache*, "tolerance begets weakness." Even the most minor infractions drew sanctions and punishment: solitary confinement, beatings, withdrawal of correspondence privileges, and reassignment of barracks. To quote Article 11, "Whomsoever undertakes political activity or communicates any information on the camp will be hanged." Article 12 stated, "Whomsoever shall protest or disobeys orders will be shot on the spot." Eicke also was named inspector of the concentration camps and headed the SS Surveillance Associations.

In one telling incident, a Jehovah's Witness spoke out against the treatment of a fellow prisoner at Orianienburg-Sachsenhausen and was subjected to the cruelest reach of these laws. The facts, recounted by Gaston Bernard (prisoner number 59249, a French Communist), are related simply as follows: "The custom whereby a condemned man escapes his fate if the rope destined to hang him breaks, is not respected by the Nazis. A hanged man must die at all cost. . . . A Dutch Jehovah's Witness protested from within our ranks when another rope was taken to replace the one which had broken. The condemned man was rehung and the Dutchman along with him."

NOTES

1. The authors of this book made repeated attempts, in 1990 and afterward, to obtain additional information from the Jehovah's Witness associations on the situation involving Balzereit. Their two sources remain the Watch Tower Society's "1974 Annual" and an analysis done by Deltef Garbe.
2. Eike later became chief of the dreaded "Death Heads" unit.

3

If We Are Ready to Answer "Yes"
If we answer "yes" upon being asked to betray our beliefs,
then no salute for us.

—Milena Jesenska

In July 1933, the Prussian interior minister issued a circular ordering that the "German" (Nazi) salute be given on duty hours in all office buildings by raising the right arm. Failure to perform the Nazi salute would signal a lack of professional duty. The Jehovah's Witnesses of Prussia responded that they refused to give the salute or say "Heil Hitler" because none other than their God could be so hailed. They cited the Acts of the Apostles IV, wherein the apostle Peter wrote, "For there is no other name under heaven given to me by which we may be saved."

Gerard Sandoz wrote, "In 1933, at the time Germany was invested by National Socialism, this sect, which numbered some 6,000 adherents, was infused with its mission in proclaiming the 'imminent return' of Christ. . . . They challenged all authority not emanating from God, refusing to serve in the Army and obstinately rejecting the German salute." He remarked on their courage, even if they were rightly or wrongly treated as fanatics, and went on that, despite being banned in February 1933, "the Jehovah's Witnesses do not dream for an instant of following this measure." He also notes the "little illegal flyer" distributed in mailboxes in the city of Dortmund in the Ruhr. Several extracts of *Wachtturm* are quoted: "We refuse military service. God has ordered us not to kill our fellow man; we will not say 'Heil Hitler!' as according to God's word we cannot accept this salute as owed to man." The word "heil" in biblical language means the same as "deliverance." Only God can determine who possesses the attributes of a "savior."

The Witnesses could not accept hailing a mortal. They invoked Psalm 146, which reads, "Put not your trust in Princes, in a son of clay, in whom there is no salvation!" They refused to give the Nazi salute or to salute the Nazi flag. For them to come to terms with those requirements would be to renounce their faith. Psalm 118, "Hymn of Thanksgiving to the Saviors of Israel," reads, "It is better to take refuge in the Lord than to trust in man. It is better to take refuge in the Lord than to trust in princes. . . . I was hard pressed and was falling, but the Lord helped me. My strength and my courage is the Lord and He has been my savior."

Thus, in 1933, a Witness who was running errands in town and failed to salute the flag was apprehended by an SA member who demanded an explanation. He responded, "As a Jehovah's Witness, the Bible is my law, and I could not perform this impious gesture, and, furthermore, having atrophied arm muscles, this motion was physically impossible." He was then struck by two other SAs who dragged him along the ground. "When we were before the troops I was ordered to raise my arm, I refused, and my arm was forcibly raised." In November, Nazi leader Martin Bormann signed a circular threatening that persons saluting "Heil" rather than "Heil Hitler" would be sent to the concentration camps.

Wolfgang Langhoff, a celebrated actor and director, was arrested in Berlin for his political beliefs after the Reichstag fire. "The speedy promulgation of a new decree-law for the 'Defense of the People and the State' introduced a long-term state of alert designed to 'protect the State against acts of Communist violence which would place it at risk.' Over and above the pretext the fire provided, it allowed measures to be taken against a supposed communist threat, and they introduced a special 'alert status' would soon prove instrumental to the National Socialists in their drive for absolute power." The antifascist Langhoff was interned for sixteen months, first at the marsh camp at Boyenmoor, then at Lichtenburg. Freed, he emigrated to Zurich, where he reported atrocities suffered by a Witness who refused to give the Hitler salute in his book *Die Moorsoldaten* (published in Switzerland and France in

1935). A passage is quoted describing the willpower and courage of the man who refused to salute, a fact that impressed Langhoff:

> And at end of his being, a shattered wreck, a ghost and mere shadow of a man, he exhausted resistance in seeming acceptance, proving even more to us his strength of character and humanism in sacrifice or apparent resignation. This is the story of a man who did not want to say *Heil Hitler!* He belongs to a religious sect, the community of Strict Servants of the Bible (*Bibelforscher*, or Jehovah's Witnesses). God had forbidden him to give the Hitler salute. He was named Frank or Franke and was some kind of engineer.
>
> And since God had forbidden him to worship Hitler, no power on earth could contravene him, for the Strict Servants of the Bible are fanatics, loyal to their faith. They told anyone who would listen "Hitler has built his kingdom on blood." And because they are part of the 40,000 souls who, after the next flood, will enter heaven on earth, they were able to bear with a lightness of heart all of the suffering, deprivation, and poverty of their present existence.
>
> This brought him to Lichtenburg. He did not speak much and looked at all of us through affectionate eyes. He had blonde hair, sparse and slightly curly, crowning a smooth forehead, big blue eyes, pink cheeks, a feminine mouth and a somewhat small round chin. He could have been forty years old. He tirelessly swept the cell and the hallway and went to fetch water and was helpful to all.
>
> But he would not raise his arm to salute. He would not say *Heil Hitler!* The first time the guard noticed, he shouted: "Why didn't you salute?" "Because God forbids me to." He did not believe his ears. The witness had a dumb look upon his face: "Are you making fun of me?" "No." "In which dormitory do you stay?" "Dormitory number 3."
>
> That evening they came to get him. Solitary! For a week! Afterwards we saw him come back with swollen and black eyes. "Be reasonable" his friends told him. What does a *Heil Hitler!* matter! Do like us. We say it. He shook his head. The next day he was caught again. He went back to solitary for two weeks. When he came back he was unrecognizable. But he would not raise his arm in a salute.
>
> The fat Zimmermann then undertook to force him to salute. Accompanied by five SS they took him into the little courtyard. "Raise your arm! Raise your arm! Raise your arm!" The comman-

> dant was present at the scene. They rained blows on him. He slipped on a frozen puddle and fell. "Raise your arm! *Heil Hitler! Heil Hitler!* So, do it now."
>
> They beat him until he lost consciousness. His blood froze on the ground. We implored him. His face hardened and he took on a look of childish obstinance. He would not salute. We gave up hope.
>
> They separated him from us and placed him in a cell with "inveterate criminals." He wears their uniform. Every day he has to empty the latrine pits on the run. His hands bleed from carrying buckets. And when it's not that, it's solitary or beatings.
>
> When we met him, we gave him little salutes and raised our arms to incite him to do the same.
>
> The SS made bets about him "Will salute!" "Won't salute!"
>
> After a few weeks he returned to the dormitory. He was supporting himself against the wall. He met an SS in the vestibule. His right arm came up awkwardly. The extended hand was coated with dried blood. He murmured *Heil Hitler!*

We can only add with humility that he was only a man, but what a man . . . This man, as Olga Wormser-Migot remarked, was forced to make the Hitler salute in order to survive. Catholic, Protestant, anarchist, and pacifist movements all rejected National Socialism for religious or political reasons. "The Jehovah's Witnesses prefer to die rather than salute and utter the words *Heil Hitler!* For them, *heil*, which means glory, could only be used with God or Jesus."

Recalling this example, Protestant minister Aime Bonifas cites "the unshakable faith of the Christian legionnaires in Rome who preferred to risk chains in answering 'Christ is the Lord' when they were demanded to declare 'Caesar is the Lord.' "

4

DO NOT SUBMIT TO THE POWER OF MAN

Man's justice: more criminal than the crime.
—Francis Picabia

In December 1933, SD Chief Heydrich gave orders for the arrest of all all those who spread the doctrine of the illegal *Bibelforscher* society, these "unbelievable fanatics who shared the faults of refusing to perform the Nazi salute and service for the National Socialist State and were opposed to military service." Despite beatings, threats, and bans and despite public humiliation, imprisonment, and camps internment, the Witnesses did not allow themselves to be "reeducated" and continued their activities underground. Repression failed to prevent them from meeting, publishing, distributing their writings, and making new converts.

In February 1934, M. Laval, the French interior minister, enacted a decree branding as subversive all writings of the Watch Tower Society. French police forces were ordered to expel all foreign missionaries from the country. Polish, German, and English missionaries were targeted by this measure and forcibly ejected from the country.

On the other side of the Rhine, the various *Länder* (states) were abolished, and in January 1934, at the initiative of Reich Interior Minister Frick and his counselor, Helmuth Nicolai, a law on the "Reconstruction of the Reich" was adopted that modified the Constitution. This law provided that "the popular (democratic) representations of the *Länder* are abolished. The sovereign rights of the

Länder are transferred to the Reich. Regional governments are subordinated to the central government. Governors are placed under the administrative supervision of the Reich Minister of Interior." According to statistics, in this unified Reich there were already a total of 7,000 inmates in concentration camps.

On March 9, 1934, Hitler ordered the dissolution of the *Bund für Bibel und Bekenntnis*. The Gestapo and the Prussian Interior Ministry drew up a list of the association's members, they had the names of its leaders, and they knew the amount of the association's bank. Beginning in 1934, Hitler ordered the persecution of the Witnesses for their refusal to bear arms and their opposition to him. Regarding Hitler, the Witnesses pointed to Daniel's judgment of the tyrant in the Bible: "He has no reverence for the love of a woman or for any God since he has revolted against all, his only religion is for the God of Fortresses."

The Witnesses also launched an opposition campaign and sought to void these unconstitutional measures. A Berlin lawyer, Ernst Fraenkel, provided a scathing analysis of Hitler's efforts: "Another major problem is [the danger] the decree—the law of February 28,1933 which is based on Article 48 of the Weimar Constitution—can also suspend fundamental rights, of which is not provided for in Article 48 (subpara. 2) and which are therefore designated in constitutional law terminology as 'invulnerable to dictatorship.' Freedom of religion is another one." During the time the Witnesses were already under the ban, they objected that their freedom of religious expression was a fundamental right that could not be suspended in accordance with Article 48 (subparagraph 2). On March 26, they obtained a favorable ruling from the special tribunal at Darmstadt. However, this was an isolated and largely ineffective victory, and the Nazis soon had an answer. On September 24, 1935, the Reich tribunal, basing itself on Article 137 jurisprudence, declared that its application "does not cover the existence and activity of a religious community incompatible with good order of the State. The verdict placed fundamental rights supposedly 'invulnerable to dictatorship' under the authority of the police and weakened the constitutional protection of freedom of religion by referring all interpretations of the constitution to the Executive Branch."

German Witnesses who did not participate in the Reichstag elections of November 12 continued to be persecuted. On March 29, 1934, Witness Ludwig Stickel, a civil servant and treasurer of the town of Pforzheim, received a letter from the town mayor announcing that "a process will be undertaken against you aimed at removing you from the position you hold." On August 20, he was dismissed from office.

In April 1934, several decrees are issued in Germany concerning *Schutzhaft* (preventive detention), which laid the legal groundwork for the establishment of the concentration camps' judicial framework. The Reich interior minister decreed that all incarcerations would be held in concentration camps or in sites controlled by the police. The decree of April 26 authorized officials to order detention under *Schutzhaft*. The Gestapo was thus empowered to order confinement in concentration camps across the country.

Hans Buchheim, speaking to the concept of justice and the state, would make this analytical observation: "The title 'President of the Reich' was abolished by decree on August 2, 1934. Hitler was 'only' the *Führer* (Chief) and Reich Chancellor. His denomination as *Führer* and Chancellor was a revolutionary innovation which constitutes the key to understanding the structure of National Socialist domination in general and, in particular, the evolution of the SS within the power structure." By officially qualifying himself as *Der Führer* and Reich chancellor, he realized his ambition to impose his will across the life of the entire German state. "The manifestation of the *Führer*'s will over the vital law of the German people enabled him to be carried along by acquienscence of the National Socialist movement."

In August 1934, to the oath administered to the German soldier was added, "I swear this sacred oath before God that I will unconditionally obey Adolph Hitler, *Führer* of the German Reich and people and supreme Army Commander, and that as a brave soldier I must be ready at all times to lay down my life for this oath."

In 1939, Ernst Rudolf Huber wrote, in his *Constitutional Rights in the Greater German Reich*, "The *Führer* unifies all of the powers of the Reich. . . . We should not speak of the State's powers but of the powers of the Chief. . . . The *Führer's* power is vast and total . . . it touches all our compatriots who are compelled to be loyal and obedient to the *Führer.* The *Führer* could use the enormous power of the laws of the State to achieve his will . . . but he could also choose extra-legal means which were exclusively legitimized by his historic mission."

Anything and everything was useful in furthering repression, and the participation of every citizen in the May Festival drew special attention from the Nazi authorities. The Heidelberger newspaper *Heidelberger Tageblatt* published an article under the title "Fired for having failed to take part in the May Festival": "An important labor tribunal decision was published by the German Labor Front. According to the latter, it will be possible to dismiss anyone who does not take part in solemn May 1st festivities. The case precipitating this decision will be of interest to members of the International Association of Bible Students." The Witnesses, wanting only to honor their God, were fired from jobs for abstaining from participation in these national holidays. The tribunal considered that there had been a breach of the work contract by a display of disobedience to the plant manager. "By not voting on August 19,1934, great difficulties befell me," reported another man. On August 20, the construction company for which he worked received a notice ordering his dismissal from the National Socialist Party.

An order issued on January 22, 1935, by the Reich and Prussian Ministries of Interior decreed, "On-duty functionaries, employees and public service workers must henceforth give the German salute in all installations and official buildings by raising the right hand—the left hand in the event of physical handicap—and distinctly pronouncing *Heil Hitler!* at the same time."

Ernst Fraenkel's personal experience provides insight into the Nazi regime: "Though Jewish, I was able to continue as a member of the bar even after 1933, since I was a veteran. The ambiguity of my civil existence made me particularly receptive to contradictions in Hitler's regime. According to the law, and as a member of the bar having the same rights, I was nonetheless subjected at every step to pettifoggery, discrimination, and humiliation which invariably came from the 'party supporting the State.' "

5

THE ASSEMBLY AT BASEL

> Man's greatest freedom . . . his choice of attitude confronted by circumstance.
>
> —Bruno Bettelheim

During early September, the Jehovah's Witnesses organized a major assembly in Basel. A thousand Witnesses from Germany managed to attend the meetings and were able to testify to their situation as well as describe the cruel persecutions to which they were subjected. A discussion followed, during which plans were finalized and it was eventually agreed that they would meet in groups in Germany on the morning of October 7 and disclose their position by releasing the following letter:

> To Government officials: The word of God Jehovah, recorded in the Holy Bible, is the supreme law and constitutes our only God for we are devoted to Him and we wish to be true and sincere disciples of Jesus Christ.
>
> During the past year, in contradiction of God's law and in violation of our rights, you have forbidden Jehovah's Witnesses from gathering to worship God, to study His word and to serve Him. For His Word commands us not to abandon our assembly (Hebrews 10:25). It was to us that Jehovah laid down: "You are my witnesses that I am God. Go forth and convey my message to the people" (Isaiah 43:10–12, 6:9; Matthew 24:14). There is a conflict between your law and God's. Following the example of the Apostles "we must obey God rather than men" and that is what we will do (Acts 5:29). You are hereby advised that at any cost we will obey God's commandments, will meet together to study His Word and that we

will worship and serve Him as he has commanded. If your Government or agents of Government inflict harsh treatment on us because we obey God, our blood will be on your hands and you will have to render account to God, the All-Powerful. We take no interest in political affairs but we are dedicated to an unswerving attachment to the Kingdom of God and Christ the King. We will harm no one. We will live happily in peace and extend kindness to all men when we can, but since your Government, and its representatives, continue to attempt to force us to disobey the supreme law of the universe, we are obliged to inform you that, by the grace of God Jehovah, we will obey Him, in full confidence that he will deliver us from all oppression and all oppressors.

On the same day, the following telegram was sent to Hitler's chancellery:

To the Hitlerian Government in Berlin,
The ill-treatment which you inflict on Jehovah's Witnesses shocks all good men and dishonors God's name. Refrain from further persecuting Jehovah's Witnesses or God will destroy you and your national party.
The Jehovah's Witnesses at . . .

Thousands of telegrams, worded such as this one, were sent from the United States, Canada, Switzerland, Great Britain, Czechoslovakia, the Scandinavian countries, France, Hungary, the Netherlands, and other European nations. In Budapest, for example, Martin Potzinger declared, "The telegram was accepted, but the next day I was called to the main post office. . . . I was informed that Hungary could not forward the telegram and I was reimbursed."

In the Netherlands, where Kaiser William II lived in exile, the post office initially refused to send the telegram. Later its sender, Hans Thomas, was informed that it had been transmitted and its receipt in Berlin confirmed. At first, Berlin postal authorities refused to accept these telegrams, stating that, in accordance with paragraph 26 of the World Postal Convention, they could not be sent to the addressee. They later reversed their position and accepted the messages. In France, where there were about 1,000 missionaires, all congregations sent the protest telegram, insisting that they be transmitted by the post offices when telegram companies refused. In those cases, registered letters with the identical text were mailed.

Karl R. Wittig, a plenipotentiary adviser attached to General Ludendorff, testified to the effect that these telegrams had on Hitler in a notarized report that he signed in November 1947 at Frankfurt am Main: "When it became time to discuss measures taken by the National Socialist regime against the International Association of Jehovah's Witnesses in Germany, Dr. Wilhelm Frick handed Hitler a number of telegrams from abroad protesting persecution of the Bible Students in the Third Reich, and he said, 'If the Witnesses do not fall into line we will employ the most severe measures against them,' at which point Hitler bounded to his feet with his fists clenched and yelled hysterically, 'This mob will be exterminated in Germany!' Four years after this meeting, and during the seven years of my detention in the hell of the concentration camps of Sachsenhausen, Flossenburg and Mauthausen—which ended when the Allies freed me—I realized that Hitler rage was not a vain threat."

The mailing of these telegrams touched off a wave of arrests across Germany. In Hamburg, the Gestapo arrested 142 Witnesses in the days following transmission. Kurt Kessler, arrested at Steinpleis in August 1935, was initially incarcerated at the Sachsenburg concentration camp before being brought to trial. Sentenced to a year in prison for having taken part in the October 1934 campaign, he was transferred to the Weimar prison and later to Ichtershausen, where he died.

As stated in their messages sent on October 7, the Witnesses continued to prosyletize, meet, and study. Many were arrested and tortured along with their families. A father arrested in December 1934 with his wife and son saw his family sentenced to prison terms after they were brutalized by their torturers.

Another Witness, arrested by the criminal police, signed the criminal registry under the heading "religious martyr." Initially freed by the investigating judge, he was later rearrested and transferred to a concentration camp. He recalls his arrival at the camp, where he was taunted with threats and insults: "Among other things they called Jehovah's Witnesses 'heaven's jokes,' 'Jesus-catchers,' 'birds of paradise,' and other such clever appellations." He also remembered threats that an SS officer made against him: "The head cook took out his revolver, placed it against my temple, and told me I would die if I persisted in remaining a Witness."

Freed, having served his term, he fled persecution and emigrated abroad.

6

SURVIVAL

> There was earth in them. They dug. They spent their days and nights digging.
>
> —Paul Celine

On June 30, 1934, during the "Night of the Long Knives," 1,000 SA officerswere killed, along with their chief, Ernst Rohm. Thereafter, concentration camp administration, which had been in the hands of the SS, was assigned from to the inspectorate of concentration camps through December 1934. Theodor Eicke, former commandant at Dachau, assumed responsibility for camp organization.

An internal order, dated August 1934 at the Esterwegen camp, stated,

> The inmate will have plenty of time to think about the reasons which brought him to camp; he will have the opportunity to make honorable amends to his homeland and compatriots, and to recognize the merits of the National Socialist regime, unless, from a purely personal point of view, he prefers to die for the shameful ends of the second or third judeo-marxist international of a Marx or Lenin.
>
> No prisoner will be authorized to wear civilian clothing inside the camp. . . . All new arrivals will have their head completely shaved. . . .
>
> No matter what their origin, their profession or social standing, all camp inmates are considered inferior. All whether young or old, must on arrival submit to military discipline and rules.

> All SS, up to camp commandant, have the upper hand over inmates who owe them strict obedience without any discussion. . . .
>
> Prisoners will be required, in conformance with discipline, to display the respect to all SS ranks that is owed military personnel; they must stand at attention as soon as an SS address them. . . .
>
> All prisoners, without exception, are assigned manual labor. Their origin, personal situation, or profession will not be taken into account. Whomsoever refuses to work or shirks or fakes an infirmity or sickness to avoid work will be considered incorrigible, with all consequences flowing from these actions. The camp commandant is the only one qualified to set the duration of work hours in the entire camp. Starting and finishing times will be signaled by a siren or bell. If the needs of the camp require and, with the approval of the camp commandant, work may continue beyond normal hours as well as on Sundays and holidays.

Whatever the camp—Dachau, Esterwegen, Oranienburg, or Sachsenburg—inmates' lives were burdened with suffering, pain, and the annihilation of their human state. Inmates were beaten on arrival and tortured. At one time, Witnesses were whipped as soon as they entered camp, immediately receiving twenty-five lashes of a steel rod. A Witness described these punitive "gymnastics" sessions to which he and fellow Witnesses were subjected while lying naked on the hard tiles and hosed with alternating jets of boiling and freezing water. He remembered during one of these "sports" sessions that one of them was carried off unconscious on four occasions.

Bruno Bettelheim, the celebrated psychiatrist at the Chicago Orthogenic Clinic, was interned prior to World War II for a year in Dachau, then at Buchenwald. He analyzed the behavior of individuals in extreme hardship, poorly housed, underdressed and underfed, exposed to harsh elements seventeen hours a day and concluded, "If one wished to survive as a man, debased and degraded, but all the same human, and not become a walking cadaver, one had to be aware above all—and keep it in mind—of one's individual point-of-no-return beyond which one could, under no circumstances, give in to the oppressor, even at the risk of one's life. This implied that one was aware that beyond this threshold, life would have lost its meaning. One survived not by having diminished respect for himself, but having none."

To survive, inmates had to have an ideal or goal to hang on to, whether it was a loved one, revenge, or the chance to provide future testimony. Bettelheim notes, "It is a fact of concentration camp life that those with religious and moral convictions survived better than the others. Their faith, and their belief in an afterlife, gave them the strength to bear an ordeal which went beyond most of their comrades." He then remarked how concentration camp prisoners, displaying great reserves and putting affective distance between themselves and their companions, maintained their former personality structure and value system throughout even the worst ordeals: "Their personality was hardly affected by living conditions in the camp. I encountered similar behavior in another group of individuals which, from an analytical standpoint, would be considered extremely neurotic and even delirious and therefore vulnerable to psychiatric disintegration in time of crisis. I am referring to the Jehovah's Witnesses. Not only did they display exceptional moral behavior, they seemed protected against the influence of the camp environment that rapidly destroyed persons that our psychiatrist friends, and even I, would have judged well integrated."

For Bettelheim, when the SS dealt with an inmate, "if he was cruelly treated and humiliated it was with conscious or unconscious intent to show him that he was no different from the other prisoners. This had the effect of distinguishing him, even as the SS underscored the contempt they felt for him. These outrages were of a personal nature because they were directed against his very person. He was not interchangeable with other prisoners. It may be that is why the self-respect of this category was not as radically destroyed as the others were. By being 'set apart' in the ways they were mistreated, was this not a way they could remain individuals?"

Franz Zurcher outlined a similar situation for the *Bibelforscher*: "As soon as Jehovah's Witnesses arrived in camp a 'special welcome' was accorded them." We can only imagine what this was.

7

THE "NEGROES" IN EUROPE

General von Blomberg, a soldier in the Reichswehr tradition, took over as war minister, navy minister, and, on Hindenburg's death, commander-in-chief of the Reichswehr under the authority of Hitler. In order to understand the events that followed under the Third Reich, it should be noted that the Reichswehr was an all-volunteer army, annihilated following 1918 and loyal to the Weimar Republic. Its soldiers were, for the most part, nonpolitical and acted with patriotic fervor for "the people and homeland."

Hitler won over the leadership of the Reichswehr, von Blomberg, and especially von Fritsch with deceit. He organized meetings between the heads of the SA and the Reichswehr in 1934. It is important to recall Ernst Rohm's wish to submerge the "gray rock" of the Reischwehr under the "brown wave of the SA."

Because of its history and development, the Reichswehr was unable to provide a solid base of opposition to Hitler; moreover, it was in a complete state of disarray since its 100,000 men were used to staff and train a volunteer army that was to become the Wehrmacht. The Wehrmacht was also under active rearmament according to Hitler's wishes. He pledged in 1934 that he considered it "his sacred duty to insure the continuity and inviolability of the Wehrmacht, and to root it as the only body authorized to bear arms." General von Blomberg imposed an oath on all soldiers of absolute obedience to Hitler as Reichsführer. The decree of March 16, establishing universal military service and the occupation of the Rhineland, violated terms of the Treaty of Versailles. The Wehrmacht was rearmed secretly but then later in full view of the victors of 1918. The victor's acquiescence would embolden

Hilter to press his campaign for domination even further in the time ahead.

Göring's March 3 circular, addressed to police authorities, authorized wide latitude for actions that constituted "protection of the State endangered by communist violence" in these terms: "In accordance with the aims and subject of the decree-law, additional measures will be applied against not only the communists, but also against all those who collaborate, support, or encourage them—even indirectly—in their criminal pursuits."

On March 21, three new decrees, which proved to be extremely important, including the Reich president's right of special exception, significantly modified the German legal system.

The first law granted amnesty for all criminal acts committed "during the struggle for the national resurgence of the German people." The amnesty decree waived all sentences handed down on National Socialists for political acts and crimes. The second law was the so-called Criminal Gossip law, which was careful to curb even verbal criticism of the new regime by prison terms and, in serious cases, forced labor. The third law created the "special tribunals." On March 15, the Jehovah's Witnesses were tried by the special tribunal in Hamburg as conscientous objectors and sentenced with the following condemnation: "That which prevails is a general tendency which characterizes the Witnesses, which infringes upon good behavior and violates the moral sentiments of the German race. . . . Germans have never wanted to a nation of servants. The doctrines professed by the Witnesses run counter to this fundamental wisdom." The Hamburg special tribunal expanded the February decree in its March verdict by stating, "The decree-law promulgated following the Reichstag fire on February 18, 1933, was not only applicable to the communist threat endangering the State but also applied against those who come from other surroundings."

On April 1, a national law was passed forbidding all the Witnesses' activities. The law also deprived them of the right of public service, denying them the opportunity to hold government jobs. This led to numerous dismissals, and many Witnesses became unable to practice their professions.

A secret Gestapo order clearly indicates that the secret police sought to crush the Witnesses: "State Secret Police, Berlin, 20 March 1935. According to *God's Battle,* writings confiscated from the Bible Students, groups of the anointed will probably meet on April 17, 1935, after six o'clock in the evening for a feast commemorating the sacrifice of Jesus Christ for the glory of Jehovah. It may be that an unannounced visit to the homes of the leaders of the Bible Students will be successful. Please advise results. Signed: Hardtmann." Another circular, dated April 3, suggested, "A surprise attack on that date against known leaders of the Witnesses should be successful. Please advise, before April 22nd, the success of your efforts."

A number of Jehovah's Witnesses "classed as noxious elements to the State" were arrested. Some were fined and others sentenced to detention for violation of the law that they voluntarily broke by meeting together. A Witness later recalled, "I was arrested during the commemorative dinner and transported to the concentration camp at Lichtenberg. I suffered greatly there." Martin Broszat also notes, "Beginning in 1935, a new category of internees placed in protective detention (*Schutzhaftgefangene*), began to make up important groupings in the concentration camps called *Internationale Vereinigung der Ernsten Bibelforscher*, or Jehovah's Witnesses. This organization of *Bibelforscher* had already been dissolved by the Third Reich in 1933, and all Witness recruiting activities had been legally banned because they were viewed a group whose goal was sabotaging the foundations of Germany's military defense."

On May 29, in conformity with the decision of the Braunschweig tribunal (Brunswick), the Watch Tower Society's publishing arm was disbanded. "In order to defend against harmful acts of communist violence against the State, it appears equally opportune to ban such associations which may, without their leaders being aware, harbor friends of the communists." Recall that on radio on February 1, the government broadcast a statement that assigned responsibility for the disorder, then reigning in Germany, on Marxist parties.

As attorney Ernst Fraenkel remarked, this verdict took no account of the principle of the right of proportionality since it was the police who evaluated that which was harmful and invoked the argument that the *Bibelforscher* might offer an eventual hiding place for Communists. Police decisions were not subject to judicial control or review, and officials reported only through police hierarchy. This duality of procedures and law remained a distinguishing feature of the Third Reich—that of a dual state as aptly characterized in anti-Fascist Fraenkel's book.

In applying the Law on Representations of Factories and Economic Associations, the labor tribunal of Onasbrück ruled on July 30, 1935, that the "Heil Hitler" salute should be considered part of the attributions and duties of all salaried employees. "Every manager is authorized to dismiss, at his convenience, employees in his establishment suspected of acts hostile to the State without their being able to appeal by invoking labor laws." Whomsoever persevered in opposing this salute was to be fired, even if the recidivist delinquent had scrupulously performed his duty for twenty or thirty years or more. Jehovah's Witnesses (railway and postal employees and government civil servants in education and public health positions or working in the private sector) were fired without indemnification and most often incarcerated.

Heinrich Dickmann from Dinslaken, who was subjected to Nazi mistreatment on the eve of the November 1933 elections, was dismissed in May 1935 on orders of the German Labor Front for his refusal to give the Nazi salute, failure to participate in the balloting, and refusal to join the Front. He was jailed as a saboteur under *Schutzhaft* for ten days as an enemy of the state. During the summer of 1935, the Nazis proceeded with numerous arrests against Witnesses in their homes and subjected them to inhuman interrogations designed to force them to denounce other believers or, worse yet, to renounce their faith. There is the case of an interrogation that lasted seven days. The first four days, the victim was beaten by his torturers during the questioning. Then, the fifth day, the protocol chief called him back to the same room as the day before, and he was not mistreated but was warned that at two o'clock in the afternoon he would have to confess where he stood. Other than the truncheon blows and the high-pressure hosings, the prisoner was bound up and had his fingertips crushed. This treatment was inflicted when the beatings did not produce the desired recantation.

During August, the local newspapers reported numerous arrests. The *Coburger Nationalzeitung* reported that sixteen Bible Students were sentenced to prison terms at Altenburg. The special tribunal ruled that "the Bible Students was not a religious community." The *Goeppingen Tagblatt* reported the appearance before the Ulm tribunal of forty-three Bible Students who had "held meetings at their homes between the first week of October and the beginning of December 1934."

Six others from Greiz and Cossengruen were also sentenced. The chief judge's ruling reads, "Persons who place their beliefs above love for their homeland are not part of the people's community and deserve to be treated as enemies. Their activity threatens the State and the homeland."

Nevertheless, the Witnesses did not allow themselves to be intimidated, and they continued practicing their faith. Seventeen of them appeared before the Breslau tribunal on October 1, 1935. They were accused of breaking the Law on People's and State Security, enacted February 28 of that year, and for having met to study the Bible. They were sentenced to fines and detention terms, and some were even sent to concentration camps. A former political prisoner at Sachsenburg who published his memoires in Prague tells of "Jehovah's Witnesses . . . 400 of them were at Sachsenburg during the summer of 1935. . . . Most often it was the new arrivals, Jews and Jehovah's Witnesses, who were assigned the dreaded jobs at the quarry and especailly a sand quarry."

On September 12, 1935, at Sachsenburg, five inmates in "protective custody" were brutally beaten with a riding crop by SS camp commandant Schmidt, who, red in the face, yelled "damned pig, go ahead and beg your Jehovah for help. Why doesn't he come to your help. Beg him to destroy us so that you can take your turn at trampling on us."

The man, after being beaten savagely, collapsed unconscious. Some SS officers threw buckets of water on the unfortunate. "Then Dr. Gebhardt, the camp doctor, approached and ordered:

Take him away." Two SS chiefs stood him up and took him away without any care like an "exhausted beast."

In July 1935, a Witness was executed at the Esterwagen concentration camp "*auf der Flucht*," or "shot during escape." The guards at the camps often encouraged or intimidated inmates to go past camp boundaries in order to shoot at them as escapees. Shooting an escaping prisoner earned these guards extra pass days.

In 1935, some internees at the Kemma concentration camp near Wuppertsal were locked up in a narrow cabinet and then tortured. Cigarette smoke was blown into the cabinet to disrupt their breathing, and the cabinet was tipped. In some camps, the internees were forced to eat salted herring in order to inflict a thirst torture on them. At a concentration camp in Hamburg, four prisoners were tied to a cross, once for five days and three nights and another time for five days and five nights. So poorly nourished were these inmates that they nearly starved to death.

At the Esterwegen camp, several Witnesses were tied up at the arm and knee joints with rope and beaten with an ox bone. Nonetheless, they still did not renounce their faith.

Heinrich Dickmann recalls, "The morning assembly call was set for seven o'clock, but before then we had to all wash up and eat in a rush. Then the *Kommandos* (work details) left for work. The jobs were senseless at Esterwegen; the only aim was to work us to death."

The Witnesses refused to sign the following act of renunciation that was presented to them by the SS and Gestapo during their interrogations and incarceration:

> I, the undersigned . . .
> born on . . .
> herewith make the following declaration:
>
> 1. I have come to know that the International Association of Jehovah's Witnesses professes a false doctrine and pursues subversive goals under the cloak of religious activities.
> 2. I, therefore, left the organization entirely and made myself absolutely free from the teachings of this sect.
> 3. I affirm herein never again to participate in the activities

of the International Association of Jehovah's Witnesses. I will immediately denounce any person attempting to win me over with the false doctrine of Jehovah's Witnesses or reveal his own membership in this sect. I will immediately remit to the police all publications which come to me from this organization.

4. In future, I wish to observe the laws of the State and to defend my homeland in the event of war, weapon in hand, and join in every way the community of the people.
5. I have been informed that I will at once be taken into protective custody if I should again act against the declaration given today.

[Date]
[Signature]

Almost all the Witnesses resisted the pressure to sign the statement. A few succumbed to the mistreatment. The ease with which they escaped punishment held an implicit threat for all Germans. A citizen could be accepted or consigned to misery: "Today a one-hundred-percent Aryan can easily become a 'Negro' in his own country if, for example, he is a socialist, a democrat, or if he holds the Gospel as a higher law than various Government directives."

8

Der Anstreicher

> Nero burned Rome to persecute the Christians. Goering burned the Reichstag to persecute the communists.
>
> —Lambert horn, political director of the KPD, 28 February 1933

All soldiers, bureaucrats, and even government ministers were required to swear an oath of loyalty to Adolf Hitler—chief of the Reich and of the German people. The reestablishment of a personal oath restored of aspects of the monarchy. In reality, however, Hitler's total power and control far exceeded those enjoyed by any monarch. The notion of "divine right" was replaced by a model in which the Führer was both a savior sent by providence and the incarnation of the unspoken will of the people.

Sentences handed down by civil and administrative courts of the Third Reich provide an snapshot of the practice of Nazi "justice." Attorney Ernst Fraenkel also cites "the case of a postal employee who had been a Witness, but who, since the organization was prohibited, was no longer participating in their meetings." Nevertheless, his religious convictions prevented him from saluting with a "Heil Hitler!" He lost his postal job. The sentence handed down on February 11, 1936, included the charge that "the accused cannot and should not invoke religious considerations."

Other verdicts punished those would not salute men as gods or those who refused to renounce their faith. In March 1936, a Reich railway worker was fired because he failed to obey an order to give the Nazi salute. "During questioning I was ordered to acknowledge that Hitler was sent by God. I answered that God had sent Jesus Christ." The worker steadfastly refused to acknowledge any other "Führer" than Jehovah and Jesus Christ.

Not only did the Witnesses repeatedly refuse to give the Nazi salute, but they persisted in their refusal to participate in the voting or to wear a military uniform and serve in the army. During the 1936 elections for the Reichstag, they refused to deposit their votes in the ballot boxes. The Nazi reaction was swift and vicious. They attacked the homes of the Witnesses with paint or attacked them personally with blackjack. They also had them fired from their jobs with no judicial recourse. One Witness found the word "Traitor" painted on the front of his home.

Another Witness attempted to explain to three SA officers why he had not voted. "Without allowing me to finish, they beat me so hard that I fell down on the floor. When my wife came running, she was also badly treated."

However, this maltreatment was nothing compared to the abuse visited on Witnesses that same evening by some uniformed SS troops:

"Why didn't you vote?"

"I have always been uninterested in politics because I have faith that God will solve all problems."

"Who is your Führer?"

"God is my Führer."

"Adolf Hitler is our God and Führer. What is your God's name?" (the SS yelled).

"My God is called Jehovah."

On hearing the name Jehovah, the four SS officers beat their victim brutally, then forced him to lick his own blood off the floor. They continued to beat him, banging his head against the wall. They forced him again to lick his own blood. They left him half dead after beating him one last time.

On April 28, the labor tribunal at Kaiserslautern heard the case of Mr. Lichtenhagen, a town employee who had refused to participate in the voting. He was dismissed for having "placed religious requirements over national requirements."

Himmler, jealous of the power that Göring's Gestapo had

amassed, was determined that the State's Secret Police would become the *only* organization authorized to decide who was sent to the camps. He used the Gestapo's growing influence to enhance his own influence. The suppression of provincial autonomy, strengthened centralization, the unification of the police forces, as well as the increasing privileges accorded the Gestapo strengthened Himmler's powers. On June 17, 1936, he became head of the German police forces attached to the Interior Ministry and chief of the SS (Reichsführer SS).

An ordinance dissolving the Association of Jehovah's Witnesses was issued several days later. It was based on Article 48 of the Reich Constitution and predicated on the notion to "defense against acts of communist violence endangering the State." A tradeswoman who was close to the Jehovah's Witnesses was refused her request for a license. The Bavarian administrative tribunal justified its refusal by alleging, "It has not been proven that Maria S. is a member of the forbidden Association of Jehovah's Witnesses. On the other hand, it has been proved that she conforms absolutely to this association. . . . She has . . . also refused to state that she will not act on behalf of the Witnesses in the future. This mindset and its spread is hostile to the State . . . because she has insulted the State and the Church, alienated the people and the State and serves the cause of pacifism which is incompatible and in absolute contradiction to the heroic ideology and daily life of the State and people."

In June 1936, a special budget was set up for the Reich's concentration camps. Their network was centralized under the auspices of the inspectorate of concentration camps. In August, the Sachsenhausen concentration camp was established, succeeding the Oranienburg camp, which was disbanded in 1935.

"On July 7th Eicke ordered the transfer of 150 inmates from Sachsenhausen, 75 from Lichtenburg and 75 from Sachsenburg, to be chosen by *Obersturmbannführer* Koch, to the new camp at Buchenwald, Koch's new command. Initially, 149 common law inmates arrived at Ettersbeg. The first roll call was held on July 19, 1937. The next day, 70 more prisoners arrived, followed eight days later by first political prisoners from Sachsenburg. Among these were seven Jehovah's Witnesses."

Jean Bezaut described how the first fifty inmates arrived from Esterwegen in mid-July and had to clear brush, level the site, and build the new camp under appalling conditions, with no limit to hours worked. "When the camp was under construction, there was no regulated work day. Work hours were unlimited, with breaks only at noon and in the evening for meals. On several occasions the inmates were given only four hours of sleep. The work proceeded at an insane pace. Any slackening resulted in immediate assignment to the disciplinary company."

On June 24, the Gestapo created a "special command" whose mission was to infiltrate several groups of Witnesses. Informants had told the Gestapo that a Witness congress was scheduled for Lucerne during the first week of September.

A confidential secret police memo dated August 21 gave the following order: "[They] must be stopped from leaving the country. Their passports must be confiscated."

A wave of arrests followed. On August 28, thousands of people were rounded up: "During the summer of 1936 at Wiesbaden, the SS began persecution of Jehovah's Witnesses. They were subjected to terrible and exhausting questioning. A 25-year-old woman was interrogated for forty hours over a period of several days—once for eight uninterrupted hours."

Other inmates were beaten until they fainted. At the Steinwache prison at Dortmund, Gestapo agents, especially Knoop and Theiss, inflicted ceaseless cruelties. The latter, during his interrogations, employed methods worthy of the Inquisition, and his actions would leave indelible memories on the victims.

Hitler believed in the "laws of nature" and the eternal struggle of races and in the "law of the strongest."

9

YOU ARE ACCUSED OF TEN THOUSAND CRIMES: YOU KNOW NOTHING

> You have been accused of 10,000 crimes. You learned to open your eyes to emptiness, beyond which only God exists.
>
> —Jakub Deml

Because of the campaign of harassment and arrests, only a third of the expected Jehovah's Witnesses were able to travel to Lucerne in early September. The rest were interned. The some 300 Witnesses in attendance confirmed the persecution. A resolution supporting the Witnesses and protesting the cruelty was drafted and sent to both Hitler and the pope. As many as 3,000 copies were sent to the Reich leadership. The mailings were sent from Bern on September 9. Registered receipts show these were delivered. On the afternoon of December 12, more than 300,000 copies of the text were distributed. The statement was handed out in broad daylight by 3,500 Witnesses in the cities of Berlin, Hamburg, Munich, Leipzig, Dresden, Freiburg, and all the main cities of the Ruhr. At the end of 1936, theWitnesses also sent 10,000 letters to prosecutors and judges in the Third Reich accompanied, as an attachment, by the statement and brochures.

The Gestapo continued to track the Witnesses down, and arrests continued. On December 12, a female Witness was arrested in Dortmund and taken to Steinwache prison. Brought before

Theiss and accused of passing out the Lucerne statement, she recalls how the enraged Theiss erupted: "We will not tolerate foreign Gods in our midst. We will crush them under our boots."

The same day in Munich, Gertrud and Martin Potzinger were arrested. Gertrud had been detained but was released in February 1937 because no proof against her could be found. "The detention itself was not as hard as those cruel interrogations. For me that was a true torture." According to the report of the prosecutor-general of Karlsruhe, 382 sentences were handed down against the Witnesses in 1936 in the Baden grand duchy, twice as many as during the preceding year. One of them, Hermann Emter, arrested because of his activities after the Lucerne Congress, was deported from camp to camp: Dachau to Mauthausen, back to Dachau to Flossenburg, and finally to Buchenwald (it should be noted that until July 29, the Buchenwald camp was known as Ettersberg), and his wife did not return from the concentration camp.

Witnesses were also arrested in Germany at funerals. In Bielefeld, twenty-three appeared before the tribunal after one of them had given a speech over a fellow member's grave. To Nazi authorities, burials represented an occasion to arrest Witnesses for violating the ban against public meetings.

The Nazi Party organ, the *Angriff*, demanded the firing of Witnesses in all German firms. Three members of the Jehovah's Witness community in Chemnitz were dismissed without judicial recourse.

On December 4, 1936, an administrative tribunal in Saxony refused to issue a work permit to a midwife suspected of being a Witness. The court, having proved nothing, concluded that her demeanor and profession of faith "supports efforts designed directly to harm the people."

When Mayence cemetery worker Gertrud Franke learned that contributions for the German Labor Front had been withheld from her pay, she protested and was fired. Refusing to affiliate herself with the Front, she was unable to collect any unemployment insurance and could find no work.

It should be pointed out that some company heads and magistrates courageously came to the rescue of Witnesses under duress. Carl Gohring, fired from his company for refusing to sign up with the Front, found work at M. Kornelius's stationery shop in Weissenfels.

As Eugen Kogon noted, "The Jehovah's Witnesses were 'exported' from the United States to Europe around 1880. After World War I they had spread considerably until they were banned for refusing to bear arms or swear an oath of loyalty in 1933, as well as the fact they deemed all public institutions as 'the Devil's work.' " They saw the Front as one of the "Devil's works." The Jehovah's Witnesses refused to wear the military uniform and bear "Satan's arms." At the end of December, Gestapo headquarters sent a circular to its members concerning Witnesses: "They refuse to perform military service and try to influence the youth. To this end they handed out tracts which began with these words: 'I am obliged to make you aware of my intention that I will not take part in exercise of a military nature. Bearing arms would be contrary to my convictions.' "

Explaining their refusal to serve a kingdom other than Jehovah's, their attitude can be compared to Daniel Parker's: "When then will Christians understand that one of their most urgent and most essential tasks is to prove to men, their own brothers, that it is impossible to fight against evil with violence, lies and war?" Despite his reservation about the Witness doctrine, Parker felt that "we should render well deserved homage to the Jehovah's Witnesses: sustained on this point by a very firm doctrine and by the support and prayers of the little communities to which they belong, they remain unshakable in their faith in Jesus Christ. . . . More than 24,000 conscientious objectors were executed in prison on Hitler's orders. Most had their heads severed by ax. Among those were a great number of Jehovah's Witnesses."

It should be noted that the Witnesses were and are in conflict with the authorities in many countries. In the United States, for example, they were not recognized as conscientious objectors because they refused the use of force utterly: They were awaiting the battle of Armageddon, the final combat when Satan would be vanquished.

During the first three years of Hitler's reign, many decrees were enacted. All these laws betray the Nazis' desire to disguise the illegality of their actions. Condemnation of the Witnesses was thus justified by a torrent of decrees and decisions referring one to another. In January 1937, Himmler wrote of their role and that of the concentration camps: "First and foremost be convinced that no person is wrongly interned in concentration camps." The SS and the Gestapo could always find a specious justification to detain adversaries.

On January 19, the minister of foreign affairs provided his staff with the list of concentration camps. We know that the Nazis centralized the unofficial camps (opened in 1933 and 1934) under the direction of the SS and the Gestapo. Dachau, Lichtenberg, Sachsenburg, Sachsenhausen, and Salsa were among the camps effeted by this centralization. Two weeks later, Hitler announced that inmates would be subject to forced labor during his speech at the Reichstag.

The Witnesses were not only interned in concentration camps but were also being held in insane asylums and psychiatric hospitals. In August 1936, the wife of a Witness was informed that her husband had died in a lunatic asylum. His body was riddled with punctures from injections. On January 20, 1937, another Witness under lockup in the police prison was transferred to an asylum where he was chained up and beaten.

10

"ALLE JUGEND DEM FÜHRER"

By law, all German youths aged ten to eighteen years old were required to join the Hitler Youth. Commenting on the persecution of the witnesses, Eugen Kogon wrote, "It was a shame of National Socialism that families were broken up, children taken away from their families and that parents were sent away to camps for adults." The National Socialist state extended an iron grip over everyone; even children had to belong, body and soul. Many Witness children and adolescents were taken away from their parents, separated from their relatives, and subjected to intense pressures—sent to reformatories, entrusted to Nazi families, and even deported or shot. The Nazi goal was global domination. In order to achieve that, destruction of German families was necessary. The world would be German, and in Hitler's eyes, that which was not Nazi could not be German. In 1938, Erika Mann wrote, "If the world was to belong to the Nazis, Germans had to belong to the Nazis—not to God, family, or even themselves." Under the merciless gaze of the Nazi power structure, utter loyalty to Hitler became the supreme commandment.

As early as 1932, Hitler was exhorting his political allies to keep a watch over children's education: "I wish to say, comrades, this will be the future social order: there will be a master class, a class with an historic mission emerging during the struggle with the most diverse of elements; there will be a throng of party members, organized hierarchically—they will make up the middle class; and there will be the anonymous masses, a community of servants. . . . Lower down there will also be the subjugated class of foreign races, lets us simply refer to them as the class of modern slaves.

. . . There must be only one education for each class and in its way for each particular level. Full freedom of education is the privilege of the class of elites and those admitted into it. . . . And, consequently, we will allow the large mass of the inferior classes the well-being of illiteracy."

During a speech at Weimar in June 1933, Hitler stated, "If there are still those in Germany today who say: we will not submit, then I respond: you will *disappear*—and after you will come a youth that will know nothing else."

The "training" of the youth and all educational programs were closely monitored by the Nazis. Bernhart Ruse, an NSDAP member, was named minister of religions in 1933 and was charged with responsibility for the Ministry for Science and Public Education in April 1934. The number of school years was reduced as was the duration of the school day. Teachers had no say in the changes. In mid-July, decrees were issued calling on teachers to break off all contact with the Social Democratic Party, observe the common cause, and draw their inspiration from Hitler's screed *Mein Kampf*. Nazi committees were formed to keep an eye on "good order," and school books were reviewed, revised, and rewritten along ideological lines.

The Law on Hitler Youth evinced the control that the NSDAP had over German youth and the value that Nazi leaders placed in this issue. "The future of the German people depends on the youth. All German youth must be prepared to undertake their future obligations. Consequently, the government of the Reich has taken its legal decision and promulgated the following:

> 1. All German youth inside Reich territory are rallied together in the Hitler Youth.
>
> 2. All German youths are to be educated bodily, morally, and spiritually in the spirit of National Socialism: in their parents' home; at school; and in the Hitler Youth for service to the people and the people's community.
>
> The task in educating all German youth inside the Hitler Youth is entrusted to the Chief of the Reich's Youth of the NSDAP. He also becomes "Chief of the Youth of the German Reich" with headquarters in Berlin and reports directly to the Fuhrer and Reich Chancellor.

4. Legal arrangements and administrative decrees of a general nature necessary for the application and amendment of this law will be promulgated by the Führer and Reich Chancellor.

On June 17, 1933, Baldur von Schirach was appointed Führer of the Reich German Youth. By the end of 1934, the Hitler Youth had 3.5 million members. On October 4, 1934, Baldur requested that Secretary of State Heinrich Lammer invite all Reich ministries "to grant, if possible, the request of the Youth Führer who wishes to be consulted before decisions are taken on laws affecting German youth. On March 4, 1937, the German Youth chief issued the slogan "Alle Jugend dem Fuhrer" (All German Youth for the Führer), reflecting unconditional submisiveness to Hitler.

In 1941, that phrase was changed to "Unser Leben Ein Weg zum Führer" (Our life—a road toward Hitler). By that time, National Socialist propaganda was pervasive: German youth were subjected to propaganda in school, in the Hitler Youth movement, in youth camps, and during courses in self-defense. The entire system was oriented at encouraging youngsters to use force and believe in the superiority of the Aryan race. The December 1936 law on the Hitler Youth included the organization as a part of the state structure. It also invested von Schirach, the national leader of the Youth movment, with a position of supreme authority in the Reich.

A conversation that Erika Mann had with a young German woman in St. Gall, Switzerland, explains the dilemma in poignant human terms. The woman, married to a doctor, wanted to flee Germany because of her son. She wanted "this little boy to become a man—a man and not a Nazi." This mother pondered the education her son would receive if they were able to leave Munich: "He wouldn't learn about *Rassenschande* and how we do our best to wipe out the French, the Jews, and the *Bibelforscher.* He would know about justice and who is just and not what we are taught. He would learn to *be* somebody when he grows up, and he wouldn't practice target shooting. He wouldn't denounce me and would like me to talk with him and would listen willingly. He would love and serve the country we emigrate to, but he would learn, so to speak, to be filled with the love of freedom and justice."

Three weeks after speaking with the woman, Erika Mann learned that the couple had been arrested in Munich. "For having spoken out many times and denigrating the system being built by National Socialism," her husband was deported to Dachau, and she was arrested. Mann relates, "Little 14-month-old Franz M., son of the guilty couple, was placed in a State children's home. A newspaper of the day reported, 'It is to be hoped it will succeed in making the child a good national socialist.' "

Ernst Frankel cites a ruling of the regional tribunal of Hamburg in June 1936 that took several Witness children from the care of their parents and who were not allowed to grow up in their parents' faith for fear that "the spiritual well-being [of the children] would be gravely imperiled."

Pursuing the same policy, the government of Saxony and its minister of public education addressed a circular to public education advisers requesting them to draft "a report on observations teachers have made regarding the children of Witnesses. It would be helpful to note whether these children, as a result of family influence, display any hostile behavior against the State and passively resist all attempts to bring their thinking around." Children's education was closely supervised, and the grounds given for a decision taken by a pupil's council, handed down on March 7, 1937, read, "The National Socialist State can only harbor elements attached to its principles. It cannot tolerate a display of divergent opinions by others, and it must take proper care of German children's education—even if the children are their own." This charge derives directly from Hitler's own words, which have already been quoted. Walther Hamel, a Nazi constitutional law "expert," wrote in one of his books in 1935, "If education, that is to say the establishment of national conduct, is the duty of the State, then the police should have at their disposal the means of education—including the strictest detention."

By the end of May 1937, a Witness named Max Ruef fled to Switzerland with one of his children to prevent that child from falling into the hands of the Nazis. Since 1934, the Nazis had unleashed their full fury on the family. In May 1934, they were forced to sell their property, and in December 1936, Ruef was sentenced to six months in jail by a Munich special tribunal for breaking the law forbidding prayer and hymns in his home. He left behind a wife who was six months pregnant and two children, ages nine and ten.

On March 27, 1937, Ruef was granted three days of freedom because his wife had died. Part of the nursing staff at the hospital at the clinic where his wife went for the birth advised him to file a complaint, as she had been in perfect health at the time of delivery. Returning home, he found that the newborn baby had also died, and he then decided to escape. He left one child with his in-laws and went into exile in Switzerland with the other. Unfortunately, Ruef's escape to safety was a rare occurrence.

11

A LYNCHING OF CONSCIENCES

Among snakes of the earth, there is no peace.
—Max Jacob

Many Witnesses lost their children for refusing to perform the Nazi salute. Their children were sent off to schools to be reeducated. A statement signed by a Mr. Mergenthaler, dated April 1937, decreed that the *Kulturminister* sent from Stuttgart be responsible for dealing with failure to perform the Nazi salute in public schools. Such failure, said the statement, could never be permitted for reasons of personal conscience "that it was impossible not to give the German salute and at the same time wish good health to the Führer and Chancellor of the German Reich." In plain language, students who refused to give the salute were considered troublemakers. If the children refusing to salute were of school age, "immediate supervised education is indicated in conformity with para. 67 of the Reich law for the social providence of the youth stated the proceedings of the cantonal tribunal referring to the decree."

Children were required to make the Nazi salute at all times. A ministerial decree of January 5, 1934, ordered that "Heil Hitler" be repeated at the beginning and end of catechism classes. Erika Mann estimated that children uttered "Heil Hitler" up to 150 times a day. She conducted her own tally of those places where the phrase was repeated: on the way to school, among friends, at the beginning and end of the day, and at the beginning and end of each course. Civic employees were also encouraged to repeat it:

"The mailman, the train conductor and the saleslady at the shop where they bought their notebooks all used the phrase." Even at home, there was the risk of denunciation if they did not make the gesture and say "Heil Hitler!"

Young boys and girls in the different Hitler Youth groups also had to say "Heil Hitler." "The children's evening prayer ended with *Heil Hitler!* . . . They had to raise and extend their arm while uttering *Heil Hitler!*"

Willi Seitz, a child born on March 11, 1932, in Karlsruhe, told how he was segregated and forbidden to talk to his classmates: "In other words, I was hated and made fun of as though I was a mangy dog." His mistreatment at the hands of his fellow classmates can be traced to the sentence handed down by Karlsruhe Court B III: "Willi Seitz was expelled from the public school because he refused to take part in school patriotic holidays, and to sing patriotic songs such as *Deutschlandlied* and the *Horst Wesellied.* It was alleged that he would only give his loyalty to the God who created heaven and earth." His parents were notified by the tribunal that for these reasons he was being assigned to the reeducation center in Flehingen.

The civil tribunal of Karlsruhe explained its reasons in the sentence

> Re: parental authority over Willi Joseph Seitz, born March 11, 1923: He stated to the school principal that he would not become a soldier, and also gave his views on current events in two homework assignments. This minor child is not able to feel German or to acquire an understanding of the grandeur of the German people. A violation of these obligations on the parents' part should be considered a subjective offense accordance with para. 1666 RGBl. Contrary to the father's depositions, the court is convinced that the son's attitude is due to the parents' influence. The father admits to being a Jehovah's Witness.
>
> Signed: v. Frankenberg.

Willie's father did his utmost to keep his son from going to the Flehingen reformatory and to keep him from being sent to an SS *Obergruppenführer* later. He managed to get him a passport and sent him to the Alsace-Lorraine section of France. In June 1937, he arranged for the son to cross the Weiseburg border and enter Bern in Switzerland.

In January 1936, Willi's father lost his jobs in the public baths' administration and at the municipal hospital because he refused to perform the Nazi salute. Although he had served for twenty-three years, he was denied retirement benefits, and unemployment insurance was withheld from him for sixteen weeks. He was sentenced to four months in lockup by the special tribunal in Mannheim for meeting with other Witnesses, and on his release he resumed his activities. Rearrested, he was deported to Buchenwald. His son was safe in Switzerland.

Adolf Muhlhauser was in the *Schutzhaft* from June to November 1936 and then held at the Mannheim prison from November 1936 until May 1938. Later, he was sent to Dachau and finally to Mauthausen, where he died. His wife, Emma, was already in *Schutzhaft* for five months from March to August 1936 in the Mannheim prison. After four months of imprisonment at Gotteszell, she was deported to Ravensbrück for over five years, which ended in May 1945. Fritz, their son, who was twelve in 1939, was summoned before the Youth Office and sent to a reeducation center despite the fact that his parents had entrusted him to his adult sister. It should be also noted that the Muhlhauser family plot was taken from them. As Jehovah's Witnesses, they were adjudged unworthy of cultivating German soil.

Gunter Strenge, whose father was arrested and sentenced to a three-year prison term, refused to learn patriotic songs at school. His school principal, Mr. Hanneberg , threatened to "hit him on the finger until it became so bloody and swollen that he could not stick it up his [rectum]." When the principal asked this child of ten whether he would do his military service, Gunther refused, instead reciting biblical verses.

After the boy was sent home, the police laid siege to his household. His mother was arrested and sentenced to eight months in prison. The special tribunal at Elblag appointed a tutor for the children, and Gunther was sent to a family to be raised according to National Socialist ideals. His fifteen-year-old sister was assigned to a labor camp.

12

FAMILIES DESTROYED

> Antoine: But it is the truth of the doctrine that makes a martyr.
>
> —Gustave Flaubert, from *The Temptation of Saint Anthony*

Austria's Jehovah's Witness children were also being wrenched from their parents. In one case, a boy named Gerhard was placed in guardianship because "it is dangerous to leave him under the responsibility of his father, a Witness, who forbids his son to give the Hitler salute or to sing patriotic songs." Gerhard was sent to a children's camp at Lienz in the Austrian Tyrolian Alps.

The same treatment was meted out to eleven-year-old Hermine Obweger when she was placed in a reformatory before being shifted to a convent for her fierce refusal to give the Hitler salute or to wear the uniform of the League of Young German Women.

Christa Appel, age fifteen, and her ten-year-old sister, Waltraud, were initially placed in a youth center and then with the director of a placement center to be educated according to Nazi principles. Their father Walter, a printer in Suderbrarup, was condemned to death and decapitated on October 11, 1941, along with three other Witnessess, for their refusal to wear a military uniform.

Walter Appel's son was originally assigned to a youth center, then was removed from the school and placed in an apprenticeship in Hamburg. Called up for military service in 1944, he followed his father's example and refused to serve. He was beheaded without a trial in eastern Prussia. He was seventeen years old.

Another German family was atrociously persecuted by the Nazis. The family of Franz and Hilda Kusserow had eleven children. The three youngest children were torn away from their parents. Elizabeth, one of the girls, stated, "I will never forget that day. It was during the spring of 1939. The school principal accused us of being spiritually and morally negligent, and he arranged for the court to take us out of school to an unknown spot. I was eleven, Hans-Werner nine, and Paul-Gerhard was only seven." The children rejected demands by their teachers to utter "Heil Hitler," salute the flag, or sing Nazi hymns. They were taken to a supervised education center in Dorsten and then were transferred to another establishment near Minden before being separated and assigned to different locations. Despite their age and the terrible ordeals they were subjected to, the children remained faithful to their religious principles.

Two of the older Kusserow sisters, Anne-Marie and Waltraud, were imprisoned. On August 1940, between two prison terms, the father, Franz Kusserow, returned briefly to his home in Bad Lippspringe. His wife, Hilde, and daughter Hildegard were also jailed before being transferred to Ravensbrück. Despite being just seventeen years old, Magdalena was sentenced to solitary confinement in a prison for juvenile delinquents in Vechta. After six months of refusal to recant and sign the renunciation statement, she was subsequently transferred to Ravensbrück, where she was reunited with her mother. On April 26, 1940, Wilhelm, the eldest son, was brought before a firing squad and shot in the Münster prison gardens. His sister Magdalena, who with her mother was able to visit with him shortly before he was executed, recalls the "calm and determination" of her brother before his death. "Hitler turned down Wilhelm's third appeal, and signed the death sentence in his own hand. Nonetheless, when his eyes were being blindfolded Wilhelm was given a last chance to renounce his faith." He refused, expressing as a last wish "that they shoot straight." The court lawyer sent the family a letter: "He faced death standing tall, he was killed instantly. His attitude profoundly impressed all of us and the tribunal. He died in accord with his convictions."

The mother claimed the body from the authorities so that Wilhelm could be buried at Bad Lippspringe. "We can bear witness to the people who knew him." The mother asked that his father be given a four-day pass for the funeral, and "to our great astonishment the pass was granted." During the burial, the father recited a prayer. Karl-Heinz, Wilhelm's younger brother, shared thoughts and some insights he had taken from the Bible before the large crowd. For that gesture, Karl-Heinz was deported to Sachsenhausen and then to Dachau. Wolfgang, the third son, refused to serve in the army and was beheaded in Berlin in March 1942. His sister Magdalena remembers thinking, "Hitler decided that a firing squad was too soft a punishment for conscientious objectors."

Thirteen-year-old Helmut Knoller was singled out at school for special abuse:

"Knoller, come here! Why won't you make the 'Heil Hitler!'?"

"It's against my conscience, Sir."

"You swine! Outside, insolent—and quickly. Traitor!"

Knoller recalls, "Then they changed my class. On March 17, 1940, I was called up to military service."

At the public school in Stuttgart, Knoller was frequently subjected to this type of harassment by his instructor when he refused to perform the Nazi salute. Later at a recruitment center, he refused to swear the oath. He was imprisoned and subjected to harsh questioning by the Gestapo before being sent to Dachau in *Schutzhaft* custody on June 1, 1940. "My first days of detention in Dachau were very hard. As I was twenty I was one of the youngest of the new arrivals. I was assigned to a special team which worked even on Sundays. My guard was particularly tough on me. I had to do the most difficult tasks, which I wasn't used to—and on the run. I collapsed constantly, and each time I was revived and taken to the basement, where they put me in water up to my hips and poured water over my head. I suffered so much I finally went to see the camp chiefs and agreed to sign the statement that I would disassociate from the Witnesses. I was told that I *could* sign the statement first because it didn't mention the Jehovah's Witnesses but only the Bible Students, and then because it wasn't wrong to fool the enemy in order to go free and to better serve Jehovah on the outside."

Transferred to Sachsenhausen, other Witnesses covinced him

of the errors of his ways. He was baptized at Passau at the end of the war after having been shunted from Sachsenhausen to Alderney, only to end up at Steyr in Austria. He was freed by the Allies in May 1945.

Some children whose parents were arrested were placed with families who did not belong to the Witnesses, and these youngsters succumbed to pressure and renounced their faith. This is understandable, considering their ages and the great strain they were under. A boy named Horst Henschel from Meissen recalls that he was beaten at age twelve for refusing to give the Nazi salute. His oldest sister was arrested and died in prison, his father executed in jail, and his mother incarcerated. Sent to his grandparents, who were not Witnesses, he ended up recanting. He joined the Hitler Youth a few months before the end of the war. Horst Henschel explained his recantation with the wrenching logic of a troubled child finally accepted by his hosts: "All of a sudden they all became extremely nice with me. The teachers didn't punish me anymore, even if I didn't salute saying *Heil Hitler!*, and the members of my family became particularly kind to me. It was then that I changed my mind. Today I can affirm that brutal outside persecution tests our faith, but that Satan's indirect attacks are also dangerous."

Eight hundred more cases of children torn from their families were collected in Germany, and this total is undoubtedly only the tip of the iceberg.

13

THE CHURCH AND THE STATE

> The Pope? Why the Pope, poor Abraham—innocent dreamer? Tell me brother, suppose you had succeeded? Suppose the Pope had courageously taken Joshua's side against Christ: would you have won the battle? There would have been one more Jew in the world that another Pope would send to the pyre.
>
> —Elie Wiesal, *Le testament d'un poète juif assassiné*

For years, the Vatican had regarded Hitler as "representing a solid bulwark against pagan bolshevism." On July 20, 1933, Franz von Papen and Eugene Pacelli, the future Pope Pius XII, signed a concordat guaranteeing "freedom of denomination and public practice of the Catholic religion."

In Germany, nominations for the post of bishop were to be submitted to the Reich for approval, with the proviso that candidates should not "present any drawback from a general political viewpoint." Before taking office in his diocese, each bishop was required to swear an oath of allegiance to the Reich. His "duty" was to ensure "the interest of the German State." Von Papen, referring to Pius XII, stated that the pope was pleased to see the German state headed by a man "committed to fighting communism and Russian nihilism."

After the victory of the NSDAP in the March elections, a large part of the Catholic population represented by the *Zentrum* were in favor of strengthening ties to Hitler. The Church hierarchy had no objections, and even certain senior Church officials, such as

Cardinal Faulhaber from Munich, were to revise their earlier pastoral judgment on "National Socialist errors." This shift in Catholic thinking facilitated achievement of Hitler's goals.

Beginning in 1933, Hitler had attempted to curry favor within the hierarchies of the Catholic religion with promises to "respect treaties signed." The *Deutsche Christen,* the German Evangelical Church, was infiltrated by the NSDAP. Ecclesiastical authorities raised no protest despite unrelenting Nazi attacks against the Witnessses and all other smaller sects that had their headquarters in the United States. Their attachment to the Old Testament also fueled Church prejudices and to stigmatize them as disciples of Karl Marx. Better yet, the Jehovah's Witnesses' petit bourgeois environment, their messianic message, their fanaticism, and their skill as propagandists made them, in the eyes of the Nazis, a new party organization. At a Bishop's Conference in Fulda in March 1933, earlier official warnings and prohibitions against the National Socialist movement were discussed, but the Conference concluded that the Catholic population was ready to collaborate positively with the new Reich.

A Lutheran minister's address in Saxony on April 20, 1933, referred approvingly of Hitler's persecution of the Witnesses as a fight for "morality" and the "moral sense of the German people." The organized Church hierarchy was not idle: "When Jehovah's Witnesses were banned in Bavaria, the church acquiesced when charged by the Ministry of Education and Religion to reporting any member of the forbidden sect who continued to practice the religion. A growing totalitarian State apparatus catered to the special interests of Catholics as a whole and, under these conditions, the church found little difficulty in seeking out a path of reconciliation." The Church's opposition was, in truth, hesitant and replete with compromise. The Catholic Church began to actively support Hitler.

On October 10, the Catholic bishop of Freiburg, Conrad Grober, was wildly applauded when he offered total support to the new government and new Reich. In November 1933, Gau-Obmann Krause at the Sports Palace in Berlin proclaimed that the Old Testament was a "book for ploughmen and pimps."

During discussions with the American consul, a member of the German Watch Tower Society, and a Dr. Fischer (a counselor from the Interior Ministry), Fischer stated, "The Bible is not trustworthy, Jehovah is not acceptable. We must get rid of the Old Testament." The Nazis idealized Hitler as a messiah and, according to a circular issued by Martin Bormann, stated flatly that "Nazism is an act of faith." Martin Mutschmann, the SS governor of Saxony, went quite a bit further when he declared, "Our faith is the Führer's ideology and nothing else. No one can serve two masters." German Labor Front Chief Robert Ley also offered unconditional submission to Hitler: "Our only design and goal should be to observe the doctrine of Adolf Hitler, which represents the gospel of the German people."

Nazi ideology became the gospel for all of Germany. A cult grew up around Hitler: his portrait was displayed on a background of crosses and swastika flags draped across church pulpits. Indoctrination began early during school years where catechism classes started and ended with "Heil Hitler." If the Nazi's considered Hitler as their heaven-sent Führer and spiritual guide, the Witnesses saw a Satanic envoy. For Alfred Rosenberg, the NSDAP "ideologue," "Nazism is a movement of a religious nature which inspires politics, the Sate and the army." From 1941 on, he would be informed by Reinhard Heydrich of police measures taken in the Reich and in the occupied territories against "ideological enemies" and especially against "institutions of worship."

Ernst Fraenkel stated that Nazi orthodoxy "recognized no absolute religious values, nor absolute ethical values based on legislation. A religion's value is judged not on its metaphysical worth, but on its political opportunity." In addition, just before the signature of the concordat, Hitler advised a cabinet meeting, "This *Concordat*, the content of which in no way interests me, benefits us in our implacable struggle against international Jewry by establishing an extremely useful climate of trust." This confirms what Alfred Rosenberg wrote in his *Myth of the Twentieth Century:* "Any man who does not consider nationality and love of his homeland as supreme values loses all rights to protection. Only prison and death are suitable for traitors to the homeland and to the nation."

In Nazi Germany, there could be no higher values than homeland and Hitler—and full acquiescence was demanded. This put the Witnesses on a collision course with the state, as their values were completely oppositional. The Witnesses were committed to St. Peter's precept to "obey God rather than man."

Thomas Mann questioned the Nazi beliefs in a radio address thusly: "You believe that he is the man of the century and that he has come to replace Christ, to replace the sacred doctrine of God's human fraternity by a murderous and violent doctrine of body and soul."

Nazi aspirations for spiritual hegemony inevitably met with some religious opposition. The Holy Synod declared on May 31, 1934, that "we reject the false doctrine which provides that the State may overstep its specific tasks and can and should become the sole and total organization dominating the lives of men, thus supplanting the mission of the Church." In March 1935, the synod of the *Bekenntnis Kirche* condemned Nazi racism, and on August 26, 1936, the provisional leadership of the Protestant churches held up for criticism "outrages against Christian faith" in Nazi writings and stood up to "such oppressions of conscience," including "hypocrisy and servile spirit." However, the main churches did not really take a stand against Hitler. Gilbert Badia quotes the bishop of one of these groups who complained in November 1936 of an "order which forbids the SS to appear in uniform at weddings and the display of flags at funerals." This same bishop required during the spring of 1938 that all his diocese pastors take an oath to Hitler.

Not all the Catholic hierarchy agreed with this position. According to Cardinal Gerlier and Pastor Boegner, "The duty to obey the State must be absolutely subordinated to our faith in God," and the bishop of Munster preached, "Remain firm! Remain constant! it may be that obedience to God and faith in one's conscience will cost you your lives, your freedom and homeland. But it is better to die than to sin."

While much of the Catholic hierarchy remained silent, the leadership and members of the Jehovah's Witnesses continued to resist. Ersnt Fraenkel would write during the late 1930s, "The astonishing growth of the Jehovah's Witnesses these past few years is all the more remarkable. The group's members, whose pacifism brooks no compromise and whose worship of Jehovah induces a rejection of all secular authority, constitutes the prototype of a community living according to its principles of absolute natural law. None of the outlawed German groups rejected National Socialism more fervently than this defiant body. Its rapid growth was a reaction against undermining the Third Reich of all of the principles of natural law. It can only be this fundamental contradiction which explains the National Socialists' hate for Jehovah's Witnesses, who have become martyrs of the religious wars in today's Germany." Christine King asserted that "the theological position of Jehovah's Witnesses is unshakable . . . and the more the Nazis persecuted this sect, they stronger became their convictions." She underscored that any compromise was impossible, for "any renunciation would have called into question the whole basis of their lives and its understanding . . . the Witnesses belong to a community with a very strong belief system which has given them meaning and a goal in life. Failure to embrace a single precept would have been to reject the whole." In an article on German opponents of Nazism, Michel Bosquet wrote, "Even the Catholic Church, through the *Concordat* it signed with Hitler, denied legitimacy to that part of the clergy which offered resistance."

Hitler's opponents were forced to choose higher values than those of patriotism and place their ethical and political ideals over loyalty to the homeland. Compared to the uncompromising resistance of the Witnesses to National Socialism, the attitude of the *Bekennenden Kirche* was not unequivocal. Yet it should not be overlooked that 800 *Bekenntnis Kirche* priests, as well as many Catholic priests, were interned in concentration camps. In March 1937, the pope issued an encyclical protesting against "more or less open violations" of the concordat, and he accused the Nazis of "sowing the seeds of suspicion, discord, hate, calumny, and hostility against Jesus Christ and the Church, secretly and in the open." By contrast, the Italian clergy encouraged the repression of Jehovah's Witnesses by Fascist authorities. Its newspaper *Fides* declared, "The Jehovah's Witness movement is an expression of atheistic communism, and an open attack against the security of the State."

While Pope Pius XII addressed a message of sympathy to leaders of nations invaded by Nazi Germany on May 10, 1939, the Episcopal Conference of Fulda wished the Führer every success during the 1936 Spanish civil war "in defeating the Bolsheviks," and, at the time Austria was annexed, its bishops called on their flocks to become active Nazis. In 1938, a League for German Christianity was formed, and its dean, Leffler, viewed Hitler as "a prophetic figure . . . the sole savior of the cause of Christ in Germany." It should be noted, moreover, that the "official" established religions preferred to seek out accommodations with the regime rather than put up fierce opposition.

Roger Manvell and Heinrich Fraenkel take note of these major reservations and place the blame for the Vatican's compromising stance with regard to Nazism and Fascism unambiguously on the pope. "The Pope could have carried on a spiritual struggle. What were the reasons preventing him from threatening Hitler with bolts of God's lightning if he did not give up his policy of extermination? Nonetheless, he continued to believe that Stalin was a much more dangerous enemy than Hitler."

As Hitler himself claimed before the cabinet, "The dissolution of the Zentrum must be considered definitive by the *Concordat* agreement . . . after which the Vatican ordered its priests to keep away from party politics."

Dachau, however, stands in mute testimony to the large number of Catholics incarcerated there. As Martin Broszat remarked, "The Protestant Church was never considered, in principle, an ideological opponent, and the scope of political persecutions against it was also quite different. Although there were hundreds of Catholic priests in concentration camps, some of whom spent years in jail, we know of very few cases of Protestant pastors who were imprisoned for any length of time."

14

1937, THE YEAR OF "ORDINARY" REPRESSION

> And like cranes who draw long strings in the sky singing a plaintive call, I saw shadows trailing the lamentations carried off by this tempest.
>
> —Dante

By the beginning of March 1937, numerous sentences were being handed down against the Bible Students by tribunals in Silesia, Saxony, Prussia, and so on, and the daily newspapers made much of these events. Charges against the Jehovah's Witnesses for violations of the law and resulting in prison terms included holding meetings and distributing literature. Hundreds of thousand of pounds of tracts and publications were confiscated.

Hans Marsalek provides insight into the SS's attitude to the Jehovah's Witnesses: "If clergymen were incarcerated for national, political or religious reasons in the Mauthausen concentration camp, there was a group of prisoners who were persecuted strictly on the basis of their faith and pacifist views: they were Germans, some Austrians and Poles who were members of the *Ernste* Witness group. However, the Polish Witnesses deported to Mauthausen were also often jailed for nationalist, not simply religious, reasons. But according to the Poles, 'every Witness is a preacher chosen personally by Jehovah'; they, too, considered themselves persecuted clergy."

A Swiss journalist wrote, "In Germany 4,000 Witnesses were

imprisoned. It must be admitted that these Christians have to be considered among the most courageous. They take very seriously the command to obey God rather than man." The journalist continued his analysis by reproaching Protestants and Catholics for a lack of bravery and concluded in his article: "But the Churches bent before the God-State as well as the economic gods and self-interest."

Under the headline "Heavy Penalties Imposed on Bible Students," extracts of a major trial were reported: "Leipzig, April 30th. One of the largest trials ever held before German courts began last Thursday before the Saxony Tribunal. The court heard charges against 186 Witnesses from Leipzig and surrounding areas. Thirty defendants, including 24 women, were questioned *in camera*. . . . Their activities, beginning in 1934, consisted of meeting in small groups, meditating together, obtaining illegal writings and contributing dues. On Friday, May 7th, the Special Tribunal sentenced the 36 defendants."

Renewing their public awareness campaign of December 12, 1936, the Witnesses decided on another effort to get their word out. Joseph Seitz was freed from Buchenwald by the Allies in April 1945. He recalls distribution of an "Open Letter" in June 1937: "During those days we also handed out a tract 'To All Men Who Love Christ in Germany.'" The tract denounced atrocities inflicted in concentration camps and the ill-treatment afforded the *Bibelforscher* and how they were tortured and beaten to death. Faced with the number of tracts distributed, especially in Karlsruhe, the SS ordered its henchmen to collect all copies. "According to a police superintendent they collected about 300." For this activity, Seitz was rearrested in February 1938 and sentenced to eighteen months in jail by the special tribunal in Mannheim.

Placed in a detention cell after his arrest and treated as a common criminal, he was then transferred from one prison to another, and "they refused my request for a bible or religious material."

Eighteen months after his release from the Esterwegen concentration camp, Heinrich Dickmann also distributed the "Open Letter." He was arrested for the third time and deported to Sachsenhausen.

Gertrud Potzinger also participated in passing out the "Open Letter"; she then found herself in Silesia, where, after a wave of arrests, she renewed contact with Jehovah's Witnesses in Frankfurt, Dresden, and other cities around the nation. Arrested for her propaganda efforts in Dresden, she was transferred to Breslau, where she was placed in *Schutzhaft* beginning on September 24, 1937.

Accusations against her included the following:

> 1. For having continuously contravened the *1937 Silesia edict in Silesia* enacted by the regional administration in application of the Reich Presidential Law the protection of the people and the State of February 28,1933 and the Prussian Ministerial order of June 24, 1933 for the same offense.
> 2. For having intentionally distributed false assertions which are of a nature to cause great harm to the well-being of the Reich and to the prestige of the Government of the Reich.

The statement of charges specifically refers to the tract and even quotes extracts:

> In early August 1937 the accused received from Lohr a large number of copies of the tract: "Open Letter! To the People of Germany Who Believe in the Bible and Love Christ!" which deals with the ban on the International Association of *Bibelforscher*. The letter makes among other statements: it is an appalling fact that the present German rulers have cruelly defamed, slandered, and persecuted all sincere Witnesses who publicly profess their faith in God and serve Jehovah. . . . For many years, we the Jehovah's Witnesses, previously known as *Bibelforscher*, have taught the Bible and its comforting truths to our German compatriots and full of self-sacrifice we have spent millions to lessen material and spiritual misery. The present Austrian Government is the enemy of the Bible and has the audacity to declare the Roman Catholic Church and the Church of State as the only religions entitled to exercise a certain freedom of expression and that no freedom of belief or conscience will be accorded to the other Christians. The consequence of these positions are prison terms of up to five years. Evil treatment reminiscent of Inquisition tortures occurred in the concentration camps and other locations in the Ruhr region, in Prussia and eastern Ba-

> varia. We have in our possession specific facts and the names of about eighteen cases of Jehovah's Witnesses who were badly treated and killed. For example, at the beginning of the month of October in 1936, Jehovah's Witness Peter Heinen, residing on Neuhuller Street, Gelsenkirchen, in Wesphalia, was beaten to death by State secret police officials at the City Hall in Gelsenkirchen.

In the summer of 1990, Gertrud Potzinger was interviewed by an author of this book at Selters, Federal Republic of Germany:

Author: What happened after your transfer to Breslau?

GP: I was sentenced to three and a half years of prison cell lockup at Breslau. The isolation was only broken from time to time, and always for very brief periods, by the company of other inmates who remained for a short time in my cell. The cellmate who stayed the longest was a prostitute.

Author: Why a prostitute?

GP: I think it was some kind of test. The authorities wanted to see how I would react to all of the insanities and perverse stories that prostitute was going to tell me. And to me who had only been married for three and a half months!

Author: How did things go in Breslau?

GP: At the Breslau Prison I had to work; I had to paint wooden toys, little soldiers. The inmates had to finish a hundred forty-four figures a day and, if not, it was the bunker.

Author: Were you the only Jehovah's Witness?

PG: No! There were other Jehovah's Witnesses jailed in Breslau. I saw some on the daily walks, and we made furtive signs of recognition to each other. This visual contact was comforting.

Author: How did you live out your imprisonment?

PG: Every day I tried to rejoice in something: On Monday, it was a new work day, Tuesday was mail day, Wednesday we had a piece of sausage, Thursday a shower, and so forth.

Author: Was there any event which was particularly striking?

PG: Yes, because at one time I was able to have a Bible and I read passages on Saturday. And even though the prison pastor refused to give me one, a fellow inmate got me a copy which I was able to keep for a time. This woman, who briefly shared my cell, was sentenced to six months because she was on public assistance and took a small job—without declaring it—to earn some extra money.

Author: How did you occupy yourself during your detention?

PG: During my cell detention in Breslau, moments of joy were, of course, limited, but I was able to stand those three and a half years pretty well because I knew why I was imprisoned and my conscience was clear since I hadn't betrayed anyone or done anything wrong. I tried to stay occupied spiritually. Each day I assigned myself a topic of reflection: love, justice, empowerment, hope, the government, consolation, et cetera. I compared what I had read in the Bible with what was going on around me and I tried to make an analysis of certain spiritual values.

Author: And what did you feel?

PG: I often told myself that this solitary imprisonment, this isolation would have been intolerable and would have been spiritual torture if I had to myself to blame for it.

Author: Was there a particular memory which left its mark on you?

PG: I remember when the special tribunal in Breslau sentenced me that I was alone on the defendant's bench. . . . The court even asked me what I would do if I had to perform military service. So I answered that as a woman it wasn't a question which concerned me. The tribunal then asked me what I would do if I were a man. I answered that I couldn't think like a man, but that I could only think like a woman.

Author: How did that day end?

PG: When I was taken back to my cell it was already nighttime, and the attendant took me by the hands and thanked me and told me that my attitude had given her back the strength to believe in God. That also gave me lots of strength during my imprisonment.

In Fritz Poppenberg's documentary *Frauen die Nicht Vvergessen,* filmed by *Fries Berlin* television in 1989, Elfriede Lohr and Ilse Unterdorfer also recalled the "Open Letter" and the atrocities that ensued. Accompanied by television journalists on the train that took them back to Ravensbrück after an absence of forty years, they spoke of "a certain person, Theiss at Dortmund, and Tennhoff and Heinemann, who were members of the secret police of Gelsenkirchen and Bochum who would not hesitate to beat women with a riding crop and rubber truncheons and who were especially sadistic with the Witnesses."

Ilse Unterdorfer also spoke of a trip she made to Prague to obtain stencils and of being arrested when she brought them back to Berlin. She underwent interrogation at the Moabit prison on Alexanderplatz before being interned under *Shutzhaft*, initially at the Lichtenburg camp. Since the first copies of the "Open Letter" had been intercepted by the Nazis, Elfriede Lohr was awaiting another shipment. It arrived in the form of a suitcase consigned in accompanied baggage and filled with tracts that she then distributed in Liegnitz. She was arrested several weeks later and deported to Ravensbrück.

The "Open Letter" unleashed a wave of arrests. Two Witnesses who had printed at least 70,000 copies were arrested by the Gestapo and harassed by the secret police, who subjected them to terrible cruelty during interrogation. Although the wife of one of them was sadistically tortured at the *Steinwache* in Dortmund, she refused to tell of her husband's whereabouts. Because of what she had endured, she spent several weeks in bed, her body wrapped in alcohol-soaked bandages, and came away from the ordeal with a pronounced limp.

A harmonium owned by Heinrich Schmidt was even characterized as an "enemy asset of the people" and confiscated in Streipt by the Prussian state. The seizure was reported in an article that appeared in the *Nationalzeitung* in Basel, and the reporter noted that "in handing down such a sentence in Prussia, a country of precision and correctness, no less than two laws and a decree were required to give it a semblance of legality."

As early as May 1937, Gestapo orders decreed that Witnesses across Germany could be held in concentration camps for mere suspicion—formal charges were not required. "Whoever supports the aims of the International Association of Bibelforscher (IBV), an illegal organization, is to be placed in protective custody and immediately handed over to the courts. As for those already interned as soon as their prison terms were completed, they are to be automatically transferred to preventive detention in concentration camps."

The following is the final passage of a Gestapo order dated August 1935:

> 1. If a Witness is acquitted during a penal procedure, or if his imprisonment has been declared served by the *Schutzhaft*, he should not be brought to court but placed instead in necessary protective custody.
>
> 2. If the authorities responsible for carrying out the sentence announce an imminent release of a witness, I must be consulted immediately on measures to be taken by the State Police concerning his transfer to a concentration camp as soon as his term has been completed.
>
> 3. If the transfer to a concentration camp is not possible immediately after the completion of their jail sentences, the Witness must be held in a police jail.
>
> In all cases an immediate report must be submitted.

It will be noted that procedures in exquisite detail were in place to ensure, at all costs, the appearance of legality.

In this regard, a Colonel Wheeler, in sworn testimony before the Nuremberg War Crimes Tribunal, stated, "We have already provided proof through Document #D-84 showing that the members of this group were not only prosecuted before the courts but also arrested and placed in concentration camps even after completion or reduction of sentences levied against them."

In July 1937, the Buchenwald concentration camp was opened and then directed by Commandant Koch. It had formerly been known as the Ettersberg concentration camp. In the days following, the first prisoners were shipped in from the Sachsenhausen and Lichtenburg camps: 149 and then 70 professional criminals were also sent from Sachsenburg during the third week of July. On July 27, the first political prisoners arrived, among them seven Fundamentalists. By the autumn of 1937, the numbers of Witnesses had grown at Buchenwald to about 160. That number swelled to 450 by the autumn of 1938.The camp population was

2,561 on December 31, 1937, so that approximately one in ten inmates was a Jehovah's Witness.

At the women's camp at Lichtenburg, Jehovah's Witnesses were subjected to a more severe prison regimen. Ilse Unterdorfer reports on Hitler's visit to the Lichtenburg camp in 1937 and on his words to the Witnesses: "You, too, will surrender. We will humiliate you: we will withstand longer than you." Everything was done to force them to sign a statement renouncing their faith. Unlike Jews and other pariahs of Nazi society, they were "voluntary inmates" who, if they signed, could be integrated back into the national community. The deal that the Nazis held out was a simple one: sign, or face extermination.

Unterdorfer spoke of the torture that was used in an attempt to break a Witness at Lichtenburg: "One day, Sister Elisabeth Lange, who came from Chemnitz, was called before the director. She refused to sign the statement, which earned her a lockup in the dungeon of this old castle. The cells were black holes with a narrow window with bars, the bed was stone, and most of the time one was obliged to lie down on this cold and hard 'bed' without even a straw mattress. Sister Lange spent six months alone in that hole." Yet Witnesses rarely signed the statement, and a number of those who did—from exhaustion, harassment, or fear—would later challenge their signatures and demand invalidation of their statements.

August Dickmann (the brother of Heinrich, cited previously) succumbed to the pressures of his torturers and, on completion of his prison term, signed a statement. His gesture was futile; it did not prevent him from being sent to the Sachsenhausen concentration camp. When confronted by fellow Witnesses, he asked that the statement be canceled as having been signed in a moment of weakness.

The fact that some did sign did not bring them relief. As Karl Kirscht explained, "Some signed, but in most cases they had to wait more than a year before being released. During that period they were often insulted in public by the SS, who reviled them as hypocrites and cowards, and forced them to take a 'tour of honor' around their brothers before being authorized to leave the camp."

From Mauthausen camp are these descriptions: "From 1939 to 1945 the Jehovah's Witnesses were given many an opportunity to gain freedom if they renounced their faith. Very few took advantage of this because there were only six Austrian or German Witnesses who were released from the camp at Mauthausen. We [H. Marsalek] were unable to obtain details of these releases."

Willhelm Roger recalled the case of a Witness who signed a statement and who had to stand before the camp gate for a full day. Then the camp commandant forced him to stand on a stool placed in front of the courtyard when his fellow Witnesses came in: "Knittler then directed our attention to the brother and gave us a piercing look and said: Look at this coward: he signed without telling you!"

It should be understood that the tortures endured during interrogation and later in the camps must have been horrific and might have broken many more Witnesses were it not for their depth of faith. Emil Wilde was arrested early one morning and taken along with his wife to the police station. However, the interrogations and torture did not begin until ten days after he was arrested. He protested several times on hearing his wife's screams as she was being brutalized for twelve consecutive hours. Silence returned only after she was taken from police headquarters and transported to a psychiatric hospital. "On October 3rd, Classin the head Gestapo guard came into my cell in the early morning and told me my wife had died in the psychiatric hospital. I told him to his face that they were responsible for her death and the day of her burial I filed murder charges against the Gestapo. They attacked me for defamation."

In 1937, at least 122 of the 234 inmates in Gestapo *Schutzhaft* at the Fuhlsbuttel police prison were Witnesses. By January 1937, there were 132 of 258 who were Witnesses: they made up the largest group of Gestapo inmates. This large penitentiary in Hamburg had been under Gestapo direction since 1936. During the census of 1933, 345 city inhabitants claimed to be Jehovah's Witnesses. A member of the Socialist International, Helmut Kalbitzer, who was an inmate at Fuhlsbuttel, remembered that some Witnesses resisted the established order that reigned inside the penitentiary. He mentioned one who refused to speak for the six months of his incarceration and another who refused to come out of his cell and noted further that six weeks of solitary confinement could not change his mind.

A former policeman, Karl Zietlow, arrested in September 1937 and sentenced to at least three years in prison for "continuing to believe in false doctrines of the Jehovah's Witnesses," was also jailed at Fuhlsbuttel and then assigned to detention at the Wolfenbuttel prison, of which a fellow inmate would say, "I never suffered more from hunger than at Wolfenbuttel."

15

THE CONCENTRATION CAMPS

"Mauve (violet)": That was the color of the *Bibelforscher*, those internees whose religious convictions led them to resistance of the Nazi regime. It was especially the Jehovah's Witnesses. In addition, it was astonishing that many of them also wore the golden triangles of the Jews.

—Evelyn Le Chêne, *Mauthausen ou la comptabilitè de l'horreur*

In January 1938, Reich Interior Minister Frick issued a memo authorizing protective arrest as to protect the state and its citizenry against all hostile intentions directed against them by those whose behavior threatened public safety. Adversaries of the people and state were thrown into concentration camps for an unlimited duration. They could hope for release only if "the means achieved its end," and the concentration camp was considered an institution of behavior modification—a place for reeducation.

Author Germaine Tillion provides the following analysis on the handling of inmates: "The question of rhythm in dealing with human material in the camps was absolutely essential: not only did it create between men and women, but also between nationalities, a kind of grading system in their march towards death by sheer wear and tear. There were camps where one could survive from two to five years, like Buchenwald and Ravensbrück, and those where one could live for only a few months, like Ravensbrück and certain work details in Auschwitz. At the harshest camps, like Bergen-Belsen, the Jugenlander, and Block 25 at Ravensbrück, lives evaporated within weeks. . . . Death resulted, of course, from an agonizing process, since in death by sheer exhaustion there is necessarily a more or less long period of agony during which no output could be derived from the poor human beings."

All camps had disciplinary companies in which work parties were subjected to measures of extreme severity. Isolated in special barracks and never allowed out, they worked in the quarries. These underfed inmates had to remain on their work site, and camp management kept them on the job even on Sundays, performing the most tiresome and disagreeable tasks. They received no pay, were permitted to write only one letter every three months or never, and were subjected to punishment details.

Life in these companies was a life of utter despair. Egon Kogon wrote, "Jehovah's Witnesses had to endure all kinds of tribulations in the camps. At the beginning, in all the camps except for certain specialized workers, the violets were thrown into disciplinary companies. They couldn't write or buy anything. From 1939 they were allowed to send just one twenty-five word letter a month to their relatives."

That letter was a standard text: "Your letter has been received; thank you very much. I am well, in good heath and vigorous." On several occasions, relatives got these letters after receiving a death notice. All correspondence from Witnesses bore the following stamp: "This prisoner is more than ever an obstinate Witness and refuses to renounce his heresy. For this reason he has simply been denied normal correspondence privileges." This notation, which demonstrated their continuing belief, was helpful to recipients because it meant that their relatives had not renounced the faith. "In fact it wasn't the content of the letter which interested us—for what could one say in five lines?—but that stamp always provided us with joy." Gertrud Potzinger still has several letters that she exchanged with her husband, also imprisoned. These few slim sheets of a few penciled lines that Martin Potzinger managed to save were for the most part torn and cut up by the censors.

In March 1938, Sachsenhausen camp commandant Hermann Baronowski engaged in his own pitched battle against the Witnesses. He confined them to the barracks of the disciplinary work details and isolated them from the rest of the camp by a palisade of planks and barbed wire in a group of barracks known as the *Isolierung*. This "little camp," as it was known to inmates, became a theater of incredible brutality, and initially the sadistic *Strafkompanie* corps of disciplinary troops were assigned there. The Witnesses were also grouped there into a special block. Heinrich Dickmann, who was transferred a year later to the camp, confirms that "at Sachsenhausen, we Witnesses were cut off inside the concentration camp. Around our barracks (35 and 36—I was in the latter) a wall with a gate was built so that we had no contact with the other inmates."

These measures were equally applied at Dachau. A sworn statement given by Matthias Lex before the Nuremberg War Crimes Tribunal bears rereading. A former vice president of the National Union of Shoemakers, he described his three-year experience at Dachau: "When I was released and got out there were about 20,000 inmates in this camp. In my estimation the number of political prisoners was about fifty percent. I include the Witnesses among the political prisoners and I would estimate they numbered more than 150. . . . The following groups were completely segregated: the *Strafkompanien*, or disciplinary work parties who found themselves back in the camps for a second time; and the Witnesses. Members of 'disciplinary companies' were prisoners who committed minor infractions against camp rules. The following groups lived separately but could mix with others during the day, whether at work or during walks in the camp: political prisoners, Jews, antisocials, Gypsies, inveterate criminals, homosexuals and, before 1937, also the Witnesses."

Pierre Durand provides an astute description of the state of mind of the SS and among others of Else Koch, the wife of the commandant at Buchenwald: "The wife of the SS General was herself a member of Hitler's party and was a racist who thought she belonged to the 'master race' superior to all other categories of humans, and because of that used to reigning over 'sub-humans.' Among them were communists, Jews, and all those assimilated under the heading of too soft (Jesuits, Jehovah's Witnesses, Freemasons, homosexuals, and democrats of all types) and who must be 'broken'—morally and physically diminished and eventually simply killed."

According to Friedrich Frey, a Jehovah's Witness from Rot and a member of the disciplinary company at Dachau, "It is hard to describe the hunger, the cold and the torment endured. One day an officer kicked me in the stomach provoking a serious illness. Another day I was beaten so severely that the bone in my nose was all deformed to the point that, even today, I have difficulty breathing. And another time an SS caught me eating a few crumbs of dry bread during work hours to satisfy my hunger. He kicked me in the stomach and I collapsed to the ground. As further punishment I was hung from a three-meter post with my arms chained behind my back. This abnormal body position and its weight caused blood circulation to be cut off and horrible sufferings. An SS grabbed both of my legs and swung them forwards and backwards and yelled, 'Are you still a Jehovah's Witness?' But I was incapable of answering since the sweat of death had soaked my forehead. Since that day I suffer from nervous spasms."

Martin Potzinger, arrested at the same time as his wife, was first interned in the hell of Dachau. He, too, was hung from a post:

> My *Schutzhaft* arrest warrant was handed to me on my birthday, and I arrived in Dachau by the next convoy. I will skip some details, but I would like to stress that each Jehovah's Witness was called to the Gestapo office every three months to submit to questioning, and three questions were submitted to him for signature:
>
> 1. Recognize the faith of Jehovah's Witness as a heresy.
> 2. Recognize the German Government as the "supreme authority."
> 3. Defend the homeland, under arms, in case of war.
>
> The first question brooked no discussion and was, therefore, unacceptable because it would have been denial of the truth of the word of God and a calumny against Jehovah himself. Because I was unyielding, I was sentenced to be hung from a post (*Aufhangen an den Pfahl*) for thirty minutes. But, as was usual, fifteen extra minutes were added. . . . They were twelve condemned to this punishment. Hung with their hands tied behind them and attached to a hook "in such a way as both arms were dislocated backwards and

> the body slumped gradually lower which caused horrible pains. All the inmates cried out terribly which was understandable. Some died from it. They [the guards] were particularly attentive to see how we [Jehovah's Witnesses] would bear up. . . . [Because Potzinger remained silent, an SS delivered a terrible kick and made his body swing and reignite the pain.] The SS was waiting for me to cry out. But he heard nothing.

Jean Amery, a member of a Belgian resistance group, was arrested by the Gestapo in July 1943 for disributing tracts. He was remanded to the SS and found himself "in the reception camp at Breedonk," where he fell into the hands of his torturer, SS Lieutenant Praust. "From the bunker's ceiling hung a chain partially rolled up around a pulley; on the bottom extremity was a big bent iron hook. I was taken under the apparatus. The hook was passed through the ropes tying my hands behind my back. Then I was hoisted by the chain until my body was hanging about a meter above the floor. Suspended by the hands behind the back this way, one can only maintain the strength of one's muscles for a short time to remain in a more or less vertical position. During these minutes while one has expended his last forces and the sweat is rolling of your brow and lips and breath grows short, one is in no state to answer any questions. It was at this moment that a cracking in my upper back happened, as well as a tearing of my body which to this day I have never forgotten. I fell into emptiness and my body was now hanging at the end of my dislocated arms . . . at the same time blows delivered with a beef sinew rained down hard."[1]

NOTE

1. It was on July 23 that Amery experienced his torture. Because of his Latin origins, when recounting his suffering he called it *torquere*, or "twist," the root word for "torture." He added to his remarks the comment, "What a lesson in etymology!"

16

THE INVASION OF AUSTRIA AND THE PLEBISCITE

It is appalling for a man to misdirect a traveler who doesn't know the road, and to follow and allow him to continue on his way in error.

—Kierkegaard, *The Journal of a Seducer*

On March 11, 1938, Hitler's armies crossed the Austrian border. After the *Anschluss*, or annexation, of Austria—which generated only feeble international condemnation—numerous Austrians adjudged guilty of being dangerous elements were sent to concentration camps, where they were registered and labeled German subjects. "Included in the category 'German and Austrian political prisoners' were German Jewish and Austrian political and religious prisoners as well as the Jehovah's Witnesses from Germany and Austria."

On April 10, 1938, the Austrian population were called to the polls to vote on annexation. For several weeks, the electorate had been "prepared," and billboards exhorting "Say YES to Hitler" were plastered all along the walls. All inhabitants were required to fly the Nazi swastika flag from their windows. A Jehovah's Witness from Knittelfeld, Madame Altenbuchner, refused to do so and was expelled from her lodgings.

Various detachments of the Security Service received precise instructions before and after the April elections. We located the following document, signed by SS *Oberscharführer* Helfer, in the SD detachment records in Erfurt:

> Special Order
> Strictly Confidential
> To all rapporteurs and Base Chiefs
>
> All Base Chiefs must report by Thursday, 7 April 1938 at the latest on all individuals in their districts who admit that they will vote "No" (with 100% likelihood) in the coming election. (Do not overlook the International Bibelforscher!)
>
> Rapporteurs must provide all possible assistance to Base Chiefs in this task. . . . The list of names should include: surname, first name and an exact description of the address and a brief mention justifying why the concerned individual will probably vote "No" and which members of the family, of voting age, will defend the same position.
>
> Special attention must be paid to turnout and results of the 10/4/38 [April 10, 1938] elections in small towns and villages. Should the case arise, it is appropriate to carefully examine to which group the hostile adversaries belong: Marxist circles, or circles professing other philosophies and religions.

On the day of the plebiscite, all people whose names were listed were carefully watched, intimidated, and even had their ballots secretly checked. Johann Viereckl from Vienna left his home in the early hours of the morning of the vote and went for a walk in the Viennese woods, only to return late in the evening. His neighbors informed him that they had seen members of the voting committee call on his home five times during the day.

A report of the Weissensee SD detachment of March 1938 named Witness Robert Siering and his wife: "They came to the voting booth at Grietstedt on Sunday morning and turned in their ballots after having been advised of their electoral duty by the Police at Gunstedt who threatened to seize their child in case of nonparticipation. It was noted that the envelope they placed in the ballot box was empty."

The same detachment at Weissensee filed another report, dated March 28, 1938, on these same elections: "The workman, Otto Wiegand from Sommerda, Enfurter-Strasse #17 had to be invited four times to present himself on election day, and finally voted under pressure. The above named person is a member of the former International Association of Jehovah's Witnesses."

Another entry reads, "A married woman, Frieda Schreine, maiden name: Troster, from Sommerda, Salzmannstrasse #5, did not vote even though an invitation to do so was reiterated. This woman is a fanatical member of the former International Association of Jehovah's Witnesses. Her husband, master mason Paul Schreiner, who shares the same opinions and has been the subject of judicial pursuit in this regard, did vote. Since he presented himself to the ballot box, we can be sure that he did so only because he was afraid of being rearrested."

After the Austrian annexation and "the perfect unity of the German vote which was secured with support from the security services and the body of political leadership," the Nazis issued a decree "ordering all men who served in the army during the First World War to take part in three days of military exercises." Johann Rainer, called up to the Innsbruck barracks, refused to swear in before 800 men. He was questioned, imprisoned, and hauled before the regional tribunal. Thanks to assistance from the boss of the wholesale grocery where he worked and who intervened on his behalf, he was released and returned to his job.

On April 1, 1938, DEST, a company formed to exploit the land and quarries, was founded as an SS consortium to provide production of building materials. On May 3, 1938, the Flossenburg concentration camp was set up nearby a granite quarry and located close to the Czech border, and various work details were assigned to installing underground galleries, factories, and warehouses.

According to *British White Paper Number 2*, presented to Parliament by the secretary of state for foreign affairs by order of His Majesty and titled "Documents Pertaining to the Treatment Inflicted on German Nationals in Germany," testimony from a former inmate of the Buchenwald concentration camp is quoted. It concerns "Mr. X, a well-off Jewish businessman," who was imprisoned during the summer of 1938 and was freed only after he could prove that he was in a position to leave Germany (it will be noted that this document appeared in Paris in 1939, explaining why the names of the witnesses were not mentioned). Of the 8,000 men in the camp when he was there, "there were 1,500 Jews and 800 *Ernste* Witnesses. These 'Bible zealots' wore a violet insignia and were denied all communication with the outside but their rations were not reduced. Mr. X spoke of these men with the greatest respect. Their courage and religious faith were remarkable, and they themselves affirmed they were ready to go to the extreme limit to bear up under what they regarded as an ordeal God had imposed."

Another prisoner was also transferred to Buchenwald on June 15, 1938: "We had barely set foot on the platform when a hail of punches, kicks, and rifle butts shoved us into the tunnel which lead to the road. There we were greeted by Rodl, the camp superintendent, in the following terms: 'Some of you have already been in prison. What you experienced there is nothing compared to what you will know here. You are going into a *concentration camp,* and that means you are entering hell. You will be shot, without trial, if you put up the least form of resistance to the authority of the SS guards. We only know two kinds of punishment in the camp—the whip and death.' "

There the prisoner encountered inmates wearing violet stripes on their uniforms, "the Witnesses, a religious group which draws its doctrine from the Bible and has a large number of adherents in all parts of the country, but had been forbidden by the SS because its members refused to do military service. These unfortunates were treated almost as badly as the Jews." According to "Mr. Z," also an inmate at Buchenwald, the Witnesses were nicknamed "Bible mischief-makers." In August 1938, a decree was published providing the death penalty for refusal to serve under the flag. "This refusal was an article of faith for the Jehovah's Witnesses; they were almost all condemned to death. Many were executed. Some were sentenced to serve with the troops and others were locked up in asylums; many were sent to Dachau."

Alfred Rosenberg appeared before the Nuremberg War Crimes Tribunal on April 16, 1946. Rosenberg had special responsibilities as keeper of the Nazi Party's spiritual and ideological flame and as chief of the foreign affairs services of the NSDAP as well as editor of the Nazi newspaper *Volkischer Beobachter.* According to Rosenberg, "I cannot say if it was before or after the declaration of war that Himmler himself took up the question of the Witness who qualified for religious persecution which had been raised by the Public Ministry. Himmler only told me it was impossible, given the situation in the Reich, to tolerate refusal of Army service which would have terrible consequences. He had often spoken personally to these types of inmates in order to try to understand them and to convince them eventually to change. But that was not possible, given that they answered all questions by quoting bible citations, which they knew by heart, and that nothing could be done with them. From Himmler's statement, I concluded, since he was telling me these things, that it was impossible that he was planning to execute the Witnesses. . . . Since I have been under detention, an American chaplain graciously gave me a religious journal from Columbus. I found out that the United States also held the Jehovah's Witnesses prisoners during the war, and that in December 1946, 11,000 were still inmates in a camp. I suppose under the same conditions each State punishes refusal to perform military service in some way or another. That was also my view, and I cannot fault Himmler on this subject."

Recalling the Witnesses at Buchenwald, Egon Kogon recalls that "on September 16, 1938 the SS offered them an opportunity to reclaim their freedom by signing a statement repudiating their principles, that is to say especially their refusal to swear the oath and bear arms. Only a very small number of them did not resist temptation. And from this moment, a terrible oppression crushed the others to render them more docile."

They were also the object of persecution at the camp at Sachsenhausen. "During the autumn of 1938 I was working as a mason on construction when *Blockführer* Sorge and *Blockführer* Bugdalle came on the job site and ordered a group of prisoners to dig a hole to the depth of a man, and they put in a Witness whose name was Bachuba and buried him up to his neck. Sorge and Bugdalle laughingly made sport of him. Then when there was nothing left but his head above ground they urinated on his head. They left him for another hour in the grave. When he was dug up and pulled out on the ground he was still alive but he couldn't stand on this legs."

This statement by a witness during the trial of the hangmen from Sachsenhausen at Pankow was confirmed by *Blockführer* Gustave Sorge's response to the prosecutor during the same trial: "I admit in 1938 I participated in executing men buried in the ground. We did that to [sect members]. To my knowledge they were brought to the camp because they didn't want to serve in the German army out of religious conviction. During the autumn of 1938 a [sect member] was buried on my personal orders in the field where we were uprooting stumps in the camp."

During 1938 alone, there were between thirty-five and fifty executions carried out in this fashion. According to Bruno Roer, a Witness at Sachsenhausen, when he arrived in camp there were about twenty inmates arrested for their religious convictions. "In 1938 and 1939 the number reached 500. For us the living conditions were worse than for the other camp inmates. Between 1938 and 1942, among the inmates who had been arrested for their religious convictions, more than 200 died in the barracks." On September 8, some six months after the annexation of Austria to the Reich, the Mauthausen concentration camp was "inaugurated." Mauthausen was situated near a granite quarry.

By the end of September 1938, a portion of Czechoslovakia was incorporated into the Reich in an agreement with the French and British governments, which had signed the Munich Accord.

On March 15, 1939, in violation of the Munich Agreement of September 1938, Czechoslovakia was invaded by Hitler's troops. Bohemia and Moravia were placed under a Reich protectorate, while Slovakia was declared independent. On March 30, the Gestapo confiscated property of the Jehovah's Witnesses in Prague, but despite the Nazis' rapid advance, the printing equipment was dismantled, and three presses arrived in Holland, where they were immediately put to use by Dutch Jehovah's Witnesses.

17

AUSTRIANS IN THE SPIRAL OF REPRESSION

Tyrants become skillful by trading with the skilled.
—Euripides

The Mattischeks were a family of Jehovah's Witnesses living in Austria. The father, a brick mason, emigrated in late 1918 and worked for ten years in the Ruhr coal mines. It was during his stay in Germany that he and his family became members of the *Bibelforscher* association, and they later returned to Austria with their children.

In 1938, Franz, the eldest, refused to appear for military service; he was interned for a year at the Germersheim Forest on the Rhine and later beheaded on December 2 at Berlin-Plotzensee. Shortly after his son's arrest, the father was picked up with other association members and interned for six years at Buchenwald. Ernst, the youngest brother, was taken in by a peasant family, and the mother was imprisoned at Ravensbrück for five and a half years.

In March 1939, Hubert Mattischek was arrested by the Gestapo, even though the search of his residence yielded nothing. Two Gestapo agents questioned him:

"What would you do if you were called up to serve in the Army?"

"I would refuse to take the oath and to have anything to do with the war."

"Do you know what that would cost you?"

"I know it very well and I have for a long time."

Willi Mattischek was arrested the same day, and both brothers were brought to the police prison in Linz. Their refusal to serve under the flag would have consequences. After six weeks of preventive detention and without trial, both brothers were placed in *Schutzhaft*, loaded in a cattle truck with other Austrian Jehovah's Witnesses, and sent to the Dachau concentration camp, where they arrived in May 1939.

Both brothers were assigned to barracks 15 (part of the disciplinary company, along with barracks 17 and 19), where there were already 150 Jehovah's Witnesses. Hubert, inmate number 33502, and Willi, number 33501, first worked in the gravel pit and had to push heavily loaded trolleys full of gravel and pull the so-called Moor Express.

By the end of September 1939, the Mattischek brothers, along with 1,600 other inmates, were transferred to the Mauthausen concentration camp, where they were to remain for five and a half years. SS officer Spatzenegger "welcomed" them in the harshest terms: "No Gypsy or Bible Student will come out of here alive." Hubert and his brother refused to renounce their faith or sign the statement given them, and they told Ziereis, the SS camp commandant at Mauthausen, and August Eigruber, the *Gauletier* of Upper Austria, as well as other high Nazi officials, "We do not wish to be unfaithful to God Jehovah and our beliefs." From the onset of *Anschluss*, the Austrian Jehovah's Witnesses were subjected to the same harassment at their coreligionists in the Reich.

Hubert Mattischek recalled the situation of inmates sent on an outside work party near Sudelfeld: "In order to construct a sport's training camp in the Bavarian hills near Sudelfeld they chose a group of pretty sturdy Jehovah's Witnesses. They only took Witnesses because they thought in *this* area there might be an escape, and there was no danger of that from our brothers. The SS concluded that anyone who took on, more or less voluntarily, camp life for just religious reasons would probably not escape, even at Sudelfeld. There were only a few guards there, which was practical for the SS because it saved personnel. The brothers selected also had better rations, more substantial because of the nature of the work, and because the SS wanted their sports complex built in a hurry. The brothers told us they had a real human relationship with the guard. I say this intentionally because to this day very few things are known about us, and most times people have erroneous images, and so biased views are the consequence."

They were freed by the Americans on May 5, 1945, and Hubert Mattischek had the impression on liberation of "having come back from the dead. . . . For having a strong will to live, we rotted for years more as animals, without thinking much . . . since we lived with death by hunger, cold and weakness before our eyes. Only our hope in the promises of our God gave us the strength to persevere."

Franz Wohlfahrt, aged twenty, was called up for mandatory service for the Reich, but he refused to wear the uniform and belt and also refused to salute the Nazi flag or perform the Hitler salute. "A high official from Berlin whose name was Almendinger personally intervened to make him change his mind. 'You have no idea where this situation can lead you,' he remarked during a conversation. 'I am well aware. My father was beheaded for the same reasons just a few weeks ago.' Almendinger gave up. Finally, Franz Wolhfahrt was sentenced to five years of imprisonment at the Rollwald Camp in Germany."

On March 27, 1939 an order from the Reich Justice Ministry mandated that the Witnesses must be locked up in concentration camps upon completion of their prison sentences. In addition, on April 27, 1939, referencing its circular of December 15, 1937, the Düsseldorf Gestapo Bureau forwarded the following circular concerning *Schutzhaft* of the Witnesses: "Recently, and only many occasions, Jehovah's Witnesses have been released after having completed their sentences without first obtaining the required approval here. That is why you are being reminded of my order of May 12th, 1937 and further I draw your attention to the following:

1. As a matter of principle, all the Witnesses after having fulfilled their sentences will be put in *Schutzhaft;* a request for *Schutzhaft* with the required documentation must be filed with the IID Service.

2. If, for whatever reason, and contrary to general practice, the Witnesses are to

be released after having served their terms a detailed report is warranted—with supporting documentation, if needed—and presented to Service II B; this office will file a report with the Gestapo. If, in such cases, no response has been received by the expiration of the prison term, the Witnesses must be put in temporary *Schutzhaft;* further directives should be awaited, the Gestapo reserves upon itself exclusive authority on all decisions on the release of Witnesses who have completed their jail sentences.

What is stated in 2, above, is also applicable law when the Witnesses have furnished a trustworthy statement to refrain from future participation in these activities or even if they have signed a Statement of Agreement.

I ask adherence to the above directives.

Signed: Sommer.

Arrests of Witnesses continued in Germany, and on April 4, 1939, while the Witnesses were celebrating the Commemoration of Christ, the Nazis initiated searches and arrests in Bad Ischl and Braunau Molln. Those arrested were then transferred to concentration camps: women to Ravensbrück and the men to Dachau.

Alois Moser (who came from Braunau) and Josef Buchner (who came from Ranshofen) were arrested at that time, and they remembered well their arrival at Dachau and the reception given them by SS commandant Grunewald: "Henceforth you Witnesses will be the *raw* material in Dachau. You will *rot* here in this camp. The only way you will get out is through the chimney."

However, they would remain for only a few months at Dachau and were transferred to the Mauthausen camp on September 29, 1939, along with 141 other church members. The reception was similar: "Mauthausen is not a sanitarium like Dachau. You will all be *exterminated*. . . . For the first three years, the brothers, without exception, were forced to do tough physical work in a quarry." It should be recalled that the quarry was the notorious *Steinbruch* at Mauthausen.

Jean Laffitte described one of the longest-serving inmates at Mauthausen: "Emil was Polish of German origin. Even though he wore the green triangle he never struck anyone. In his *Kommando*, which at the time was comprised of thirty men, there were fourteen Spaniards. The rest of the crew was made of Germans, Czechs, and Poles, as well as five Austrians classified as Witnesses."

Laffitte depicted Mauthausen as a hellish place, "a wall of rock two hundred meters high and five hundred meters long. At the base there were holes dug in from here to there into the walls from which seven tunnels had been sunk into the white rock. The inmates dug holes in the rock. They were covered with a white powder which made them look like ghosts. One couldn't see their eyes and they looked like statutes in stone convulsed by the vibrations of the machines." In the evening, the detainees had to climb the 426 steps carrying twenty- to forty-kilogram chunks of rock. As Evelyn Le Chêne aptly remarked, "The atrocities which occurred on these steps is beyond description. No account of the tortures that were endured would be sufficient and no photograph of this sinister place would be able to convey, however remotely, the sufferings of the deportees."

Moser and Buchner were then assigned to the work party responsible for gathering up bodies of dead inmates in the camp. Several years later, their cadaver cart hauled away the body of August Kraft, one of the leaders of the Austrian association who had been arrested by the Gestapo on May 25, 1939. "On Easter Sunday 1939, the camp inspector at Buchenwald made a renewed attempt to convince the Fundamentalists to 'recognize the State and Hitler,' and were welcomed with a few sarcastic nicknames like 'celestial comics,' 'Bible gnawers' or the 'Sheik of the Jordan.' The results were zero. On Pentecost, all of the Fundamentalists' barracks were again called out on the parade ground. After a speech by Hackmann they were made to perform an awful punishment exercise in two sections. They had to roll on the ground, jump, crawl, and run for 75 minutes while being pummeled by the barracks' chiefs."

The women's concentration camp at Ravensbrück was opened in May 1939 with "867 prisoners (180 Germans and seven Austrians); many Witnesses came from the Fortress of Lichtenburg and retained their former I.D. numbers. The numbering system at Ravensbrück began at 1415. Some Witnesses came in from Moringen."

"Some of them had been living in prison since 1933. Their stay in the concentration camp had to be of unlimited duration since they were to be 'reeducated.' "

Therese Schreiber from Vienna and Madame Stadtegger from Wels were among the Austrians deported to Ravensbrück by the end of 1939. The former, arrested for passing out biblical literature, never came back from Ravensbrück. Schreiber, who mimeographed and distributed *The Watch Tower* periodical, was first sent to Ravensbrück. She was brought back to Vienna by the Gestapo to be tried before the regional tribunal for her participation in the reproduction and distribution of copies of *The Watch Tower.* First sent back to the concentration camp, she was "lucky" to be transferred to a work camp where she survived in detention for five and a half years. Anne Dickmann, the mother of August and Heinrich, was first interned in 1937 at the Moringen camp in Harz and then at Lichtenburg (Elbe) and had ID number 267 at Ravensbrück.

Ilse Unterdorfer and Elfriede Lohr were part of the first convoys of women sent to Ravensbrück. "On arrival it was sandy desert and every two meters someone was posted. We had to dig sand, an assembly line job with shovels that were too short. Never stopping, always continuous and for nine hours a day during the hot summer with the sun beating down on this desert of sand."

As a matter of fact, the first arrivals at Ravensbrück had to undertake all the excavation work and it was these women who leveled and built roads and filled in and dried out the marshes. "The first inmates transformed the sand desert on which naked barracks had been thrown up into a 'city of barracks' crisscrossed by 'streets' and surrounded by a group of pretty little houses and small gardens for the SS."

Beginning August 8, 1939, by order of the Reich chancellor's office, prisoners placed in protective internment were henceforth to be under the authority of the chief of the SS and no longer under the Justice Ministry.

The Reich and Russia signed the Pact of Non-Aggression on August 23, 1939, and on September 1, Germany launched its invasion of Poland. Territories occupied by Hitler's Wehrmacht were either directly incorporated into the Reich or reconstituted as a "general government."

18

WHILE FRANCE IS ARMED . . .

> While France is armed, and a venomous war disturbs its rest and mine, the best I can do, as winds blow contrary, is not be drawn into it. I let the storm roll along; lightning passes overhead. If I have to die, I am ready: I resign myself to fate and trust whatever heaven ordains. His will shall be done.
>
> —G.Durant de la Bergerie, *Saturé Mé Nippée* (1550–1615)

Britain and France declared war on the Third Reich on September 9, 1939, but in France it marked the start of "The Phony War." At Buchenwald, SS officer Rodl assembled all the Witnesses on September 6 and gave them orders to fight against France and England, threatening death for refusal. As none of them obeyed, "the SS fell on the 'violets' and took all their money. A grotesque scene." The Witnesses were dispatched on work parties in the quarries and during this period were denied access to the infirmary.

A German Witness, interned at Buchenwald since November 25,1937, related that in early September, "they asked us to sign a statement attesting that we renounced our faith and that we were ready to denounce people who actively supported the teachings of the Bible Students." For three days, the Nazis threatened them: Those who signed would be released and the others shot. At that point, "total silence ensued. No one gave in. Some who had even signed earlier revoked their agreement. So, when they were reassembled, an SS commandant said, 'I think the best thing is to sur-round them and yank them around.' But that was only a strategy to sap our morale."

Author Jean Bezaut wrote, "The first public execution took place on September 15th inside the camp. August Dickmann, a Witness, was hanged in the presence of all the inmates assembled in ranks on the parade grounds. Despite this example, only ninety Witnesses out of the 450 imprisoned at Sachsenhausen signed the renunciation of faith agreement presented to them by the SS."

August Dickmann, a Dinslaken youth, had signed the statement while he was still in jail, but despite that, he was sent on to the camp at Sachsenhausen in October 1937. There he retracted his signature and asked that it be voided. Three days after war was declared, the camp commander, SS *Oberführer* Hermann Baranowski, nicknamed *Vierkant* (the square, or sturdy, one),. called him into the political section. He was holding Dickmann's commitment papers. Since the latter refused to sign and, moreover, told his brother before going that "they can do what they want with me. I won't sign and I won't make any more compromises." Baranowski threw him into the camp bunker and asked Himmler for authorization to execute him publicly. He hoped this example would break the Witnesses' spirit and cause them to renounce their religion.

Himmler agreed. The *Vierkant* prepared for Dickmann's execution on Friday, September 15, 1939. Inmates received orders to stop work an hour early, and Witness Paul Buder remembers the words of an SS officer: "Today is Ascension Day. One of you is going up to heaven." Security measure were quadrupled. SS guards were posted everywhere, perched on the walls and on the bars of the camp gate. All Sachsenhausen inmates were assembled in the courtyard, and the Witnesses were lined up right behind the firing squad. The condemned man was brought out, surrounded by several SS officers with his hands bound in front of him. The SS *Oberführer* spoke over the loudspeakers: "Listen up, Prisoners! Prisoner August Dickmann from Dinslaken, born on January 7, 1910, refuses to do his military service maintaining he is a 'citizen of the Kingdom of God.' He has said, 'Whoever spills man's blood will have his own blood spilled.' He has outlawed himself from society and in conformity with SS Chief Himmler's orders he will be executed. An hour ago I told Dickmann that his miserable life will be taken from him at eighteen hours [6 P.M.]."

A deathly silence fell over the the camp. The commandant addressed Dickmann one last time, snarling, "Turn around, pig!" Three SS officers fired, and one delivered the coup de grâce—a bullet in the back of the neck. After removing his handcuffs, four Witnesses were designated to remove his remains. Then the other inmates were allowed back to their barracks. Baronowski told the Witnesses to remain in the ranks, and he demanded that they sign the statement renouncing their religion and accepting military service.

Gustav Auschner, who was present at the execution, remembers, "They shot Dickmann and warned us that we would *all* go before the firing squad if we didn't sign. We were to be taken to the quarry in groups of thirty or forty, and we would all be shot. The next day, the SS gave us all a sheet to sign under penalty of being shot."

Dickmann's brother Heinrich, who was sent to Sachsenhausen in March 1939 after being sentenced by the special tribunal in Düsseldorf, was present at his brother's execution. Three days later, it was his turn to be called in to the political section. Two Gestapo officers had come from Berlin to gauge the effect of his brother's execution execution. He was interrogated:

Agent: Did you see how your brother was shot down?
Heinrich: Yes!
Agent: What lesson did you learn from that?
Heinrich: I am a Jehovah's Witness and I will remain one.
Agent: You will be the next one shot.

During the interrogation, since he had quoted the Bible, a Gestapo agent said, "I don't want to know what is written down—I want to know what you *think*." They again demanded that he sign the statement. He refused, saying, "Signing this statement recognizing the State and the government would be for me to approve of my brother's execution. I couldn't do it." Heinrich Dickmann was then transferred in early 1940 to the Wewelsburg (where his other brother Friedrich was also imprisoned), then to Buchenwald in April 1940.

A former deportee spoke of the Sachsenhausen-Oranienburg: "At Wewelsburg, near Padeborn, about 120 Witnesses were working at the camp at Sachsenhausen-Oranienburg in 1940. Some Dutch Witnesses were also brought into our midst. All without exception were strong believers in their faith and would not submit. Many were sworn at, struck, and beaten. One of them (in 1939 before my presence) was shot in public. Many died in the camp but remained faithful to their religious convictions. Glory to all the Witnesses!"

Rudolf Hess, deputy camp commander at Sachsenhausen beginning August 1, 1938, referred to the Witnesses in his prison memoirs that he wrote in prison before he was hanged in Auschwitz on April 7, 1947: "I knew many religious fanatics. But the *Bibelforscher* at Sachsenhausen, and in particular two of them, exceeded anything I had seen until then. Those two affirmed they would have nothing to do with the military state. Those two wouldn't stand at attention, wouldn't keep their spacing, wouldn't hold their hands down along their pants' seams, wouldn't raise their caps. Their only hierarchy was Jehovah."

Isolated, then beaten on several occasions by SS commandant Eicke, "They were condemned to death by the SS Reichsführer. When they were informed in their cells they were full of joy and ecstasy: they could hardly wait for the moment of their execution and wouldn't stop shouting: Soon we will be near Jehovah, what a joy that we have been chosen." Hess recounted and continued in these terms: "This was how I imagined the first Christian martyrs in the arena, waiting to be devoured by wild beasts. All of the onlookers, including the firing squad, were affected. Some who had already signed the statement by which they renounced to spread their faith retracted their signatures—they wanted to continue suffering for Jehovah."

At Ravensbrück the declaration of war also had consequences: Elfriede Lohr and Ilse Unterdorfer recalled the speech that Commandant Kogel made in demanding they sew little sacks for the soldiers. Since they refused all work connected with the war effort, they were made to stand all day without moving behind the bunker in the freezing cold. "And to give themselves courage they taught each other psalms."

The Nazis occupied Danzig in September 1939, which, according to the Versailles Treaty, had officially been a "Free City" under a League of Nations mandate.

From that moment on, the "Heil Hitler" salute was mandatory on territories under Nazi domination and on all job sites. Harald Abt, an engineer in the Danzig port administration, refused to salute "because I felt it was not right to attribute so much glory to a man." He was fired on the spot by the deputy director. "Several days later after the German armies had conquered Poland, Hitler came to Danzig. He proclaimed his victory in a fiery speech which he gave on the main square not far from our home. All the inhabitants were supposed to hang a flag from their window, but we didn't do it." Abtlater took his family into hiding in Lodz with his pregnant wife. A daughter was born on September 24, 1939.

It should be noted that twice, on January 21, 1937, and January 15, 1938, Judge J. F. Rutherford, head of the Watch Tower Bible and Tract Society in Brooklyn, New York, sent a petition to the League of Nations in the name of Danzig's Jehovah's Witnesses to protest violations of the city's constitution. By that time, the association had already been banned and dissolved and had its assets confiscated. Despite the petition, Jehovah's Witnesses had been attacked in the streets.

On September 20, 1939, Reinhard Heydrich sent a Gestapo demanding that the Witnesses be made to pay for their resistance: "[We must] come to grips with all those who risk thwarting the combative spirit of the nation by suppressing or interning them. This would be known as Operation *Gitteraktion.*"

The behavior of two men called to appear before the tribunal during the trial in Salzburg made a strong impression on the judge, who observed, "These men are neither criminals nor traitors, but a group of believers who do not number two or three but attain the hundreds and even thousands." The same judge brought a Bible to them in their cell since it was their final wish. These two Austrians, Joseph Wegscheider and Johann Pichler, were shot on

September 26, 1939, at the military camp at Glanegg near Salzburg for refusing to do their military service. They even objected to having their eyes blindfolded, and it was only after a second order and under threat of disciplinary measures that the firing squad obeyed and executed the men. Over 300 people attended the funerals, one of which a Gestapo agent interrupted, saying that the prayer was too long for his taste. The SS considered that this affair had caused too much commotion, and similar cases were no longer dealt with at the local level but transferred to the penitentiary at Berlin-Plotzensee.

The authors have already noted that on September 29, 1939, 403 Witnesses were moved from Dachau to Mauthausen. The camp was closed temporarily during part of October 1939, and inmates were assigned to other camps. According to Hubert Mattischek, the Austrian inmates (their homes in parentheses) were Alram (Vienna), Ignatz Bachmayr (Wilfsegg, Upper Austria), Anton Bodenwinkler (Innsbruck), Franz Braunstein (Graz region), Joseph Buchner (Braunau), Fritz Burger (Salzburg), Franz Desch (Maurach, Tyrol), Johann Desch (Jenbach, Tyrol), M. Estl (Freistadt), Wolfgang Fritzenwallner (Pongau), Anton Greisberger (Salzburg), Johann Gruber (Friedburg, Lendgau), Josef Heckenbleiker (Jenbach, Tyrol), Thomas Hohlrieder (Worfl), Fritz Kampar (Salzburg), Karl Killinger (Hall, Tyrol), August Kraft (Vienna), Hubert and Wilhelm Mattischek (Attnang, Puchheim), Alois Moser (Braunau), Josef Obrist (Maurach, Tyrol), Franz Rothauer (Bad Ischl), M. Spiessberger (Molln), Valentin Steinbach or Valentin Eder (Molln), M. Steindl (near Steyr), Adalbert Strasser (Carinthie), Josef Sturmayr (Wolfsegg, Upper Austria), Rudolf Thamannsbock (Inn region), Franz and Josef Unterbrunner (Molln), Karl Weiroster (Maurach, Tyrol), and Eduard Wohinz (Graz).

Hans Marsalek reports, "We don't know if the Jehovah's Witnesses were liberated after April 20, 1944, but it's very unlikely. Initially German and Austrian Jehovah's Witnesses were mainly assigned to the quarry and camp construction."

Evelyn Le Chene provides the following numbers: "By December 1st, 2,772 inmates were present at Mauthausen, of which 628 were political prisoners, 143 Jehovah's Witnesses, 51 homosexuals, 13 immigrants, one Jew, 946 criminals and 930 antisocials."

On October 26, 1939, an ordinance from the Central Office of Reich Security (RSHA) directed all personnel not to reveal the length of detention in concentration camps: "If the SS Reichsführer or Chief of the German Police has determined the length of detention, it must not be mentioned in any case. For external consumption the length of detention in concentration camps must be 'until further orders.' Nevertheless, there should be no drawback in serious cases, when the establishment of a skillful whispered campaign can increase its persuasive effect, by informing the inmate we learned he will not be freed for two or three years because of the severity of his case." From then on, inmates of concentration camps were never freed by the Gestapo, and toward the end of 1939, SS officer Richard Glucks was named inspector-general of all concentration camps.

At Ravensbrück on December 24, 1939, Elfriede Lohr, Ilse Unterdorfer, and other Witnesses were locked in the bunker. They were given nothing to eat for four days and emerged no more than skeletons. However, they found the strength to sing, which helped, and they impressed the SS that they had been unsuccessful in breaking them. Fifteen inmates, including Ilse and Elfriede, were assigned to the penitentiary block. Certain inmates became completely apathetic, awaiting death. Those were the feelings that Elfriede Lohr experienced a bit later when, ill with pneumonia, she ended up in the infirmary. There, among thousands of patients with typhus and other infectious diseases, she lost the will to fight. Not wishing to see her friend's body transported to the crematorium, Ilse Unterdorfer brought her back to the penitentiary block (even though that was strictly forbidden), where an inmate Russian doctor administered a type of treatment to her that burned her skin but saved her life.

In France until 1939, the main activity of the Jehovah's Witnesses consisted of passing out biblical literature. At that time, the community was a small one, numbering perhaps 1,000. Before World War II broke out, there were ninety-four congregations in France, thirteen German-language groups in Alsace-Lorraine, thirty-two Polish (for the most part in the north and Pas-de-Calais), and thirty-nine French-language groups. In total there were about 1,000 members, or an increase of 19 percent from the previous year. By mid-October, or about six weeks after the beginning of the war, the Jehovah's Witness organization was banned in France.

Mr. Knecht, head of the French Association of Witnesses, addressed a final letter to his fellow Witnesses: "We inform you that by order of the Interior Ministry, the Watch Tower Association, and the Association of Jehovah's Witnesses in France are no longer authorized to exercise their activities, and, consequently, the office of the Watch Tower, located at 129 Faubourg Poissonniere in Paris, is closed. We will endeavor to defend our cause and work and to justify the worth of Jehovah's Witnesses' activity, especially against the tendency to consider us Communists."

By mid-October, the association was dissolved in France as a foreign organization by order of the government. The Bethel was abolished, and the faithful were no longer permitted to exercise their religion. Arrests were made, especially in eastern Alsace and northern France. The following examples are typical.

Joseph Hisiger was jailed at Thionville on September 3, 1939, charged as a conscientious objector. Louis Piechota was first arrested in September 1939 while he and five others were preaching in a small village on the Normandy coast. Because of their equipment and accents, some locals assumed that they were spies. They were taken off to prison in Dieppe. After twenty-four days of detention, Piechota was taken across town chained to his detention mates and brought before the court in Dieppe, then released. He was rearrested by the end of October and, this time, sentenced to six months in jail for illegal preaching, the association having been banned in the interim. He was incarcerated in the prison at Bethune in cell detention. He asked for a Bible. "I gave up hope to get one. One morning the door opened and the guard brought me this much-hoped-for Bible. Once I was in possession of it, my helplessness vanished. I had occasion to read it four times. I learned hundreds of verses and several entire chapters by heart. These passages fortified me against the hardships I had to endure later, and, even today, I can quote texts which I learned in the prison at Bethune. The guards were pretty well disposed towards me. They made a distinction between the majority of prisoners who had committed crimes, and us. As to the inmates, they sympathized with us. I never had any problems."

A Mr. Queroy was already imprisoned by the time the Germans arrived in France. The Nazis sent him off to a prisoner-of-war camp. In one of the camps in eastern Prussia, he received biblical literature hidden in packages of macaroni that his sister sent him.

19

IL DUCE'S OPPONENTS

Silence of the earth, mouths sewn shut by tears: and death cloaked in silence along a front of men under a compact sky.

—Mario Luzi, *The Coming of Night*

In Italy on August 22, 1939, the Interior Ministry published a memo on the "Pentecostal and assimilated religious sects," taking note of the appearance of "various evangelical religious sects introduced from abroad, and especially from America," with "doctrines contrary to all established government." The memo stated that "the Pentecostals are extremely active and tenacious propagandists. Even after recent measures taken against them, the continue efforts to meet everywhere they can, even in the countryside. They are in principle against the use of arms. It is, therefore, necessary to oppose these sects with the greatest resolution." The memo also mandated an investigation: "All legal measures must be taken against anyone who is found taking part in a meeting, in religious rites, or in propaganda activities." The interior minister recommended all practitioners be kept under strict surveillance and that they be personally searched on the least suspicion. "All brochures confiscated from members of the Pentecostal sect, have been translations of American works, mostly written by a certain J. F. Rutherford, and edited by the Watch Tower and Bible Society, International Bible Students Association, Brooklyn, NewYork, United States of America."

The memo then quoted the titles of works published by the

American Society and advised, "The introduction and distribution of this type of brochure must be stopped on national territory."

A similar memo appeared on April 9, 1935, from the office of the secretary of religion in the same ministry. It invoked an immediate ban on all associations conducting activities "contrary to our social order and harmful to the physical and mental well-being of our race." On September 21, 1939, the Interior Ministry drew up a list of subscribers to *The Watch Tower*, and it was forwarded to all provincial prefects requesting further information on the activities of the subscribers to this periodical.

In the autumn of 1939, Italian Jehovah's Witnesses were persecuted, especially after the discovery in October of a postal package of biblical writings and the book *Enemies*, which had been mailed by Maria Pizzato. On November 1, the Fascist police (OVRA) searched Pizzato's home in Milan and placed her under arrest. She recalls, "Early in the morning the policed barged into my home. . . . There were seven of them, six agents and a police commissioner." They found a Bible and some publications as well as addresses of several other Witnesses. Between October and December 1939, Italian Fascists questioned approximately 300 people suspected of being members of sects incriminated by the August memo. They arrested and sentenced 140 people.

Domenico Giorgini was arrested on October 6 in the province of Teramo. "While we were down in the vines bringing in the harvest, I saw a truck approaching the house with a couple of carabiniere officers. They took me to the Teramo jail, where I remained for five months. Then, I was sent into three years exile on the Isle of Ventetene. I found myself in the company of five other brothers and about 600 political prisoners. Among the latter were a number of well-known personalities, including a man who later became President of the Republic and whom I was privileged to give testimony on the Kingdom of God. Since the fascist government considered many of these prisoners particularly dangerous, the island was under very strict surveillance with a motor launch fitted out with a machine gun which patrolled continuously, ready to open fire on anyone who attempted escape."

While Guido d'Angelo was "sowing corn for a family of brothers whose men were already in prison," he forgot his seeder and "was badly beaten and imprisoned." On the same day that Maria Pizzato was picked up, Santina Cimorosi was arrested in Abruzzia. Her father, Domenico Cimorosi, was put into solitary confinement at the same time at the police station in Roseto. The next day the were jailed in Teramo, where they found themselves in the same cell with four other Witnesses, including Caterina de Marco. She was twenty-five years old at the time. "I was arrested by the Fascists the evening of November 1, 1939, because I was a Jehovah's Witness. My refusal to support the war made me a dangerous citizen." After several weeks at Teramo, her cell mates were transferred, and she found herself alone in a dark and very cold cell. "From time to time I was taken to the police station for questioning. They tried to intimidate me with shouts, threats, and insults to get me to deny my faith. They assured me I would never get out of jail. I was not permitted to meet with other Jehovah's Witnesses who I knew were being held or to speak with anyone. As I was considered dangerous, I was completely isolated. My guards wanted me to do the Fascist salute, but I didn't want to. I settled for saying good morning and good evening."

Prison authorities set up an altar in front of the door to her cell. "They put it there and for several weeks the priest said mass at that spot. The door to my cell was left wide open in the hopes of seeing if I would come back to the Catholic Church or if I would disturb the religious service, which would have gotten me an extra sentence. But I remained in my cell quietly as though nothing was going on outside."

The altar was eventually removed. A guard slipped her a little pocket Bible, which she hid under her coat and read when she could. In February 1940, she was sentenced to two years of house arrest in her village, and the carabineers came often to check on her whereabouts. She regained her freedom only at the war's end. The authors asked her what she thought of Fascism: "Fascism means nothing to me except another period of persecution which nothing could justify."

Dante Rioggi, who was arrested under horrible circumstances during the same period, reported, "From November until late

February I shivered in the cold because the cell was unheated and because the window didn't have any glass. It didn't take long for me to become an appalling and repulsive creature, infested with parasites. I received two or three visits from priests who assured me I would be freed if I returned to my parents' religion. I wrote to the *questura* and obtained a Bible."

Vincenzo Artusi, the father of three children, was arrested in November while on his way to work. The police searched his home and found a Bible and a copy of *Enemies*. He would be exiled to a province far from his home.

The most significant trial occurred on April 19, 1940, when the Fascist's Special Tribunal for State Protection tried twenty-six of the faithful (twenty-two men and four women, including Maria Pizzato, Albina Cumineffe, and Mariantonia Di Cenzo) who had been arrested on October 29, 1939, as recipients of packages confiscated by the police. Half of these so-called agitators were from Abruzzia, prompting Raffaele Colapietra to say, "In Abruzzia, no political party, not even the Communists, could claim to have as a large group hit harder than these quiet and inoffensive peasants of the coastal region." The tribunal sentenced all defendants to prison terms running from five to eleven years. The verdict was final and could not be appealed. Guerino d'Angelo recalls proudly, "Only one of them renounced the faith and signed a statement of allegiance to the Fascist State." Moreover, the renouncing signer was sentenced along with the others, with the judge adding, "This man is worthless to you *and* to us." Charges levied against Maria Pizzato and her companions were as follows:

1. Belonging to an "association contrary to the national interest with conspiratorial political goals"
2. an offense to the dignity and prestige of the Fascist "Duce" [Benito Mussolini]
3. an insult to the sovereign pontiff
4. an offense to the dignity of a foreign head of state.

Albina Cuminetti and Mariantonia Di Censo were condemned to eleven years and served out their sentences in the prison at Perouse. A common-law inmate asked Mariantonia the reasons for her incarceration and added, "They gave you eleven years because you refused to kill your fellow man and they gave me ten years for killing my husband! Either I'm crazy or they are."

During the first three months of 1940, between the mass arrests and trial, the Fascist Italian government introduced significant measures against Jehovah's Witnesses, including a law banning their association on March 13, 1940. This memo reinforced the earlier August 22, 1939, order and eliminated any possible doubts: "The Watch Tower and Bible Society is an independent evangelical sect commonly known under the name Jehovah's Witnesses, or Bible Students. An examination of statements provided by several of its members under arrest warrant, as well as a review of published material found in their possession, have enabled us to carefully define the distinctive characterize of this sect. The Jehovah's Witnesses claim that The *Duce* and Fascism have both come from the Devil and, after a short period of victory, these phenomena will undoubtedly end in their downfall. Since they are supported by printed materials published by the Bible Society, you are authorized to undertake energetic measures to confiscate, whenever possible, these publications or to intercept them in case they are sent by the post." Their characterization of the Fascist regime as a "Satanic emanation" was also emphasized by the general superintendent of the Avezzano police, Pasquale Andriani. Andriani sent a report to the Special Tribunal for State Security in which he stated, "The sect is particularly dangerous from a political viewpoint. In brief, it can be said the *Duce* is to equated with Goliath, and that 'the totalitarian regime under and arbitrary and absolute dictator is a hateful monstrosity' supported by the Roman Church, 'the grand prostitute.' The report clearly stipulates the will behind the Christian commandment they put into practice: 'Thou shalt not Kill.' They refused to take up arms and requested exemption from military service." The report added, "The youths refuse to serve their military duty periods and when put in jail for their position, they again refuse when they have served out their jail terms."

The authors have obtained copies of letters dated January 3, 1940, from the ORVA and February 1, 1940, from the Interior

Ministry containing lists of names and addresses of individuals denounced for their membership and activities. The ORVA memo of January 3 advises that they should be "handled in the same way as political subversives and they should be distrusted and followed constantly with a watchful eye." The Italian Bethel advised that it was 140 members strong at the beginning of the war and that "they were all simple people—farmers, working people—of modest economic circumstances and of limited education. They were jailed and exiled, but not deported except for one, Narciso Riet, who died in Germany."

Narciso Riet was born in Germany of Italian parents from the province of Udina. Obliged to flee Muhlheim, were he was passing copies of *The Watch Tower* into concentration camps, he hid in Italy on the shores of Lake Como. He continued these activities, particularly translating publications. Captured in 1943 by an SS officer, he was deported to the Dachau concentration camp in Germany, where he suffered the worst tortures. "He was chained like a dog in a narrow cell where he was forced to stay hunched over day and night." He was sent to other camps and finally put to death along with other inmates before the liberation of Berlin by Allied forces.

Giuseppe Neviconi, who was freed in 1943 after spending sixty-one months in prison because of his religious convictions, was a unique example. This man met up with Jehovah's Witnesses after his liberation and was baptized at that time. He recalled,"I got a hold of a Bible for the first time in March 1935. Rapidly the news made the rounds in the little village of Castellana (in Pinella Province). It reached the ears of the village priest, who was quick to pass it along to the local *carabiniere*. I was arrested in April because I possessed a Bible which was then forbidden. I spent sixty days in jail. Naturally, the Bible was taken from me.

"At the end of my detention, I had no job and was considered a dangerous man and a traitor to the homeland. I insist that during this time I didn't know of the Jehovah's Witnesses. My only crime was to have read the Bible." He was arrested a second time in August 1935 on the basis of defamatory comments. Some neighbors claimed that he mistreated his wife. She was interned in a psychiatric hospital, and he was jailed. "One of my neighbors, out of generosity, took some bread to my five children who were alone in the house. He was sentenced to thirty-nine months for his gesture."

Guiseppe Neviconi appealed to the Supreme Court, which reduced his sentence to eleven months. "On April 28 I was drafted into the military, but I refused to show up because of what I had read in the Bible." He refused to take his medical exam in August 1939, preferring instead to remain home to feed his family. He was arrested again on All Saints' Day 1939, locked up in the jail at Pescara, and transferred to Rome, where he was sentenced by a Fascist special tribunal to eight years of imprisonment: "From Rome I was sent to the prison at Modena, where I spent fifty-six months. All this for reading the Bible and for learning that God condemns violence."

20

THE DAILY HORROR

A man banished is at the mercy of others.
—Robert Badinter

The Berlin-Plotzensee penitentiary, along with the central prison in Brandenburg, was the site of more executions than any other in northern Germany. There, the Nazis executed more than 2,500 by guillotine or hanging. Franz Reiter sent his mother in Austria the following letter: "I am convinced I made the right choice. I can still change my mind, but that would be unfaithful to God. If I had taken the [military] oath I would have fallen into a sin deserving of death." He would be guillotined on January 7, 1940, at the age of thirty-six along with five other Witnesses.

In 1940, Louis Piechota was transferred from the Bethune jail to a camp at Vernet. The camp was located in Ariege in southern France and was originally set up as a "disciplinary camp" for the internment of foreign Communists, Spanish Republicans, and members of international brigades. Although the majority of inmates were being held for their political views, there were also individuals sentenced for common-law violations, as "suspects" and people interned without grounds as well as foreign refugees.

The authors interviewed Piechota to speak with us about his experiences: "There were already other Jehovah's Witnesses interned before us. They came from different regions in France: the north, the Pas-de-Calais, and from around St. Etienne. Our relationship with the other inmates was normal. We took advantage of our free time by witnessing the Kingdom of God to the other inmates to such an extent there were complaints and a sign was posted forbidding all talk about religion. In the camp there was a flag ceremony which was held at the gate. Two ranks were drawn up: one with the mobile guards and the other of inmates selected at random. One time I was invited to participate along with other Witnesses. During the ceremony, to everyone's consternation, we broke ranks to show our nonparticipation. The result: three days in the black hole with a loaf of bread and rats running over us when we sat down on the planks. During the spring of 1941, a German commission came to the camp to requisition labor. Since I was a miner, I was released for work in the mines, and I was sent back home to the north in the Occupied Zone."

In March 1940, the Dachau concentration camp was reopened. When it was closed in October 1939, most of the inmates were transferred to Mauthausen. Under the leadership of SS officer Eicke, Dachau was used as a training ground for the SS's dreaded Death's Head Units before they were sent to the front.

Hans Marsalek, a Communist in the Austrian resistance and an inmate at Mauthausen, was impressed, as were many of the deportees, by the Witnesses' conduct. "Until the end of 1941, before, during and after the review commission's visit, the *Bibelforscher* (we also called them *Bifo*) were regularly subjected to maltreatment, especially since they were easily recognizable by their violet triangle. For example, a recruitment commission also came to the main camp during the month of February 1940, and for the 143 *Bifo*, the consequences were as follows: in January 1940, the census showed ten deceased; in February, fifteen; in March, nineteen; and in April, nine. Of the 143, twenty-five were lucky enough to be repatriated to the concentration camp on February 18, 1940." Their systematic liquidation was stopped because "in March 1940 the first foreigners, the Poles, were massively assigned to the concentration camp at Mauthausen. From April 1940 onwards, the SS almost excessively concentrated on the new arrivals, who were Slavs." The following Mauthausen statistics reveal an accounting of horror and confirm Marsalek's observations: On January 1, 1940, out of 2,606 inmates present, there were 143 Witnesses, but by May 1, 1940, out of 2,803 inmates, there were only 66 Jehovah's Witnesses left." Hans Hildenbeutel, a tradesman from Karlsruhe, was one of them, but he died in early 1940. Another native of Karlsruhe, Adolf Muhlhauser, the father of three sons and a wife in Ravensbrück, also died in the same camp on March 20, 1940.

The death ledger conserved in the Mauthausen archives records for April 12, 1940, contains the following entries: a German *Bibelforscher auf der Flucht erschossen* (shot during an attempted escape).

When Margarete Buber-Neumann arrived at the Ravensbrück concentration camp on August 2, 1940, it had already been open for fifteen months. She described the camp for Milena: "Ravensbrück is located in Mecklenburg, eighty kilometers to the north of Berlin. By 1940 the Gestapo had locked up about 5,000 women: political detainees, Jews, Gypsies, criminals, and antisocials." By the end of the war, about 25,000 women were incarcerated in Ravensbrück. In the beginning, there were sixteen barracks built level with the ground; as the years went by, their number expanded to thirty-two, and the women were just jammed in. The first year there were relatively few of the regime's declared political adversaries aside from German, Polish, and Czech political detainees and the Jehovah's Witnesses.

The camp had already registered prisoner 4208. Buber-Neumann's case is particularly interesting: She had been a Communist Party of Germany (KPD) delegate who arrived in Moscow in 1931 with her husband, Heinz. As a KPD leader, she was arrested by Stalin's henchmen in 1937 and deported to Siberia. After the Nazi-Soviet Pact, she was transported back to Fascist Germany. Shortly after her arrival at Ravensbrück as a red triangle, she was appointed *Blockalteste* (barracks chief) in barracks 3 by *Oberaufseherin* Langefeld, who told her, "You should know that barracks 3 is allowed visits. You have to be very attentive to maintaining order. Take your things and get going now to barracks 3!"

"At that time," Buber-Neumann remembered, "Milena was still one of the new arrivals. I took interest in them which was only possible because I was the *Blockalteste* of the Jehovah's Witnesses barracks."

It was with mixed feelings that Buber-Neumann reported to barracks 3, which was on the right-hand side of the camp road across from barracks 1, where the political "veterans" were housed. She described the minutiae of the scene and was impressed by the silence and cleanliness evident in the barracks. "I didn't feel at all at ease, and it was with some hesitation that I opened the door leading to the *Tagesraum* [dayroom] on the A side. Immediately, a big blonde got up and invited me to sit down, took the mess tin I was carrying and filled it to the brim with white cabbage. Most of them looked like peasants, with tanned, emaciated faces worn by the wind and sun." Buber-Neumann ate while continuing to observe in their expressions "a strange mix of well-being and submissiveness." She noticed that they responded to tasks before being asked when, even before the midday whistle was sounded, they were already well along down the camp road headed toward their work details. Speaking of their gray-green shoes and jackets, she added, "But the winter clothes of the Witnesses, who came in during the first days of the camps, were made of better cloth and were, therefore, warmer." Buber-Neumann knew that the Witnesses had been in the camp for years because "they had on their sleeves the lowest numbers which they wore with pride. Some 275 Witnesses lived in this barracks. In block 5, next door, there were 300 others. They had all the camp rules memorized."

She described how everything was cleaned and scoured: "The stools, which were impeccably washed, were all lined up. Each Witness wearing shoes knew and followed the rule: It was forbidden to rub your feet against the stool legs lest you get polish on them." Pushing sadism to the extreme, the female SS guards "climbed up on tables to check the cleanliness of the beams. A detention camp chief put on special white gloves when she inspected the barracks and passed her hand along under cupboards hoping to find dust." The sinks and dormitory were impeccably clean. The straw mattresses and covers tied up by a cord were all folded up in the same manner. "Every bedstead had a little board with the name and number of its owner." On seeing these visiting barracks where the Witnesses were interned, Buber-Neumann thought, "And I have to keep an eye on all this? It gave me the shivers and made me nauseous."

At Ravensbrück, as has been described by Gertrud Potzinger and confirmed by Buber-Neumann, inmates were allowed to buy letter paper at the canteen bearing the legend "Ravensbrück Concentration Camp." There was even special paper for the Jehovah's Witnesses, over and above the usual rules, which carried the inscription in green letters "I am still a Jehovah's Witness."

In looking back on the Communist and religious women inmates, Marie-Elisa Nordmann-Cohen, who was part of the January 24 convoy[1] deported to Auschwitz and subsequently transferred to Ravensbrück, wrote, "They 'held on' because they all had the faith. Admittedly, my Catholic and Protestant friends found strength in their beliefs, which enabled them to accept death with serenity. Our sisters, whether believing in heaven or not, all died with admirable courage for loving their homeland and freedom more than life itself."

NOTE

1. This was a special convoy of women in the French Resistance who went to Auschwitz. A large part of this convoy was transferred to Ravensbrück. By doing this, Himmler wanted to make a deal with the Allies (especially the United States), hoping to succeed Hitler.

21

A PLAGUE SWEEPS ACROSS EUROPE

What meaning today of yesterday's disputes? The same as yesterday: they are true, except that blood flows—drop by drop—in rivulets dug between the huge stones of the law.

—Franz Kafka

Germany invaded Denmark and Norway on April 9, 1940. The 1,373 Danish Jehovah's Witnesses were not harassed during the Nazi "protectorate." A number of members of the Norwegian association were arrested and imprisoned, and all its publications were banned in July 1941. Yet they were released one week later, and Norway's 462 members continued their activities clandestinely without too much interference or ill-treatment.

On May 10, 1940, Hitler's armies launched the invasions of France, Belgium, the Netherlands, and Luxembourg. When the Wehrmacht invaded and occupied Luxembourg in mid-May 1940, the twenty-three Witnesses in the grand duchy were arrested and jailed in the Luxembourg and Trier prisons. Almost all were released a few months later and were forbidden to preach, but despite the ban, they continued to recruit disciples and celebrate baptisms. Two were deported, including Victor Bruch, and their wives and the children were sent to Germany. The women were put to work in German officers' homes, and one of the sons rejected the draft and was jailed. His five-year-old brother was expelled from school for refusing to perform the Nazi salute, and no other school would accept him. Bruch, who was converted and baptized in 1935, was deported to Buchenwald and described his jailing and deportation in these terms:

> In the Trier Prison we were given the usual forms to sign. By signing, I would have admitted following a wrong doctrine and given up my faith. I would also have admitted never having had in my possession any Watch Tower Society publications. I would have to pledge never to distribute any of its writings and to denounce anyone who asked for them as well as to respect all German laws. The Gestapo tried everything they could to get us to bow to them. Since I persisted in refusing to sign the forms on January 2, 1941, the Gestapo sent me to the concentration camp at Buchenwald near Weimar.
>
> At first my friend and I were kept in penitentiary quarters. . . . On our arrival at Buchenwald our heads were completely shaved, and we were made to cross an icy street at a dead run to the baths and then back across to our barracks. There, in front of a long counter, a prisoner issued our prison uniforms, piece by piece. Behind that prisoner was another inmate who was facing me. Several times he asked me for news of the outside, but I turned a deaf ear. We had been told that Gestapo men would often disguise themselves as prisoners with the aim of spying. Finally, I told him, "You won't get any information from me." As I was getting my last piece of uniform he told me, "You can talk—I am like you." He was Brother Hassel from Saarbrücken, and later I understood his curiosity since the Brothers had been jailed and cut off from the organization since 1937.

In May 10, 1940, German army units invaded the Netherlands, and by May 14, the Dutch had surrendered. Germans who had fled National Socialist persecutions and taken refuge in the Netherlands were hunted down from the outset of hostilities. A number of German Jehovah's Witnesses were also arrested beginning on May 10, 1940.

On May 29, 1940, Third Reich Commissioner Seyss-Inquart announced a ban on the Jehovah's Witness Association, and a month later the Gestapo searched its headquarters seeking German refugees, but they were unsuccessful in finding any. The Czech printing presses continued to operate until July 6, when Gestapo agents who had taken over the headquarters three days earlier placed seals on the Association and its print house buildings.

Years later, on June 12, 1946, Seyss-Inquart appeared before Judge Biddle representing the United States at the Nuremberg War Crimes Tribunal:

Biddle: And you carried out Heydrich's orders?

Seyss-Inquart: I carried out Heydrich's orders in the area of property assets. The Bible Students sect (Bibelforscher) was one of many.

Biddle: The Bible Students were one of them?

Seyss-Inquart: Yes, they were included.

Biddle: And their property was confiscated because they were enemies of the Reich?

Seyss-Inquart: They didn't have much, but whatever they had was confiscated because they refused to take part in the war effort.

Biddle: They refused. . . . Let me make clear—it's interesting. The Bible Students had refused to fight or to take part in the war effort, and that is why their property was confiscated. Is that right?Seyss-Inquart: Not quite. The Bible Students refused to serve in the German army, and then they were banned, and later the ban was extended to all regions.

Biddle: One moment please. I am not talking about that. I am talking about the Netherlands. Did it also apply to the Netherlands?

Seyss-Inquart: Yes, but the Bible Students weren't banned because they refused to serve in the German army, we banned them because we were opposed to them on principle.

Biddle: Ah, on principle. They were pacifists; so you were against them, and you seized their property?

Seyss-Inquart: Yes.

Despite the prohibition and confiscation of the Association's property, the Dutch continued to meet in small groups and organize underground. They were able to bring out many publications and distributed the June 1940 issue of *The Watch Tower* with a report on the persecutions in Germany as well as the January 1940 issue, which featured a study on Christian neutrality. They also passed out copies of *The Informer,* the booklet *Refugees,* and a booklet named *Fascism or Freedom.* The latter printed a speech given in 1939 by Judge J. F. Rutherford, the leader of the Bible and Tract Society in Brooklyn. The following passage seems to beas the most significant in defining the sect hierarchy's position on Nazis and their allies:

> The Devil has installed Hitler as his representative in the country. This man has an unbalanced mind and is cruel, hateful, and merciless. He casts underfoot all of the people's freedoms. Along with his acolytes he has inflicted a crushing yoke and iron discipline. He persecutes Jews, who were historically the people of Jehovah's alliance. Wasn't Jesus Christ a Jew? He has jailed thousands of Jehovah's Witnesses, true disciples of Jesus, whose only crime has been to Witness the Kingdom of Christ. A large number have suffered violent death in Hitler's jails. In order to persecute the Jews and Christians and to govern arbitrarily, Hitler has been approved and supported by the Roman Catholic hierarchy.

The following extract is from an article that appeared on May 29, 1938, in the newspaper *The German Voice* under the signature of a Berlin priest:

> There is now a country in which the so-called Bible Students (Jehovah's Witnesses) are prohibited. It is Germany! This sect was not banned by Bruning, although the Catholic Church requested he adopt this measure several times. When Adolf Hitler took power and the German Church made this same request, the *Führer* responded, "These Bible Students are trouble-makers. . . . I hold them as charlatans and will not tolerate German Catholics to be sullied by the American Judge Rutherford. I dissolve the sect of the Bible Students in Germany, and I will turn over their property to the community of Germany people. I will confiscate all their written materials!" (The priest adds, "Bravo! And to think in America the Church, and even Cardinal Mundelheim, failed in having Rutherford's book withdrawn from American libraries.").

The following quote is from the conclusion of Judge Rutherford's speech: "The Fascist fanatics, the Nazi dictators helped by the Roman hierarchy, are now ruining continental Europe. Those who obey God and Christ will survive this torment." Obviously, such a message displeased the German and Dutch Nazis on Syess-Inquart's payroll.

By August 1940, the 500 Dutch proclaimers had to be especially vigilant and careful when they reproduced and distributed such literature. When Hitler's troops entered Belgium in mid-May 1940, the entire country was transformed into a veritable battleground. Members of the Belgian Jehovah's Witnesses community continued to distribute its literature despite a Belgian Ministry of Interior ban, dated May 30, 1940, which stipulated in part, referring to their publications, that "they sap the morale of the troops and the population." Banned publications included the booklet *Fascism or Freedom*, the January 1940 issue of *The Watch Tower*, and the October issue of *Consolation*, which featured a caricature of Hitler astride a ferocious beast and casting the human race underfoot.

The Belgian Bethel provided copies of *The Watch Tower* to this project and especially the issue that appeared in January 1940 on "Christian neutrality." It is important to note that this text in particular spurred members' resolve in their unwillingness to fight in World War II and their refusal to take the loyalty oath. "Christian neutrality is the abstention or refusal to take part in a fight or a war, particularly when the nations taking part conduct themselves in a hostile fashion to neutrals. Whenever there is a contradiction between the laws of nations and the laws of the All-Powerful, Christians have the duty to give preference to the laws of God rather than those of men. Christians will observe all laws of man and nations in harmony with the laws of God. We must only be soldiers of Jesus Christ but at the same time we will fight against any nation which finds itself under the high surveillance of a Demon, God's enemy. That is why a Christian does not take part in the affairs of this world. A Christian should not get mixed up in a war between nations. The recruitment of the men of any nation is not his business. He must remain neutral whatever his national origin. Nothing prevents nations from fighting each other, but Christian must be on guard against being co-opted, by word or deed, into actions which governments may undertake to raise troops or requisition was material."

Members also continued to translate, duplicate, distribute, and interpret biblical literature despite unsuccessful searches of their headquarters by the Gestapo in October 1940.

By June 1940, German troops had captured Metz in France, and it was thus at Thionville on June 17 that Joseph Hisiger was freed by Nazi forces because he was an Alsatian citizen, although he had just been sentenced to jail by a French court on June 13.

An armistice was signed by the French state and Hitler's Germany. Northern France was attached to Belgium in fact if not in law, and Alsace was reunited with Germany, more precisely to the Bade Gau, because its *Gauleiter*, Robert Wagner, a Nazi stalwart and unconditional fan of Hitler since 1923, was named by the Reich chancellor as *Gauleiter* of Alsace. The Moselle area was reattached to the Palatinate and the Saar (Gau of Westmark, or "Western market"). France was divided into two zones, the Occupied Zone and the Free Zone. French Jehovah's Witnesses organized in small groups, continued to distribute their materials, clandestinely crossed the line of demarcation, and passed on stencils, translations, and articles received from the United States, Switzerland, and so on from the Free Zone to the Occupied Zone and vice versa.

Members who worked for the railroads often served as couriers, and those living near the line of demarcation provided "mail drops." Such was the case of Adolf Koehl, who hid stencils and copies of *The Watch Tower* behind the advertisements in the window of his barber shop.

On June 8, 1940, the RSHA published the following ordinance: "By order of the Berlin RSHA, all members of the Bible Students, all persons collaborating with them, as well as all persons known to be members of the Bible Students, must be arrested. This order also enjoys the power of law for women." A surprise sweep was initiated throughout Reich territory by the Gestapo on June 12, 1940, and, coinciding with the searches and arrests, all materials belonging to the Bible Students Association were seized.

A thorough and virulent hunt for Bible Students was also undertaken in annexed countries. Some forty-three Viennese Jehovah's Witnesses were victimized by the wave of arrests, and according to the Gestapo's daily report of August 5, a complaint was filed on July 31 with the Vienna public prosecutor against the jailed prisoners. The list is almost exclusively women. Peter and Helen Golles, who owned a grocery store in Vienna, were arrested on June 12, 1940. Peter Golles had replaced August Kraft after his arrest, directing the reproduction and distribution of biblical material in Austria. The Gestapo was aware not only that he was supplying his customers with vegetables and fruits but also that he was providing "spiritual merchandise." He was first jailed in the cell block at the Vienna Palace of Justice, where he was tried and sentenced to ten years' imprisonment, with no extenuating circumstances. Transferred to prison in Stein in Lower Austria, he remained in solitary confinement until the collapse of the Nazi regime.

On June 25, 1940, two German Witnesses, Messrs. Buhler and Ballreich, where shot after sentencing by a military tribunal in Wiesbaden for refusing to wear a military uniform. Both had just been married. On July 20, 1940, Franz Zeiner was executed in Berlin. Wilhelm Blaschek, a man who had written urging him to remain strong and keep the faith, was arrested. He was sentenced himself on August 11, 1940, to four years of forced labor at a penitentiary for "demoralizing the troops."

On August 17, 1940, Johanna Burgstaller, Helene Delacher, Hilde and Katharina Entacher, Fritz and Notburga Gillesberger, Alois Hillebrand, Alois Hochrianer, Franz Humer, Agnes Spiegl, Anna Stobl, and Franz Weger appeared before the regional court at Innsbruck, where the prosecutor accused them of belonging to the Jehovah's Witnesses.

During September and October 1940, the Jehovah's Witnesses were subjected to a wave of searches and arrests in the Netherlands, especially in the northern part of the country. The Gestapo arrested Hermann Tollenaar and other Witnesses from Leersum, Eliza de Vries from the Frise area, and Ever Dost from Groningen. All were jailed at the Scheveningen prison, where they were questioned by Nazis demanding supplementary information about the organization. Arnold Werner, who was arrested shortly before September 12 by two SS officers and jailed at Scheveningen, told how he was handed writing materials and ordered to "write out everything concerning the Jehovah's Witnesses, its congregations in Holland, its leaders, and especially their supply of publications."

The Gestapo searched the home of Steve Heiwegen at Harskamp on October 18, 1940, and he was arrested. He was jailed at Arnhem, where the interrogation was more violent than at Scheveningen. Heiwegen reported that he was beaten after refusing to tell the whereabouts of other Jehovah's Witnesses, and he was then thrown into a cell where he said he was kept for forty-eight hours without food or water and made to kneel and stand hundreds of times. He was then punched and kicked and had a revolver pointed at his temple. In December 1941, some practitioners were freed, but Herman Tollemaar was deported to the Oranienburg/Sachsenhausen concentration camp in Germany and would never return. On December 4, 1940, seventeen Austrian Witnesses were sentenced by the regional tribunal in Linz to sentences ranging from six months to two years in jail.

On December 11, 1940, Johann Seibold, from Ulm, was executed for refusing to perform military service or swear an oath of loyalty to Hitler. His nineteen-year-old brother, Konrad, would follow him to the gallows on March 28, 1942.

22

REALITY IN THE CAMPS

> And they do well to hide their Hell,
> For in it things are done
> That Son of God nor son of Man
> Ever should look upon!
> —Oscar Wilde, *Ballad of Reading Gaol*

In 1940, the Nazis cordoned off the Jews in the city of Lodz and encircled their entire neighborhood with barbed wire. To this first closed ghetto would be added those of Warsaw, Cracow, Lublin, and others. The Abt family, who fled Danzig in September 1939 taking refuge in Lodz in July 1940, found themselves persecuted by the Gestapo. Harald Abt and his wife, Else, answered a summons to appear at the Gestapo offices. Harald refused to sign a renunciation and was jailed for several weeks at Gestapo headquarters in Lodz before his temporary transfer to a Berlin prison. From there, he was deported to Sachsenhausen. After having signed a statement acknowledging that "she knew she would go to a concentration camp if she continued to practice her religion," his wife was spared by an SS officer who allowed her to return home to care for her ten-month-old daughter.

Harald Abt, violet triangle 32771 at Sachsenhausen, recalls, "I was the only Witness in my group. The Jehovah's Witnesses were all locked up together in one of the barracks at Sachsenhausen, which were set up in a semicircle around a parade ground. Our meals consisted of turnip soup and sometimes had a boiled horse head in it." He remembered the barracks, the work, and especially the SS's cruelties. "At Sachsenhausen you could never be sure of staying alive. You didn't have to do much to get noticed by the guards and risk punishment. In that case you might have been forced to stand all day in front of the barracks in the glacial winter cold." The Neuengamme concentration camp, classified as a Sachsenhausen outside work camp, became established in June 1940 and held about 1,000 inmates. A large brickworks situated nearby was refurbished by with the objective of making it profitable by supplying low-cost building materials for major construction projects in Hamburg, which Hitler wanted to transform.

Transferred from the police jail at Fuhlsbuttel on completion of his sentence for refusing to sign a statement giving up his faith, Karl Zietlow was registered as inmate number 2969 at the Neuengamme camp. Initially assigned to one of the toughest work parties on to the Dove-Elbe canal works, he was then shifted to the weed detail, made up exclusively of Witnesses, and assigned the job of cleaning out the canal. Later he worked in the clay pits at the brick factory. Once the clay had been extracted (this was brutal and exhausting work), inmates were supposed to make mortar and cement into slabs and cement casings for air-raid shelters and other buildings. Hans Weiss-Ruthels also worked at the cinder-block factory, which was a veritable torment and which reserved a special hell, the disciplinary column, which had only one objective: ridding the camp of inmates specially "recommended" by the Gestapo. According to historian Joseph Billig, "These inmates who were doomed to death were doing drainage work in an awful swamp on the factory grounds which swallowed up those who fell in. That's where the Jews were finished off. They worked until they dropped dead either crazed by the team leaders' beatings or as a result of a misstep. The daily torment of these men was unimaginable. These unfortunates had to push heavily loaded metal wagons on the run, and they were just wiped out."

An Alsatian, Henri Solbach, said that he "occasionally met some Witnesses in Neuengamme. They were part of a small group spread around amongst the other deportees. They didn't really have much contact or discussions with us and they pretty much kept to themselves. Most of them were German and we didn't speak their language. They were working at the brick-works on a small work party called the *Betonkolonne,* which was making cement slabs for construction of small homes in Hamburg for citizens who lost their homes during the bombings. They weren't very outgoing. They had their own conception of the future. They had a kind of pessimistic vision of their future since they often spoke of the end of the world. Yes, their vision of the future was the end of the world. It was kind of depressing. But for them it was a consolation, given their lives as deportees." The authors asked for more details and whether he considered them Nazis resisters. Solbach responded, "So to speak—the end of the world was a consolation to them, a relief from the misery, and they displayed a kind of fatalism. Naturally, they were what we would call today pacifists. They were against the use of force. They were conscientious objectors and refused to be drafted into the German army. They submitted themselves in a fatalistic way to the wishes of the Supreme Being. We found them somewhat unrealistic. At the time we pitied their views and opinions. But what we considered as naïveté seemed to be a consolation, and their view of the future brought them peace of conscience and peace of the soul, but in a way it was too idealistic and too unrealistic. Sometimes, when they were lining up in columns before leaving for work, some of their zealots would get outspoken in their views. It was hard for me to share their opinions since I didn't believe in their views."

The following account is that of a twenty-four-year-old, arrested for being Jewish in September 1939, imprisoned for four months in the Black Forest, and then taken to Karlsruhe for assignment to the camp at Sachsenhausen: "The train was divided into two-man cells. The SS opened one cell after another, but all were full. Finally, they found one occupied by a single inmate. I was given a hard kick and land literally on top of this crouching man. During the fourteen days of transport, he and I were attached by handcuffs." En route, he learned that his companion was a Jehovah's Witness, and during their journey the Witness explained his religious beliefs. They were separated at Sachenhausen because "two isolation barracks were reserved for them. They had about 200

Jehovah's Witnesses." None of the other 50,000 inmates were authorized to cross the demarcation line under penalty of a beating.

In 1940, about thirty Jews were transferred to the camp at Neuengamme, and the camp chief declared, "These stinking Jews, we are going to throw them in with the Jehovah's Witnesses because they adore the same Jehovah." And so this young Jewish man found himself once again with the Witnesses, where he could eat a few potato peels in hiding because the Witnesses had "a few privileges. . . . Some could sleep, work, and others raised rabbits for the SS." Again transferred in 1943, this time to Auschwitz, this young man declared, "It was with great sadness that I left the Jehovah's Witnesses, who had become like brothers to me."

Fred Sedel was deported to Auschwitz-Birkenau for being a Jew. "During the wait I asked a veteran for information on the meaning of the different triangles sewn on uniforms. He explained [that] the predominant red ones are political prisoners, Nazi adversaries; the green ones are common criminals; black ones are "antisocial" saboteurs; pink for homosexuals; and, finally, the violets: conscientious objectors or members of religious sects. And we were being watched by one of them (the violets) who took advantage of the opportunity and spewed out a whispered propaganda speech. I don't know to what sect he belonged since I only cocked a distracted ear to his personal interpretation of the Holy Trinity."

In April 1940, orders were given to open the Auschwitz camp, and Rudolf Hess was named commandant. The first Poles were herded into to camp by the Nazis on June 14, 1940. It should be noted that it was the first camp outside of Reich boundaries to be listed as an official concentration camp. The camp quickly proved too small, and Hess began an expansion program. On Hitler's orders, a second camp was set up at Birkenau, which became an extermination center.

23

TWO CHILDREN OF ALSACE-LORRAINE

My favorite virtue: childhood.
—Stephane Mallarme

"Right from the beginning, in 1941, because of our Christian neutrality, my father would have no part of 'passive resistance,' my mother and sister refused to work on military clothing; and for my part I wouldn't say 'Heil Hitler' or sing the national anthem, or say the prayer for the Führer at school. Our family also refused to join the *Volksgemeinschaft* [Nazi Party]. From that moment on, the harassment began: frequent searches carried out, and often when I came home from school there was no one there since the SS had taken my mother to the *Kommandantur* for questioning. In the evenings we were waiting for my father, who didn't come home until very late if the SS interrogated him. My sister, who was twelve years older, had to put up with the same thing.

"At the time, there were about twenty Jehovah's Witnesses in the Thionville region. The interrogations were designed, on the one hand, to get us to sign on to join the Nazi Party and thus renounce our faith and, on the other, to drag the names of other Jehovah's Witness out of us and to find out the times and places of our meetings." The speaker here, an eight-year-old girl who refused to give in, suffering through the same persecutions as her family, was Ruth Danner.

After the June 1940 armistice, Alsace-Lorraine was placed

under Nazi administration. The Third Reich's "disguised annexation" reverberated across every sector of Alsatian public and administrative life, and the whole region was subjected to an all-out Germanization and Nazification campaign.

"In Lorraine, in order to hold onto their jobs, public servants were forced to sign a statement acknowledging 'the return of their country to the Reich' and promise to obey, without reservation, orders from their chiefs and place themselves in active service of the Führer and National Socialist Greater Germany." A similar obligation was imposed on Alsatian functionaries under threat of deportation or internment. These actions were in direct violation of Article 46 of the Hague Convention of 1907, the laws and customs of war, as well as general principles of international law. In the Haut Rhin, Bas Rhin, and Moselle Departments, the means of Germanization were at the outset outright annexation and were subsequently followed up all the way down to the district level.

Even in Germany, the Germanization of Alsatians and Lorrains was actively pursued. An Interior Ministry memo addressing "behavior to be adopted" with Alsatians and Lorrains working in Germany conveys the importance accorded Germanization: It recommends treating them as "members with full rights of the community of German people" and to "do everything to insure they are not considered French citizens."

Beginning in the summer of 1940, undesirable inhabitants were checked, registered, and expelled. An ordinance relative to the property of "enemies of the German people and the Reich" was published, and as early as July 1940, *Gauleiter* Wagner stated that "order and security mandate the separation of Germans and their enemies." The Schirmeck-Vorbruck camp was set up on July 2 and two weeks later received its first inmates, opponents of the regime. Their numbers had been growing since conscription orders went out on May 8, 1941, enrolling young Alsatians from seventeen to twenty-five years old in the *Reichsarbeitsdienst* (RAD), or work brigades. Even young girls were not spared, and from October 1941 on, they were also incorporated into an analogous organization.

On September 4, 1941, the Gestapo called at the establishment of Schaeffer and Company and arrested Adolphe Arnold, a colorist and artistic adviser at this Pfastatt textile printing mill. The Gestapo took him to the Mulhouse jail after searching his home and finding nothing. Two German secret police agents returned to his apartment to question Emma, his wife. Their daughter Simone, who was twelve years old at the time, remembers that day: "The two men sent me off rudely to my room and sat themselves down in the living room and insisted that my mother sit between them with her face turned to the light coming in from the window. Then they began a very comprehensive interrogation which they carefully wrote down in an enormous register. The questions rained down and were repeated tirelessly. Everything was done to extract a betrayal. After four hours, Mama learned that my father had been in their hands since that morning. Then the threats came down: 'You will never see your husband again and you and your child will suffer the same fate!' The reason? We were part of 'that mob,' that's to say, the *Bibelforscher*, the nickname given to Jehovah's Witnesses, who were supposed to be exterminated on German soil, Alsace having been annexed to Germany."

Simone described her mother's financial situation: "Without a salary, without a livelihood, Mama tried to find work. The indispensable 'Work Permit' wasn't for 'vermin' like us. The bank informed her that her account was frozen. Day and night, whenever we heard heavy men's footsteps on the building's wooden staircase, we just clinged tightly to each other."

The Mulhouse Gestapo arrested Ferdinand Saler, a building painter and the father of two children; Franz Huber, then sixty-four years old; Eugene Lentz, a young teacher and the father of five young children; and Paul Dossmann, initially interned at the camp at Natzweiler. Despite these arrests, the community stuck together and continued to meet and distribute its biblical materials. The Gestapo then proceeded with the expulsion of entire families; that was the fate of the Schaguines and Schoenauers, and their property was also confiscated.

Adolphe Arnold remained in a cell in Mulhouse with no contact with the outside world. He was subjected to interrogation by the Gestapo, which, in a effort to break him and trick him to betray others, advised that his friend Adolphe Koehl had been arrested and given up names. Arnold did not "discover this horrible lie until I got out of the Mulhouse jail." Mr. Koehl was a barber and was freed so that his shop could remain open since the Germans feared that a French-speaking Alsatian might slash their throats with his razor.

On October 17, Jehovah's Witness inmates were shifted to a camp at Schirmeck-Vorbruck (Bas Rhin), which was called *Sicherungslager-Vorbruck* (transit camp). Although it was worse than jail, it was not quite as bad as a concentration camp. Jehovah's Witnesses could escape this hell and avoid the concentration camps by cancelling their membership in the "cursed *Bibelforscher* sect"—a way out that was always available. They refused, so they were transferred on November 20 to Dachau—a trip that took fifteen days—where they finally arrived on December 5. After a ten-day stay in quarantine barracks, they were assigned to the *Strafblock* (punishment block), where there were already other Jehovah's Witnesses from Germany, Holland, and even Russia. The winter of 1941 was especially hard, and inmates dropped dead during torturous exercises standing at attention, day and night, out in the cold. They were constantly berated and warned to "*biegen oder brechen*" (bend or break) and "*nachgeben oder ausrotten*" (give in or kick the bucket). They always had "the cancellation statement" as a way out.

It was not surprising that, at age sixty-four, Mr. Huber would weaken noticably. He was receiving a daily ration of only two or three pieces of vegetable floating in bouillon and a piece of bread. Barely able to remain upright on his knees, an SS officer told him sarcastically, "Look at your exit out of here, you dirty . . ." and, pointing to the chimney, "you'll go out that way."

Speaking of hunger, Violette Maurice spoke of the pangs she experienced: "Whoever among us was not hungry must have been drunk at Ravensbrück or at Mauthausen. Hunger pangs, which twisted your insides, left you with no strength and in a state of dizziness. The black-bread ball mixed with straw didn't last long. This bread smelled moldy but we ate it with relish. As to the noonday soup, it became thinner and thinner; it was like dirty water with some debris of vegetable floating around.

"He was hoping to work outside the camp in a paint shop. But in order to get out, they suggested he paint munitions boxes. Papa refused. The SS couldn't understand how he could paint an SS's kitchen but wouldn't paint the munitions boxes. Papa, like all the Jehovah's Witnesses, drew a distinction between the man as a human being with legitimate personal needs and his contemptible ideology. The SS, annoyed he couldn't make a quick profit, referred the munitions box case all the way up to the *Kommandantur.*"

24

PLANET ASH

Himmler gave his assent to a plan for classifying concentration camps according to types of inmates and the dangers they represented to the state. Accordingly, Reinhard Heydrich issued orders regulating assignment of prisoners in three categories of camps.

The first included camps for the least dangerous prisoners, those likely to make "amends" more easily. Living conditions were less harsh, and inmates were expected to serve as the workforce. Dachau was included in this group and was assigned a special "A" classification, which set it apart from other camps in this group. Sachsenhausen and Auschwitz I were intended for men who could handle only light workloads. In the second category were camps intended for *Schutzhaftlinge,* "protective detention," whose charges were considered more serious but who, nonetheless, might be susceptible to making amends; these were Buchenwald, Neuengamme, Flossenburg, Auschwitz, and later Natzweiler. The third category included Mauthausen and, later, Gusen and Gross-Rosen, to which were sent all criminals, "antisocials," and "irreductible political prisoners" who were slated for early liquidation. Later, modifications of the classification system were introduced. For example, Buchenwald was moved up from the second category to the first in April 1944. For many reasons, general conditions were worse at Dachau, a *Stufe I* (grade I) camp, than at Buchenwald, which was a *Stufe II* (grade II) camp until 1944. In reality, the classification system had little practical effect.

Up until 1941, Gusen held an overwhelming majority of Polish political prisoners and a few Spanish, German, and Austrian inmates. There were also 2,220 inmates in "limited preventive custody" who were not jailed for criminal acts but who were, nonetheless, classified as criminals. There were also a few *Bibelforscher* who had opted against military service, some "antisocials" who had supposedly refused to work, and finally some Germans being held for past homosexual offenses. The inmate national breakdown would begin to change in 1941 and, more dramatically, in 1942 and 1943, when men from all over Europe were sent in.

In the Netherlands, arrests increased from February to March 1941. Numerous Jehovah's Witnesses were picked up by Dutch police and the Gestapo in The Hague and other towns, and the confiscation campaign of all Witness publications continued. Some prisoners were released in December, only to be reincarcerated later. Interrogation sessions were punctuated by kicks and harsh treatment, especially those presided over by Groningen Gestapo Chief Konings. Wilhelm Ketterlaing reported slipping through a police roundup one day and happening later to pass by the town jail, where he heard seventeen jailed Witnesses singing religious hymns for encouragement.

Despite the occasional betrayal, released Witnesses were able to carry on their activities: They even sent a tract to all Dutch police stations explaining their position as the Dutch were apprehending them and turning them over to the Germans. Despite all the persecution, in 1941 the Dutch Association of Witnesses managed to increase its membership by 27 percent through new conversions. Although some were freed, dozens of others were jailed and shipped off to detention centers or concentration camps.

In May 1941, two new camps were opened near granite quarries: Gross-Rosen and Natzweiler-Struthof in Alsace. The latter housed Belgian Witnesses, known as "the dogs of heaven," who for the most part were arrested in early June 1941.

In Couillet on June 7, the Gestapo arrested a Mr. Hankus, who was hiding Andre Wozniak, one of the leaders being sought by the German secret police. Hankus was first thrown in the St. Gilles jail, then transferred to the main prison in Louvain before being deported to Buchenwald.

One the same day, the Gestapo searched the home of a tradesman, Leon Floryn. Publications that he had hidden on the store's shelves with Mr. Michiels were found. Michiels was picked up immediately and sent to a concentration camp. The Gestapo returned the next day at 5:00 A.M. and arrested Leon Floryn.

To assist in responding to the authors' queries, the Belgian Bethel contacted Floryn's son, who furnished information on his father's concentration camp experiences. His father was first jailed in St. Gilles, then in different German towns, before being interned at the Natzweiler concentration camp as *Schutzhaftling* 1589 in block 2. He remained there for four months, where he endured horrific conditions. Transferred to Dachau, he balked at working on war materials, which earned him disciplinary punishment, including standing barefoot in the snow and in the cell block.

Finally, to break down weakened inmates and especially to maintain their exemplary work output, the Nazis displayed absurd determination in maintaining a facade and did not undertake exterminations at the camp; rather, they organized undercover convoys, the purpose of which was to remove all the exhausted women to a camp specialized for annihilations. In that way it is possible to say that the work camps and extermination camps were complimentary.

25

GERMAN ITINERARIES

He who has a true idea knows he has an idea that is true and no man can doubt the truth.

—Baruch Spinosa

Max Hollweg, born in the industrial city of Remscheid-Ehringhausen on December 7, 1910, was the sixteenth child in a family of Jehovah's Witnesses. In July 1930, Hollweg became a Witness. The International Association of *Bibelforscher* sent him to Prague, and after his expulsion he returned to Germany and continued to proselytize. The Gestapo arrested him on July 14, 1938, and he was incarcerated for seven years. After three months of maltreatment in a cell at the Frankfurt prison, he was sent to Buchenwald in a criminal convoy. On disembarking from the train, he was asked by an SS officer why he was there. He responded, "Because I am a Jehovah's Witness, and I want to remain one," for which he was beaten. Assigned to a disciplinary work detail, he was given inmate number 4354 and a violet triangle with a black dot (signifying the disciplinary block).

He said, "Our Brothers dependability was much appreciated by the SS. We were even kept together in the same barracks called the *Bibelforscherblock.* Brother Tollner from Meinerzhagen shared smuggled articles from *The Watch Tower* with us regularly. A Brother suffering from hunger started smoking, thus running the risk of execution. That happened fairly often when, driven by the urge, an inmate would suddenly drop out of line to grab a cigarette butt thrown away by an SS. I shared my bread with this Brother. He has overcome his dependence and survived."

He was transferred on March 8, 1940, with eighty-nine other Witnesses to the Nieferhagen camp to labor on conversion of the Wewelsburg Citadel into a school for SS leadership. He arrived at the camp on May 25 and described the living conditions: "The Niederhagen concentration camp was set up on the same model as Buchenwald. At the beginning, there were only Jehovah's Witnesses there. A rather large convoy came in from Sachsenhausen. Also, professional criminals, antisocials, political prisoners, workers from the East, Jews, and even Russians came in after that. At least as long as we were together as Witnesses we were able to make the evenings after work more bearable. An Oberscharführer had one of those crazy ideas. He ordered me to wrestle with Roland. Roland was the most vicious camp guard dog. A command was given: 'I order you to kill the dog!' I responded, 'I can't carry out this order because the dog is camp property, and I don't fight with unreasonable animals.' "

He told of the behavior of the SS toward the Witnesses: "The Jehovah's Witnesses were often terrorized by the SS and other inmates; even though we were workers, they should have been able to count on the most. Whenever they wanted to amuse themselves, and when the idea came into their heads, the *Kapos* recruited inmates from the professional criminal, antisocial, and political populations, and together, with the SS, they treated us like wild animals."

He also spoke of escapes and of the inevitable tension between his conscience and his desire to escape his torment: "A newly electrified fence with a charge of 360 volts was to be installed along the lines of the old model to make any escape impossible. The following gave me serious conscience problems: Should we create a trap for ourselves? If another of us threw himself on the wires, would we not lose another Brother? The wiring was supposed to be hooked up so that the search lights worked, but we wanted to wire it up to make sure the current didn't run through the fence. Willi Wilke and I didn't want to let anyone in on our secret except for our dear Brother, Werner Edling. When I told Werner of my thoughts, he told me in his Berlin dialect, 'You are crazy. They are going to catch us!' I said, 'They won't catch us because I am not an electrician.' He ordered me then to do this work. It was the basis of a clandestine activity for two years."

The experiences of a female prisoner, Gertrud Potzinger, are given here:

Authors: Ms. Potzinger, what happened in the spring of 1941?
GP: My jail term finished, and I was transferred from Breslau to the Berlin Alexanderplatz prison.
Authors: What memories do you have of this Berlin prison?
GP: It was an overcrowded prison where the inmates slept on the stairs and on the ground. Lice were everywhere.
Authors: Do you remember your arrival at the Ravensbrück camp?
GP: Yes, especially the delousing . . . Those who had lice were shaved. It is one of my worst memories. The humiliation of all those naked, demoralized women; hundreds of inmates who had to stand for hours, completely naked. The women were humiliated, ashamed, and didn't know where to look. A terrible beginning. . . . A doctor passed through and examined us. Then we got our clothes and went out . . . by the window, yes, by the window. We were assigned to the *Strafblock.*"

Fortunately, she remained in the penitentiary block for only a few days since a member of the delousing detail was a Witness who signed Gertrud onto a work party carrying coal. Margarete Buber-Neumann spoke of Witnesses who helped her when she reflected back on her registration and experience at being undressed on arrival at camp: "It was done by women in white smocks who were also inmates because they were wearing red and violet cloth triangles with numbers on their sleeves. The red triangle was for political prisoners, the violet one for *Bibelforscherinnen*. . . . This [the delousing] was done by two *Bibelforscherinnen.* One of them was named Emmi. . . . I had occasion to observe her perform her duties for years. For her, cutting hair became a pleasure. More than one woman prayed and begged; the more beautiful and rich was their hair, the faster Emmi, the Jehovah's Witness, used her clippers with diabolical ardor to reduce a beautiful curly head to a poor bald skull."

Authors: You said earlier that thanks to a *Bibelforscher* woman you were assigned to the coal detail?

GP: I had to carry a twenty-five-pound load of coal in a basket with another inmate to the camp staff quarters. After three years in Breslau my muscles were soft and I had to make terrible efforts to keep from dropping the load and I hung on with my fingers with all my might.

Confirmation from another prisoner was obtained on the above recital of prison labor: "The second type of work, which occupied most of the prisoners, was cartage: We used hand carts, wheelbarrows, and also our bare hands. We moved coke, briquettes, vegetables, wood, and straw. Cartage by wheelbarrow was the hardest because, empty, they weighed fifteen kilos and tipped over easily. Also, there was a lot of seasonal work, like shoveling snow and splitting wood. A special detail unloaded shipments for the camp; they were constantly on the alert and had to unload freight at top speed. The most painful was unloading the boats. This work provided a cruel spectacle: the women moved along rocking gangplanks with their wheelbarrows, awkwardly crossing each other, and often they lost their balance and fell into the water."

Gertrud Potzinger was assigned to another detail, where she pushed wheelbarrows full of rocks. Then she worked in a wood factory. This was a fairly privileged detail, as she did not have to work outdoors, exposed to the cold. She became sensitive to the cold during her time in prison. Her job in the factory was making wooden soles and heels, and one day she caught her fingers in the machine and shaved off her fingertips. Iodine burned them badly, and she was forced to take two days off.

Authors: You told me one of your most horrible memories of Ravensbrück happened on those days off. Can you tell about that?

GP: Certainly. While I was carrying a bucket of water along the camp road to the kitchen, I saw a Gypsy and her little girl coming towards me. There was also an *Arbeitsführer* who asked her inmate number and where she was going. The Gypsy answered and the *Arbeitsführer* told the child, who was hanging onto her mother's skirts, to let go. He ordered the mother on down the road. The child was kneeling, begging the guard to let her go with her mother; she wanted to die with her mother. In answer he just trampled her under his boots. . . . After roll call, when the lines for work were being formed up, the commandant saw two women supporting a third who couldn't stand. He ordered them to leave her, and she fell to the ground. The commandant then grabbed her by the back of the neck, as one would a cat, and threw her into the little duck pond by the main gate. The unfortunate bumped against rocks, hurt herself, cried out, and tried to hang on the edge of the pond. With one kick the commandant sent her backwards into the water, where she drowned. Then he turned around and stared at all the inmates to try to figure out what they were thinking. I had to make a terrible effort to remain impassive. These two scenes were all the more horrifying since they were poor creatures, completely weakened, and crushed under the boots of the stronger ones.

Potzinger then described her poor state of health when she arrived at the camp and the solidarity of her fellow inmates. She suffered awful stomach pains and hepatic diarrhea, and she had been vomiting and could not keep food in her stomach.

Authors: But how were you able get out alive?

GP: Thanks to the help of a fellow inmate, a *Bibelforscherin* who worked in the SS canteen, I was able to end my torment. She stole some oats and a little sugar which she brought me. Then I hid in the latrine and ate the dried oat flakes and the sugar. That helped me a lot. Elfriede, who was my bunk mate, worked at that time in the camp garden. She made herself an artificial bust out of tomatoes and pickles, hid some parsley under her clothes, and that's how she brought me her booty. That's how I was able to regain some strength.

Gertrud Potzinger was first assigned to block 5 in the old camp and then in the *Musterblock* (number 17 or 19).

Authors: Do you remember Margarete Buber-Neumann, and have you read her account of her own deportation. If so, what do you think of it?

GP: Margaret Buber-Neumann was an agreeable person and tried to keep us from squabbling and was not in the least bit vulgar. Nevertheless, she absolutely couldn't believe in God and stayed loyal to Lenin.

26

A REGIME OF TERROR

> Don't look for consolation for affliction. Affliction itself provides the consolation.
>
> —Stig Dagerman

On July 3, 1942, Ludwig Cyranek was executed in Germany. In Vienna, he had helped type Watch Tower stencils, for which was sentenced, among other charges, by the special tribunal on March 20, 1941, "for demoralizing the armed forces, for active support of an association opposed to military service, and for defying the ban on the International Association of Bible Students."

On July 8, forty-four Dutch Jehovah's Witnesses were deported to Sachsenhausen from the Utrecht train station. A review board toured the concentration camp at Mauthausen in mid-August 1941 to recruit inmates. Historian Hans Marsalek relates, "Among the recruits were nine German Jehovah's Witnesses. None were prepared do their military service. . . . None of these *Bibelforscher* were assigned to the disciplinary company or killed immediately thereafter. At that time it was the killings of Dutch Jews and organization of the first transports to Hartheim which saved those nine inmates."

At the Ravensbrück camp, according to chronicler Germaine Tillion, "it was Kogel who ordered the brutalities. He tortured *Bibelforscher* himself during the winter of 1941–1942. They refused to work or even show up at roll call, believing that would be a form of acquiescence with the Nazi war machine." In an ordinance dated August 1941, Himmler ordered the suppression of all freedom for concentration camp inmates and was determined to deal ruthlessly with religious fanatics, calling them "enemies of Germany as well as Communists and scum of the same type." All "ecclesiastical rascals" having subversive opinions were to be interned in the camps.

Elisabeth Holec, a young Austrian of eighteen, was deported to Ravensbrück with her mother, who subsequently died there. According to a Gestapo report dated December 17, 1941, "Elisabeth Holec persists in supporting ideas of the International Association of Bible Students and states that she has met with people who share the same beliefs. Nevertheless, she refuses to provide the slightest information on other Bible Students and declares that would constitute betrayal, something that is not done in the organization." August Hirschmann, another young Austrian, also refused to give up any information under questioning by his torturers. A Gestapo report lists the names of twenty-eight other believers arrested and subjected to questioning and judicial investigations.

On October 22, 1941, the Ried regional tribunal at Inn handed out jail sentences from four to six months to Maria Viertlbauer, Mathias Buchner, and Josef Sax.

Says Hans Marsalek, "From the winter of 1941–1942, Buchenwald SS camp management assigned the *Bibelforscher* to relatively better work parties. But the Poles were kept out of the workshops, stables, and pig sties. Germans and Austrians were interned for religious reasons. The Polish *Bibelforscher* deported to the concentration camp at Buchenwald were often interned for nationalistic reasons and not just religious ones." As Marsalek underscores, they were the only ones who had the capability to bring their detention to an end, "for the *Bibelforscher* had the opportunity to sign a statement pledging not to act on behalf of the International Association of Bible Students, thereby admitting that it spreads heresy and its activities were hostile to the state."

On June 22, the armies of the Third Reich attacked Russia in violation of the Non-Aggression Pact, signed on August 23, 1939. The following story concerns a young woman, born in 1926, who emigrated to Russia along with her parents, university teachers who moved to Danzig in 1929. She recalled that most of her friends were Jewish and added, "When Hitler began his regime of terror, Jewish families started disappearing around us, especially at night. The first day of the German-Soviet conflict many Russian families were also taken away. We were given a few minutes to dress, and we had to leave everything else behind. In the first camp I was subjected to numerous interrogations under harsh spotlights and received so many blows I was black and blue. . . . After they unloaded us from the truck inside the first camp, I never saw my father again. To this day I don't know if he is alive. My mother and I were then locked up in a cattle car. The trip lasted four days. We had to remain standing, and there was no water, food, or toilet. We hadn't the slightest idea of our destination: Dachau."

She ended up assigned to the barracks reserved for children. "That's where I saw death for the first time. Every morning some prisoners came to pick up the bodies of children who died during the night; some from malnutrition, some under torture, and others who had been bled white for transfusions for wounded soldiers. There was a pile of bodies awaiting incineration since the furnaces couldn't keep up with the demand. Why didn't I end up in the furnaces? It was because they decided I would be part of medical experiments. First I got shots of an illness, then an antidote. Sometimes these scenes lacked enough excitement for the executioners. My parents had taught me never to cry out or show emotion. My sadistic torturers picked on other guinea pigs. It's not possible for anyone who didn't live through these conditions to understand their effect on us children. But we adopted the reasoning: Hell can't be worse that what we are going through."

It was in this state of mind that she met another inmate named Else, who spoke with her about death and quoted biblical verses that, little by little, helped ease her fears of Hell. Else comforted the adolescent on the death of her mother, who had been raped, tortured, and killed by the SS. "I was fourteen, an age when one is very impressionable, and my natural reaction was to feel hate. But I can still hear Else's words ringing in my ears: 'Don't hate them. You won't touch them. You'll only hurt yourself.' The SS made Else's life miserable because she was German and would not bend to the Nazi's demands. . . . She wore a violet triangle sewn on the sleeve of her uniform. This insignia intrigued me. After surviving my internment in Dachau, I did some research to find out why the violet triangle was reserved for the Jehovah's Witnesses [Else was a Jehovah's Witness]. Shortly after my mother's murder, Else disappeared, and I never saw her again."

At the Nuremberg War Crimes Tribunal, testimony was taken on September 30, 1946, on "medical" experiments carried out by the SS at the camp. "At Dachau in August 1942, some were immersed in cold water until their body temperatures dropped and death followed. They also did high-altitude experiments, the length of time men could live in ice water, the effect of poisoned bullets and certain contagious illnesses. Lastly, they experimented on X-ray sterilization of men and women and other methods."

At the Ravensbrück concentration camp in December 1941, eighty-six Witnesses received twenty-five blows with a baton for refusing to eat some blood sausage. Margarete Buber-Neumann, a prisoner, naively thought they did not like blood sausage and offered liver sausage. She was told that it was not the blood sausage; it was a protest in honor of Jehovah. The extremists wanted to provoke SS attacks; they wanted to suffer.

For Buber-Neumann, the Witnesses could be placed into three categories or factions: "the extremists; the centerists; and the moderates. A 'refusal list' was drawn up with the names of all those who honored God's commandments, and the list was taken to the SS guards, and the SS laughed at it." Following this behavior, 100 antisocials were assigned to the Witness barracks with orders to report any acts of disobedience or "if they surprised them discussing the Bible or talking about religion." This was a hard blow for the Jehovah's Witnesses, and these measures lasted for six months. Chaos ensued: "Denunciations, theft, and fighting came up in our pacifist barracks like a wolf in the sheep pen!" However, later there were conversions: "Antisocials, Gypsies, a Polish woman, and even a Jewish woman made it known that from then on they were Jehovah's Witnesses, and they asked to have the violet triangle and to be transferred to the *Bibelforscherinnen*'s block."

The authors leave the final words of this chapter to Germaine Tillion: "To live was to fight back and not accept what they were trying to impose on us. Survival was our ultimate sabotage."

27

REJECTION OF WAR LABORS

> Any thinking man relies upon unshakable faith, his retreat and his dungeon.
>
> —Alain

Hans Marsalek described the circumstances at Mauthausen when the Witnesses refused to perform military service: "When the new recruitment commission met to consider which draftees from the classes of 1900 to 1923 to present to the review commission, there were nine Jehovah's Witnesses in the group. None was willing to perform military service. There followed insults, slaps, kicks, vicious treatment resulting in wounds. However, no Witnesses were placed in the disciplinary company, and none was killed immediately thereafter."

At Ravensbrück in early 1942, "about ninety Witnesses declared they no longer would work for the war effort." The Witnesses stopped working on the gardening *Kommandos* as well as the *Angora Kommando* since "rabbit wool was used by the army" and "the vegetables were for a military hospital." For three days and three nights, the women were forced to stand in the bunker in the courtyard and then "were put in the bunker in the dark." That lasted four days. "The Witnesses, many of whom were sixty years of age, received seventy-five blows from a baton." Berlin had given the order that all refusal to work was to be punished with seventy-five blows. "After forty-five days I saw them at the bath. They were walking skeletons covered with sores." Since they persisted in their refusal and would not attend roll call, they were brought by force.

Some of the more humane guards had them carried to the parade ground, and others dragged them to each roll call along the camp road, prompting Margarete Buber-Neumann to conclude, "A Witness in my barracks told me in confidence: 'Ill-will has taken over the extremists.' "

Buber-Neumann discovered "the name of a woman from my barracks on the list of women scheduled for extermination. Her name was Anne Luck, and she was suffering from ganglionic tuberculosis. For days I had kept her in the barracks and prevented her from going to the infirmary because I knew she was running the risk of being administered a fatal injection. But the SS doctor had noticed her. There was only one way out. I asked Milena to convince Anna Luck to sign the statement the Gestapo prepared for Jehovah's Witnesses." Buber-Neumann visited with the patient, begging her to sign the statement and warning her of the danger she was running, exposing herself to death. Another Witness, Ella Hemple, shouted angrily, "Grete, I would never have believed this of you, never thought you would go to the devil! I never thought you would throw in with the SS! You advised Anna Luck to go sign. How could you do such a thing?" Buber-Neumann was angry, too, and shouted back, "And you hold yourself up as a Christian. You would cold-bloodedly deliver your own sister to the gas chamber? Is that love of your fellow man? You are an accomplice to murder in honor of Jehovah! You are a brute with a heart of stone."

When Milena, whose health was worsening, learned what had happened, she ended her friendship with the Jehovah's Witnesses. "From that day on, the Jehovah's Witnesses lived in fear of Milena." Buber-Neumann reminded Milena of these conflicts at a much later date, and they agreed on this: "We noticed at that point a striking similarity of their attitudes and the Communists. Some were inflamed by Jehovah, the others by Stalin."

Jeanne Kemna, a young Dutch girl, explained that, after a week's "reflection" granted by Commandant Kogel, during which time the Witnesses shoveled snow, their rations were halved, and they were shut up in their barracks without straw mattresses or covers, yet despite the harassment they persisted in their refusal:

"We were each tied to a wooden horse and were beaten on our bare bottoms." Since they remained obstinate, the punishments became harsher. Some died from the suffering. Others were starved for six weeks, and orders were given the matron, a political prisoner, to keep an especially close watch on the ring leaders. "She wrote down the names of thirteen Sisters. Later we heard from other prisoners that they were hanged." Kemna managed to survive the period of trial.

Buber-Neumann also remembered, "In the beginning of '42 a big convoy of about a thousand women was sent to Auschwitz. That was the first time we had heard of this concentration camp, and no one had any idea what the name represented. Many inmates *volunteered* to go." Dounia Ourisson, who was arrested in Poitiers in March 1942 and deported to Auschwitz, spoke of an SS officer Stibitz, who was her *Lagerführer* and who beat four Witnesses to death. "In May 1942, a convoy of *Bibelforscherinnen* arrived from Ravensbrück; they were Dutch and Polish. They refused to work, prayed continuously, and sat in small groups discussing biblical readings. They didn't want to attend roll call, saying they stood before God, but not before man." Ourisson witnessed their sufferings before they were "sent to the gas chambers."

The first gassing experiments at Auschwitz were carried out on 600 Soviet prisoners and 300 sick patients beginning on September 3, 1941. In January 1942, the first mass gassing took place at Auschwitz/Birkenau. An inmate, Kogon, recalled how on New Year's 1942 all the "Fundamentalists" held in Buchenwald were treated barbarically. For their refusal to pick up linens for Hitler's troops, the camp inspector proclaimed, "State criminals and bastard believers! You will work in 20C below zero until nightfall. Take off your underwear immediately."

Victor Bruch recalled those early days in 1942 in Buchenwald and the issuance of the following order: "If a prisoner has a sweater in excess of camp issue, it must immediately be handed in for the soldiers on the eastern front." He resisted, along with all his fellow Witnesses, and they were forced to remain standing for hours on the parade ground and worked all night without a sweater. "They took away our shoes and gave us wooden shoes. Three weeks later we found our clothes, which had been removed, returned to the barracks; they were cleaned and mended with a note indicating they had been taken due to an error." A month later, twenty Witnesses were "accused of rebellion for failing to follow camp rules, bribing the barracks matron, and switching off the radio during speeches by the Reich government representative. They had to perform exercises until exhaustion in two feet of snow."

Hermann Langbein recalls a "Russian Jehovah's Witness at Dora who refused to work in the armaments factory" as well as the case of Ernst Raddatz, a German at Neuengamme who refused in 1942 to sign his draft notice and fulfill his military obligations despite promises made that he could go home and take care of his wife. "The first overall view of the camp gave me the impression of a disconcerting courtyard of wacky miracles. Here were the 'zebras,' those who worked on the outside *Kommandos* or were *Kapos* in the infirmary. And finally, here was the enormous underworld of yokels, indifferent to outward signs of wealth, the Jehovah's Witnesses with their violet triangles; the 'go-without-shoes' from the seedy barracks."

28

JOSEPH HISIGER

Man is nothing more than his own project.
—Jean-Paul Sartre

During the month of March 1942, Joseph Hisiger was summoned to the factory director's office in Thionville. He worked as a bridge builder and was cited for "passive resistance" and failing to give the "Hitler salute" required when addressing a man of the director's level. "A 'Good morning, Mr. Director' was not enough. In the face of my refusal he told me, 'The Gestapo will teach you how, go back to your work!' The next day, just after returning from work, a car pulled up suddenly in front of my door, and two Gestapo men barged in without knocking. Looking at me, they asked, 'Are you Hisiger?' They took me off in their car and said, 'We'll teach you what you have to do in the *Luftschutz* [civil defense antiaircraft].' That was the 19th of March.

"At Thionville, where the Gestapo offices were located, several Gestapo men were seated and the interrogation began. Cross-examinations and threats were made, and one of them was twirling his revolver and several times put it against my temple and the back of my neck. 'I'll bust your skull if you don't answer.' Because I remained mute for some questions, they threw out the usual insults. 'You'll never see your parents, friends and fiancée, again. We ways to make you talk.' They opened a door through which I heard screams and sobs. Seeing my impassivity, they tried another tack: 'We know all the Jehovah's Witnesses. Mr. W. didn't want to be a Jehovah's Witness, and he has just been freed and can stay with his family. If you act like him, we will give you the privilege of being the first magistrate in the town of Hayange.' It was late at night, and seeing my fatigue they took me to the jail. Presenting me to the warden with a disdainful air they said, 'This is a Witness who doesn't want to obey our Führer.' Since their was no bed available because of the numerous arrests, I was forced to sleep on the floor without covers in a wintry cold. On awakening, I was stiff and chilled to the bone. Around eight o'clock the Gestapo came to get me for questioning. After a month and despite the brainwashing, using all kinds of tricks and given my intransigence, they compiled my file which they transmitted to the Metz special tribunal. On September 11, 1943, I appeared before the court at Metz and was sentenced to three years' imprisonment. Then I was transferred from the Metz jail to the one at Saarbruck (where I remained only a few days isolated in a cell), then to a work camp at Zweibrücken. That's where I was assigned to a *Kommando* under surveillance by SS guards to whom I showed no accommodation, nor hate, because what they were doing was fanatic obedience to their satanic ideology. Every day we took the train to Alsenborn to work on the railroad tracks. We had to put out twice the work of the civilian workers. The schedule was eight o'clock in the morning until six o'clock in the evening with a fifteen-minute break to gulp down a small bowl of rutabaga soup. In the morning we had a square slice of *Kamisbrot* with synthetic margarine. The evening after work, more rutabaga soup. There were several work parties at Zweibrücken, but we couldn't associate with them. I was watched closely by the guards so that I wouldn't have conversations with other inmates, especially since I was one of the Witnesses."

Ruth Danner, whom the authors met in Paris on August 1, 1990, after an exchange of letters, remembered the last evening spent with Hisiger on the day before his arrest on March 19. He was at the home of the Danners until two o'clock in the morning. "The next day the SS we called 'the toad' came to the house. This SS busied himself with us; he was a former Jesuit who had received special training against Jehovah's Witnesses. He never wore a military uniform during the interrogations, and we first took him for a street vendor. He was very clever. He didn't use any physical violence, but he was tireless in his interrogations, which he conducted with a master's hand. He was very skilled in twisting the meaning of the Scriptures. He first consumed the buffet in the kitchen and wouldn't stop questioning Mama. He wanted us to believe that Joseph Hisiger had betrayed us. Then my mother answered, 'If Hisiger said that, let me hear it from him face to face.' We were constantly spied on by the *Blockleiter* [caretaker] who observed those who came and left the apartments. It was a real war of nerves."

29

ARTHUR WINKLER

> Who is this man? He who, because of his very existence, must bear witness.
>
> —Martin Heidegger

In the Moselle region, from January 1, 1942, and after, membership in the National Labor Service was mandatory for young men; for young women, it was mandatory from August 26, 1942, and after. This measure, applying to young men, was also adopted in the Haut and Bas Rhin, effective August 27, 1942. The 1940, 1941, and 1942 classes were called up and drafted into the Wehrmacht as soon as their labor obligations were completed. On August 19, 1942, administrative orders were issued introducing universal military service in Moselle, and on August 25, 1942, the 1940–1944 classes were drafted from all three departments, and conscription was fully applied by German authorities. All Frenchmen failing to obey these laws were considered deserters; and their families deported and property confiscated.

Mr. Sidot, one of the many PROs (Patriots Resisting Occupation, only in Alsace-Lorraine) the authors interviewed, does not recall seeing Jehovah's Witnesses in the camps to which he was deported with his family. However, he knew that "before the war, I saw a Witness from Montbronn [his village of birth]. He must have gone somewhere in the Occupied or Unoccupied Zones, because I later caught sight of him after the war in the Moselle Department."

Gilbert Tscheiller, also a PRO, was interned in "a reeducation camp on the heights of Ober-Schreiberbau located near the Czech border." Among the 300 prisoners, he noticed a Yugoslav, "a large young man who always quoted the Bible. He wouldn't give the Nazi salute when the sections formed up in squares, any more than the sixty-three other Alsatians, Lorrains, or Luxembourgers would salute any flag which wasn't their own. Several months later, after authorities deemed that Tscheiller and his fellow inmates has failed to grasp the lessons of the 'new order,' a much more dramatic incident occurred which was to have a marked effect on our adolescence for the rest of our days. [This Yugoslav fellow], nicknamed Josi because his real name was complicated, was from Nis or thereabouts, and he was older and took us, the younger ones, under his protection in the name of the Bible, which he quoted as often as he could. He became our spokesman and participated voluntarily, as often as possible, in the 'water pumpings' during punishment sessions for others. One evening he was able to get his hands on some food in the kitchen, which he had broken into, and passed it out to us. Unfortunately, one day, Josi asked that our food rations be increased. The SS officer present turned around, grabbed a stool, and delivered a violent blow to our friend's head, and he collapsed [and died]."

As everywhere, Alsatian and Lorrain Jehovah's Witnesses refused to serve in Hitler's armies. Thus, Messrs. Freyermuth, Hoffer, and Sutter were condemned to death. Marcel Sutter, aged twenty-three, was beheaded at the Torgau prison in Germany, before which he wrote a last letter to his relatives:

> My Dear Parents and Sisters,
> By the time you receive this letter I will be dead. Only a few hours separate me from death. I beg you, be strong and courageous. Do not cry, for I have *lived.* I have finished the journey, and kept faith.

On October 21, 1942, Arthur Winkler, who directed the Witnesses' activities in the Netherlands, was arrested along with other followers. He remembered the maltreatment inflicted on him by SS agents at the *Uterperstraat* in Amsterdam and especially the interrogation of November 1, 1942: "The Gestapo wanted to crush the Jehovah's Witnesses, and they suggested I show good sense and help them achieve their goal. They scoffed that Jehovah went bankrupt in Germany and the same thing awaits him in other countries. To hear them, the Führer was God-sent, and I had better change my mind. Ah, if only I would give my support to Hitler's cause and break with this wild dream, what a wonderful position I would be in! All I had to do was reveal the names of the members of the group and the addresses of the places they had taken refuge. In return, the Gestapo promised these Brothers would never know that it was me who denounced them and that those I betrayed would not all be arrested. They would only be invited to make amends and to serve the Führer's cause. Upon my categorical refusal to participate in these machinations, they closed the curtains, turned up the radio full blast, and started to beat me mercilessly. When one got tired, he was replaced by another brute, until I fell to the floor unconscious, only to come to a little later. They laughed, 'We didn't expect to find you so unreasonable. A man like you who has shown intelligence, who is a good organizer and a valiant defender of a lost cause, should have better sense. We need more of your kind. Think for a minute how your fate would be bettered if you wished. Tell us, where is your wife, and we will give you *our word of honor* she won't be beaten. If you are reasonable and collaborate with us, you will have a villa in exchange for prison and a high position, money, and prestige instead of shame and insults.' Since I remained silent, the second round began. It was *Obersturmführer* Barbie who was the first to go into action, and when he tired it was *Oberscharführer* Engelsmann who took over. They only stopped when I lost consciousness a second time. This atrocious scene went on from one o'clock in the afternoon until midnight. At one o'clock in the morning, they delivered me back to the prison guard. It was with broken teeth, my jaw dislocated, and a body covered with wounds that I was taken to a black cell."

A prison guard showed some compassion and on November 10 even brought Winkler the Bible that his wife had given the guard. Finally, Winkler would be sent to a camp at Vught before being deported to the Oranienburg-Sachsenhausen concentration camp in Germany. In this latter camp, he barely escaped the gas chamber, thanks to the help of a Swedish doctor.

The authors of the book *Allach "Kommando" de Dachau* enumerated and analyzed the camp population and stated, "Lastly, after the political prisoners, there were the Jehovah's Witnesses (violet triangle) whose religious convictions led them to oppose the Nazi regime."

30

CORPORAL PUNISHMENTS

> The battle against a loss of faith and the debasement of our spirit was our greatest battle.
>
> —Pelagia Lewinska

On April 4, 1942, the D group of the SS Principal Administrative and Economic Office sent a memo addressed to the commandants of all the concentration camps. This memo ordered that intensified beatings be administered to the naked backsides of inmates and inmates held under *Schutzhaft.* SS *Obergruppenführer* Pohl sent a letter to Heinrich Himmler regarding the mobilization of all prisoners for war-related labor in which he admitted that "the war has occasioned a profound modification in camp structure which has fundamentally altered [the camps' functions]. The incarceration of inmates strictly for reasons of security is no longer a high priority. All of the concentration camp work forces must be mobilized for war goals [increased armaments production]."

On July 12, 1942, Heinrich Muller, chief of the *Sicherheitspolizei* (SIPO) and SD services, sent a note detailing secret instructions pertaining to interrogations: "The third degree may *only* be used on an inmate if preliminary investigations indicate he is in a position to furnish important information, notably on contacts, plans, and subversive activities directed against the State or the Reich, [and who refuses to confess] and [from whom] nothing can be obtained during preliminary investigations. Under these conditions, the third degree may only be used on Communists, Marxists, Witnesses, saboteurs, terrorists, [and their ilk]. According to circumstances, the third degree may consist of, among other things, reduced food rations [bread and water], sleeping on the hard floor, a darkened cell, sleep deprivation, exhausting exercises, and also beatings [for more than twenty baton blows, a doctor's advice must be obtained]."

On August 11, 1942, Himmler instructed commandants of fourteen concentration camps that "corporal punishments must be administered in women's camps by prisoners under supervision. In accordance with this order, the Chief of the SS Principal Administrative and Economic Office, SS *Obergruppenführer* and *Waffen* General SS Pohl are ordered that, henceforth, corporal punishment in men's camps was also to be administered by prisoners. Corporeal punishment of German prisoners by foreign prisoners is forbidden."

On October 30, 1942, a memo from Glucks informed concentration camp commandants that all Aryan prisoners (except Russians) were permitted to receive mail packages. Beginning during the summer of 1942, an outside *Kommando* from Dachau was established at Unterfahlheim (between New Ulm and Leipheim). About fifty inmates (including seven Witnesses, some Poles, Ukrainians, and even some sentenced SS officers) were assigned to two barracks to work at the fish hatcheries set up at thirty-six ponds in the Biber valley. This camp was in existence until March 1945.

A Belgian, Leon Floryn, prisoner number 46522, was assigned to the *Kommando* at the SS *Fischereischule* (hatchery) in early 1944. There, he refused all work supporting the war effort and was transferred to a disciplinary company at Soudelfeld, in Upper Bavaria near the Austrian border, where he spent the last ten months of his captivity. He was freed in May 1945 by the Canadian army. His wife, Maria Floryn, who was arrested on May 23, 1942, was jailed in St. Gilles, leaving behind two children, ages six and ten. Despite being tortured, she revealed nothing to the Gestapo. After several difficult months at Ravensbrück, she was transferred to barrack 12 of the SS *Arbeitslager* St. Lambrecht (in Austrian Styria). She languished there as prisoner number 14981 until her liberation. Evelyn Le Chene recalled the farms, which were an outdoor *Kommando*, where Jehovah's Witnesses were used mainly as day laborers. The closest farms were Rimbler, Fechter, Funchsberger, and Preller. Saint Lambrecht was one of the largest and was attached to Mauthausen after the Dachau reorganization. "Some Jehovah's Witness women were sent to St. Lambrecht to cook for the agricultural workers." Its administrator, the *Standartenführer* from Munich, was a friend of SS officer Pohl.

31

BUT WHAT IS SCRIPTURE?

But what is scripture? The guardian of history!
—Alcuin

Albin Glowacz spent nine months in jail after his arrest in Charleroi in June 1941, after which he was deported to Buchenwald. "After spending seven months in that camp, I was separated from Brother Hankus and the German Brothers and transferred to Ravensbrück. In this camp there were 10,000 men and 60,000 women. There, the guard's and SS's animosity was greater than at Buchenwald. Whenever difficult work came up, it was reserved for Jehovah's Witnesses. During the night, whenever incoming transport arrived, only the *Bibelforscher* were rousted out to do the unloading. We were 175 Brothers spread throughout all the barracks. The Brothers had some writings which were well hidden. They undertook study and discussion of the texts whenever they had a chance to get together in groups of two or three." After three months, Glowacz was assigned to various outside *Kommandos* where he met inmates working on Felix Kersten's land. As Roger Manvell and Heinrich Fraenkel described, "In addition to Bernadotte and Kersten, Schellenberg aspired to have his name go down in history as one who was interested in prisoner well-being and a promoter of peace in Europe. Thousands of Jews owed their lives to Kersten, who possessed the gift of relieving sufferings caused by Himmler and who was able to secure freedom for numerous inmates."

Glowacz and 120 Witnesses were assigned to work "at a General

Paul's place to do construction work and fix up his chateau and to dry out the marsh near the chateau to create a park. We managed to get ourselves a Bible and Society literature. That way we were able to study every evening." With the help of a civilian met while boring a well in a nearby village, one of his fellow inmates was even able to send a letter to his wife in Berlin. His wife came to see him under cover of night. "The SS slept during the day since they were chasing women at night."

When she attempted to revisit him, she was identified by local farmers and "condemned to death and hanged at the Ravensbrück camp; whereupon her husband was sent back to Ravensbrück, where he was confined to a cell for three months on bread and water."

On the *Kommando* where Glowacz worked, he was told stories by Heinrich Dickmann of his family and other camps. Four months before the end of the war, both were sent out on another work party to change a film studio into a house for a general. An electrician who had already worked in the area informed them that they were within eight kilometers of Kersten's property, the man "[who] had thirty Brothers and Sisters working for him." On Christmas, with the approval of the *Kommando* chief, they visited Kersten's farm and saw that their fellow Witnesses there "enjoyed complete freedom and abundant nourishment—corporal as well as spiritual."

Glowacz then acted as a go-between by passing copies of *The Watch Tower*, which came from the United States via Sweden, along to his fellow Witnesses, who worked on job sites assigned to the Ravensbrück concentration camp. In Glowacz's *Kommando*, community organizers scrounged food, whereas over in the main camp "every day hundreds of women were dying from hunger and being burned in the crematory furnaces." In April 1945, as the camp was undergoing evacuation, it was liberated by Russians near the town of Wittenberg. "During the night the SS slipped on civilian clothes and disappeared. I immediately took off in the direction of Belgium."

Ilse Unterdorfer, another Witness detainee, also worked outside Ravensbrück. "Since we enjoyed considerable freedom where we worked, we succeeded in sending letters to our relatives without their being censored. We were also able to write our Brothers working outside or to whom the SS had given positions of trust and who, consequently, had greater freedom. Yes, we even succeeded in getting in touch with Brothers who were entirely free."

At Sachsenhausen, "the situation improved a little in 1942. . . . It was around that time we were able to get a hold of seven issues of *The Watch Tower* and a few Bibles." These publications had been smuggled in by Witnesses who worked on the outside under the supervision of one of their own: Seliger, a nurse. Thus, for eighteen months, Fritsche would be successful in getting copies of new and old issues of various publications, as well as books, into the hands of inmates. Also, 150 letters were smuggled out of camp and passed along to their families. Harald Abt recalls Bible study meetings that took place on Sundays in the early evening. Sixty to seventy members would be on lookout from the front gate to the meeting site, thereby enabling more than 200 inmates to take part in the study group. During the winter of 1939–1940, Witnesses in Sachsenhausen in the isolation barracks could read recent copies of *The Watch Tower*, which had been smuggled inside an inmate's wooden leg. These publications were read and discussed around seven tables in the isolation blocks while others kept watch. Other Witnesses received packages in which they found what they called "Elberfeld Gingerbread." Publications were hidden inside cakes, and in exchange for food the Witnesses were able to obtain publications from other inmates at the *Effektenkammer* (warehouse) who were responsible for destroying articles requisitioned during incoming searches.

The epicenter of supply of biblical materials was the estate of Himmler's masseur, Felix Kersten, an Estonian doctor and a naturalized Finn. "He took advantage of his influence over the SS Reichsführer to save Jews, Dutch, Jehovah's Witnesses, Estonians, and others." A letter sent under secret seal from Himmler to Pohl and Muller is clear proof of this, as it speaks of Witnesses, especially those working on his doctor's farm. Based on observations made by Mme. Kersten, Himmler commented that they were loyal and behaved domestics. "They are fanatics who are unbelievably helpful and ready for any sacrifice. Naturally, since they reject war, their doctrine is so harmful we cannot tolerate it under penalty of doing the greatest harm to Germany. In the future I intend to tell each one of them: You are forbidden to work. You are better fed than the others and you should do nothing." Himmler goes on in the letter to recommend that the women be assigned to farm duties or to SS families as maids.

The masseur's property was located at Gransee (Harzwalde) in the province of Mecklenburg between the Ravensbrück and Sachsenhausen camps. Kersten also owned property in Sweden, where Himmler permitted him to take a Jehovah's Witness as a domestic servant. Thus, a number of issues of *The Watch Tower* made their way from Sweden back to Mecklenburg in Dr. Kersten's suitcases. One of the Witnesses who worked on the doctor's property was also able to contact one of his fellows who worked on a detail in the forest: "One Sunday morning my Brother Kramer and I went out on our bikes to meet our Brothers. Seeing a prisoner, we waved, and he came towards us. As soon as we saw the violet triangle on his clothes, we knew he was a Brother."

32

THOSE WITH THE POWER TO INFLICT SUFFERING

In May 1942, Elsa Abt was arrested at Lodz by the Gestapo, and her daughter was entrusted to another family living in the same building. At Gestapo headquarters, there were large numbers of Jehovah's Witnesses who had also been arrested. "They had all been betrayed by a Gestapo agent who passed himself off as one of them. Questioned, she revealed nothing of the clandestine organization—no names, no places, nor the location of the mimeograph machine. After six months in jail she was deported, along with twelve others, to Birkenau. An SS officer learned she was a Witness and advised her to sign a statement of renunciation, for if she did, she could go home. When she refused, the SS warned her: Here, you are going to die."

After several days, the twelve were taken to Auschwitz: "For some time we were lodged inside the concentration camp in the basement of a big brick house with other prisoners. Then they picked me to be a maid at the home of an SS officer who lived outside the camp." Elsa was authorized to leave the camp without escort, and she then stayed in the basement at the SS's residence. There, she was able to read biblical writings circulated by Gertrud Ott and others working at a hotel or living with SS families. It was also by this route that Abt, deported to Auschwitz, corresponded with her husband, Harald, who had been deported to Sachsenhausen.

Franz Birk made arrangements for the SS and his men to come to Gransee for Christmas. They accepted the invitation more readily since the barber at Harzwalde was a Witness. "Over time, senior SS officers didn't dare go to just any barber for fear of having their throats slashed." Some Jehovah's Witness publications have attempted to put a positive spin on the trust that the SS afforded them. The authors reject that analysis, as accepting it would risk tainting the bravery of Witnesses whose treatment was brutal and whose faith was undaunted. In a meeting that the authors had with a French Witness who tried to portray the SS as anything less than savage, they clearly delivered the same message. For them, the SS's only human element was the human blood on their hands. Evelyn Le Chene (not a Witness) opined that the fact that the SS gave razors to some Witnesses without fear might have improved the chances of survival for those Witnesses, but it cost them the trust and respect of other Witnesses.

SS officer Rudolf Hess, speaking of the Jehovah's Witnesses, wrote in his memoirs, "I always considered them as poor fools who were, nonetheless, happy in their own way."

The authors also interviewed Jean Rochotte, who had been an inmate at Bergen-Belsen after having gone through Struthof. He recalled, "In the beginning our work consisted of getting the camp into shape. Then, as the days went by and the camp was enlarged, fifteen prisoners who were in the building trades were brought in. Among them were two or three German Witnesses, one of whom was authorized to keep a full head of hair. These Witnesses were separated from the others interned in that they were put up with the camp chief in a separate room in block 1. Despite the fact they were required at roll call with all the other blocks, they took no part in camp life—I mean household chores and cleanup details." He also recounted how, each time he worked with a Witness on topographical readings, he had the right to an extra snack in the afternoon that the prisoner had brought from the kitchen.

To conclude this chapter, wherein the authors have attempted to define differing points of view on the behavior of these so-called privileged ones, we quote Stanislaw Dubiel,[1] a Polish Catholic. He testified on August 7, 1949, before District Public Prosecutor Jan Sehn, who was acting pursuant to a decree for the General and District Commissions on investigations of Hitler's crimes in Poland: "During Himmler's second stay at Auschwitz, shortly before Hess was replaced as camp commander, Himmler told him in the garden he would have to leave the camp because English radio broadcasts were talking too much about prisoner exterminations at Auschwitz. During the discussion, which went on about this subject, Hess declared he was persuaded he had rendered good service to the Fatherland by his activities at Auschwitz. He said that as soon as Himmler raised the subject of killing people with gas. I heard part of this conversation, and Witnesses working for Hess told me the rest. They were two Germans, bitter enemies of Hitler's system. One of them, Sophie Stipel came from Hess's home town, that's to say Mannheim-Ludwighalen, and knew him from childhood for they both lived on the same street. She told me that Hess said—word for word—*Ich dachte, ich werde meinem Vaterlande damit einen Dienst erweisen* (I thought I was doing a service for the Fatherland). I believe Sopie Stipel now lives with her daughter in Heidelberg. Mme. Stipel and her friend always shared conversations she overheard with us, and she warned us when we had to take exceptional precautionary measures, as when there was danger of an informer. Thanks to their help, we were able to avoid trouble on several occasions."

NOTE

1. Dubiel was in Auschwitz from November 6, 1940, until January 18, 1945, where he wore prisoner number 6059. Initially, he worked as a gardener, but on April 6, 1942, he was appointed camp commander Hess's gardener. He recalls Hess hosting different Nazi dignitaries, in particular Himmler.

33

THE HELL OF AUSCHWITZ

> Such are the facts. . . . He who wants out needs luck. Without luck, no one can escape the cold, the hunger, or even men. I had a lot of luck. That is why I am still here.
>
> —Berthold Brecht

Not all the women were assigned as maids in SS residences. The following disturbing testimony was provided by a survivor of Auschwitz: "After spending three months in Ravensbrück, I arrived at Auschwitz on June 1942 along with about a hundred other Sisters. Our train trip lasted two days. Our clothes were in shreds and we were wearing wooden shoes. The whole camp was infested with lice and the curse of lice was indescribable. If someone was ill, she was immediately sent to Birkenau. It was terrible there. Whenever an inmate died, another sick prisoner was transferred to the same bed. There was lice and excrement everywhere. For six weeks the Jews had to dig a big ditch into which they often had to throw their women who, for the most part, had only lost consciousness. Then everything was burned. The men digging the ditch knew after six weeks it would be their turn. Fires in the ditch burned night and day, and there were also five crematory furnaces at Auschwitz. Nevertheless, we thought it better to die of typhus and 'fly away in smoke' than to see oneself eaten up by the rats. Just to think of it gave us goose pimples, but some Jehovah's Witnesses died from being eaten alive, literally, because they were too weak to defend themselves against the rats. The worst thing was that these Witnesses, eaten alive by the rats, were poor women with no defenses. Torture and hunger had weakened them so badly that they were incapable of defending themselves against this horrible enemy—the rat."

Others were locked up in the camp cell block: "The cells in block 11 were terrifying. Escapees who were caught had to stand up constantly. The suffering was so horrible that often the SS didn't have to execute them: They died. They committed suicide. The cell block was part of the terror organized by the SS. For two years, 1,241 political prisoners, 286 Jews, eight Soviet prisoners of war, and eight Jehovah's Witnesses were locked up there."

Eva Tichauer, a medical student, was assigned to block 24, which was the Birkenau infirmary for Germans and Aryans. "The sick person in my block 24 who I remember best was a Jehovah's Witness. At the time they were being deported for their refusal to participate in the war effort and their women, too, for refusing to do any kind of service. They were Germans. The more courageous continued in their opposition, even in the camp, refusing to go on outside work details. I saw them praying together on their knees after roll call." Later, describing the resistance of her sick friend who experienced terrible pain, she wrote of humanity's fragility: "My sick friend was gravely burned from an attempted suicide by electrocution, although it was contrary to her faith."

Germaine Tillion wrote in *Ravensbrück* (edition of 1946), "Global statistics are still not possible, but a friend deported to Dora provided the following fragmentary data. Of the thirty friends at camp they kept track of after the liberation, five of them committed suicide. Personally, among the French women deported, I know of only one case of suicide after the liberation and none before. It's true at the camp you didn't have to commit suicide in order to die; nevertheless, that fact is striking. There the *Kapos* executed young girls who put up a despairing resistance with their bare hands." This took place at the Budy disciplinary camp, an Auschwitz outside *Kommando* where the women worked on draining swamps, constructing a wall above the Vistula, or raising pigs on Hess's farm. These women, the majority Jewish, were French, from all social strata, and German black triangles. "A German *Kapo*, Elfriede Schmidt, was the fiercest." These black triangles exacerbated their own hatred and self-loathing by having sexual relations with the SS. The SS and the green and black triangles pounced on these women and massacred them. Hess ended the carnage summarily when he gave orders that all survivors be shot.

Genia Rosoff analyzed the camp hierarchy in these terms: "There was another aristocracy: the *Anweiserin*, or work party chiefs. They were recruited from the underworld—prostitutes, and so-called free workers—who had been thrown into the camp for minor offenses. They had to work hard, to be noticed for their biceps and zeal and servility to the SS. Then came their reward: another stripe."

Anyone who witnessed these events was not expected to survive. If a victim gave any sign of life, she was dragged into a room and given a shot of phenol. "The SS nurse skillfully shoved the syringe needle in under the left breast." The needle killed almost instantly. "Outside an old lady was immobile and bent over on the front steps. For years she had been interned in different camps for her religious beliefs. She was supposed to be reeducated in the spirit of Nazism and admit the 'falseness of the Witness doctrines.' She was incapable of understanding her cruel fate."

In the autumn of 1942, convoys were organized to bring women from Ravensbrück to Auschwitz. "Also among them there were all the 'extremist' Witnesses." Sometime later, Grete Buber-Neumann saw a column of Witnesses on the square near the *Zellenbau* (cell block). Pretending to have forgotten something, she approached the group, and the extremists brought over from Auschwitz recognized her. "One of them, Rosl Hahn from Ischl, called out, 'Come here Grete! I have to tell you something important! We were brought back from Auschwitz and we will certainly be executed. But before dying, I must tell you about the horrors going on at the Auschwitz camp. They are throwing men and living children, yes, you can believe me, they are throwing infant Jews into the fire. Day and night the stink of burned human flesh hangs over the camp.' " Seeing a look of incredulity on Buber-Neumann's face, Rosl vigorously persisted: "I am telling the truth, the pure truth!" Rosl had become a human wreck. "Her face, which had been pretty, was yellow." Her fellow prisoners were spiritless and apathetic: "They looked at me without saying a word." Thinking their minds deranged, Buber-Neumann did not believe them and told them, "You will certainly come to block 17 right away. This evening I will come to see you, and we'll talk some more about Auschwitz." However, Rosl was adamant: "No, they're taking us to the cell block and after that to be executed."

Buber-Neumann experienced pangs of anguish as she saw the Witnesses loaded into a prison truck. "Shortly thereafter the clothes of the inmates, with their triangle and prisoner numbers, were returned. A capital sentence was carried out for their refusal to work."

During the last six months of 1942, Hermann Langbein estimated that each month, inmates' deaths numbered a fifth of the total prison population.

The authors contacted the vice president of the International Auschwitz Committee to learn about his life in camp and of any encounters that he might have had with the Witnesses. Mr. Montagne was kind enough to respond, "Innocents—the persecuted—they remained praiseworthy and loyal to their faith. That's the recollection I have of them, even though with the passage of time it's become very fuzzy. It's enough today for me to look back upon them to that distant time with respect [for them]."

34

THE SS'S *KALFAKTORINNEN* AND *DIENSTMÄDCHEN*

Harsh is life on God's soldiers. They seek not approval of the prideful. They wish only to stay pure and to please God—to hold forever the love of their Father.

—Erich Frost

At Selters, Germany, Gertrud Potzinger confided to the authors that, apart from the kicks and punches that were part of the daily camp routine, she was not punished during her stay, and she endured an experience less tortured than during her interrogations while in preventive detention in Breslau. She remembered the Kusserow family, who emigrated to the United States after the war:

Authors: Do you know the background of the family whose members were arrested and persecuted?"

GP: The mother, Hilde, worried about her two children (nine and eleven years old) who had stayed at home. The Gestapo took them to peasant's homes—each in a different village. But, on Sunday, the children met each other halfway and comforted each other. They succeeded in getting a letter to their mother, interned in Ravensbrück, via the Naval School. Some *Bibelforscher* worked at repairing clothes at the school, not far from the Fürstenberg train station, and some were able to get letters and Bible literature through to Ravensbrück. The letter from the two young children reached their mother, Hilde, and their two sisters.

Authors: In 1943 you were assigned to Oranienburg. Why?

GP: Because I had to work at SS *Sturmbannführer* Kiener's.

Authors: What was this work?

GP: His wife was pregnant with a second child, and I had to help her with the housecleaning and taking care of the children. For the first couple of weeks, I found myself alone without spiritual support. I no longer had my fellow detention mates and the help of the little community that we made up inside the camp. I missed the contact terribly. It was very hard.

Authors: Therefore, you had no more spiritual outlet?

GP: In the beginning, no. But I met other *Bibelforscher* on the road to the dairy, and meetings were organized. I got some Bible literature; one of the *Bibelforscher* hid some under the wood pile in the basement, and I went there when the coast was clear, that's to say, when the toilet window was shut. Then I passed them along to others. A chain was formed.

Authors: And what happened to Hilde Kusserow?

GP: Hilde Kusserow also worked in an SS household. The wife was well disposed to her and even allowed her to visit her sister in Berlin. Hilde Kusserow took advantage of that to get copies of *The Watch Tower* and other literature, which was the best support for *Bibelforscher* inmates.

From 1943 to 1945, Anne Dickmann was also an SS maid. She was first assigned to SS officer Leiner's, who was a type of *Standartenführer*. She took care of children even though Nazi justice had withdrawn parental authority over her own children. In March 1945, she was working at Dr. Kersten's property at Gransee in Harzwalde. In 1943, there were still Jehovah's Witnesses at Auschwitz-Birkenau, which the administration rented out to SS officers who had houses on the camp's outskirts. They lived there in a middle-class environment with wives, children, gardens, and "maids"—and this use of Witnesses was doubtless appreciated because the camp charged more for them than for other inmates. After an exchange of a couple of letters, the authors discussed various subjects with Germaine Tillion and asked her opinion of the Jehovah's Witnesses. She responded as follows: "When I arrived at Ravensbrück in 1943, no Witnesses were working on my block, and I didn't get a chance to know them. During this period they weren't persecuted. They were excessively persecuted in 1941–1942. I met [Margarete] Buber-Neumann after the liberation. She had been a communist, and was offended by the religious side of the Witnesses and was not able at all to understand this religious aspect. At Auschwitz, all the Witnesses were horribly persecuted. Once the most courageous and outspoken had been tortured and executed, the SS grew tired of them in a way. They used those who were left to keep their children because they were especially scrupulous."

Dounia Ourisson, who was deported to Auschwitz in 1943, also knew some Witnesses: "In 1943 their situation improved a lot. A small group who managed to survive by some miracle was assigned to work for the SS as domestic servants. They lived in the same block we did." Dounia Ourisson spoke of their conversations having to do with the Bible, the war, and their willpower and faith: "I told them: I, too, want to know happiness, I want to be present for the debacle of the Germans. 'If you survive, my child', was the answer. I asked, 'Does the Bible foretell of the German's defeat?' 'Certainly, but you must be patient and try to become a better person to deserve this grace.' "

In early 1943, a Jehovah's Witness from Ravensbrück arrived at Buchenwald to take care of a jailed foreign princess; Princess Mafalda, the second daughter of Italian King Emanuel III. In the community, it was known that she was lacking "spiritual comfort." A fellow Witness, an electrician, persuaded "a sentinel to lift me up so I could watch these two people in exchange for fifty Marks." He also obtained an underground special pass. Thus was the violet triangles' solidarity in offering their fellow beings a spiritual link and support.

Erich Frost composed a hymn while working alongside forty Witnesses on a sewage system, and he asked four for their help by each learning a couplet by heart. "On their return that evening, the four recited the couplets one after another. That was the way I was able to write down the words along with the notes." Another man was able to hide the text in the stables where he worked and even managed to send it to Switzerland.

In 1938, a villa belonging to a sinister SS commandant was erected by a work party headed up by a political prisoner and comprised of "nine men drawn from the camp Witness population." Frost was part of the group building the villa for SS *Oberführer* Loritz on the shores of Lake St. Wolfgang in Austria. "The inmates worked hard clearing woods on the site and laying down the foundations, and during the night they were locked up in a neighboring town jail."

35

THE INCREDIBLE WILL FOR CONVERSION

They thought—with some reason—there could be no worse persecution than hopeless and useless effort.

—Albert Camus

In a book published in 1945, Simone Saint-Clair refers to a conversation she had sometime in 1944 with Colette, a fellow inmate at the Ravensbrück concentration camp. She described an incredible spectacle of miserable prisoner battalions and checked off the differing triangles assigned to the camp. She spoke to Colette and questioned her on the meaning of violet triangles and conscientious objectors' beliefs. Colette answered, "It's pretty complicated! This God of this sect is Jehovah. It doesn't believe in the Virgin birth but does in the Holy Trinity. According to the Witnesses the war will end on a day foreseen by their God, although he is against war."

Colette informed her that in 1943 they were split up into different barracks because the more conservative among them refused to wear prisoner numbers and attend roll call. "I remember sometimes the SS themselves had to come inside to get them; they dragged them by their hair and by their feet and beat them harder than ever. Stoic, they refused to budge." Moreover, they refused roll call, considering it a kind of military parade. Colette emphasized that they enjoyed a favorable regime for service to the SS in general and remarked that "they are fairly cultivated, but as soon as you start talking to them, they become propaganda agents, for they're constantly seeking new members for their religion."

Jehovah's Witnesses were dispersed within many of the camps, as was the case at Buchenwald. "During the spring of 1943, we had to leave our joint barracks, and they spread us around in different blocks reserved for political prisoners." This failed to break their resistance, and they continued in their efforts to convert other inmates.

At Ilse Koch's trial in Augsburg, the only cases for punishment she admitted to reporting to her husband concerned the *Kalfaktor*: "*Kalfaktor* Schurmann kept trying to introduce his family to fundamentalist religious doctrine."

After the discovery of biblical literature in the barracks at Sachsenhausen, the same policies were initiated, and camp management reacted by reassigning and dispersing the *Bibelforscher* into different barracks. "This measure ended our big meetings, but gave us more opportunity to preach to other prisoners."

Lodewijk Schockaert had been arrested in 1941 along with most of his fellow Witnesses, but the Nazis arrested him as a Communist, unaware that he no longer was one. Arriving at Sachsenhausen, he went to the camp commandant and requested a violet triangle and was given one; later, during transfer to another camp in 1943, he was murdered by the SS. Another Belgian, Alphonse Midi, died in the Hagen prison in 1943.

Hans Marsalek explained that dispersal orders were given to "break the Jehovah's Witness community, which was undoubtedly the reason for an ordinance from Pohl on September 10, 1943 according to which they dispersed the 'Jehovah's Witnesses' around the camp in such a way that mixed two or three Witnesses among the other prisoners of each block. At the Mauthausen camp, the order had no practical effect since the Witnesses, depending on work party membership, were already assigned to different barracks."

When, on April 20, 1943, Margarete Buber-Neumann was locked up in the cell block, the woman on fatigue duty was a Jehovah's Witness. Sentenced in darkness to solitary confinement for three days without food, the door finally opened, and Buber-Neumann asked the woman on duty for more paper. The latter acquiesced and just as quickly shut the door. "Yes, the Jehovah's Witnesses were correct and fulfilled their assigned tasks at the concentration camp. The only risks they took were for Jehovah, not for just any fellow inmate." Nevertheless, one morning she heard a voice call out that they had something for her from Milena. "I crawled to the door and struggled to my feet, and the Witness woman took out a little torn package from under the front of her uniform: 'Quick, take it, Milena greets you a thousand times. But, for God's sake hide this.' " However, when Milena passed along another package to Grete Buber-Neumann by the same intermediary, she begged in a tremulous voice, 'Grete, I beg you, can I tell Milena that you don't want to get such packages because it's too dangerous? I beg you, can I pass this message along from you?' Faced with such pitiful fear I could only say, 'Yes, I forbid Milena to send anything else!' "

After that incident, the Witnesses stood firm. "They refused to help, and Milena implored, reminding them of all I had done for the Jehovah's Witnesses for two years and the risks I took for them—but nothing doing. Then, in a threatening in a vengeful tone, she had recourse to the God Jehovah and gave them a lesson on love of fellow man, painting all the horrors which awaited them in the afterlife if their hearts remained hardened. Whining, they did bring me the food they had to deliver."

Despite all the obstacles, the Witnesses continued to preach during captivity. An SS *Obercharführer* berated the guards at Uterperstraat prison for failing to segregate Van de Eigkhoff, a Jehovah's Witness who had begun to make converts among his four fellow inmates. Piet van der Molen became a disciple at the Amersfoort concentration camp. Karl Krause reported that at Gusen, five Polish inmates were baptized. A guard at the Frankfurt-Preungesheim jail was converted by Hermann Schlomer, a prisoner. Franz Desch even succeeded in converting an SS officer at Gusen. Some 227 Russian women and seventy-three Ukrainians were baptized at Ravensbrück.

36

THE ARNOLD FAMILY

Nothingness is the privation of Being.
—Leonardo da Vinci

Allow us to return to the story of the Arnold family. We saw how their troubles with the German authorities began after the annexation of Alsace-Lorraine. In September 1941, Adolphe Arnold was arrested at Mulhouse. During the 1941–1942 school year and after her father's arrest, daughter Simone refused to utter "Heil Hitler."

"I was a secondary student in a private school, and I wasn't quite twelve when I was caught in the act of 'neutrality.' I was standing with my arm along my side while I was supposed to be making the 'Hitler salute.' The matter was brought to the rector's attention who generously gave me a week off for reflection. During that week I had to go from classroom to classroom and have read out a circular announcing my expulsion [although not mentioning her name] if I didn't get straight. At the end of the week the rector came to my class and gave a speech on freedom of choice everyone was offered.

"A deafening silence came over the class and breathing became heavy when the rector said, 'Let the child who recognizes itself get up and come up on the stage either to salute Hitler or to undergo an act of expulsion. Trembling, but with a firmness of heart and a deep conviction that no man has the right to be adored and that the "Heil" or hail can't be given to man, I stood up, to everyone's stupefaction. No one expected that it would be me: 'the revolted one, unsubmitting, the gangrene, the poison.' I climbed the steps to the stage—my heart was pounding and my head bursting—the rector got up from his seat and told me that he would generously accord me a five minute 'reprieve' and their under Hitler's portrait and in front of forty-five students the rector, with chronometer in hand, gave me five long minutes. The atmosphere became even more suffocating, and crushing. Finally, the silence was broken by a rousing *Heil Hitler* uttered by the rector and dutifully followed by the students now at attention. In my mind, in my heart, there was a single thought: 'Take the act of expulsion, an act which is the expression of your faith in God's law which says adore God only.' On Monday morning, I had to contact the director of the public school. Mr. Ehrlich made an enormous scandal. Obliged by law to accept me, he laid down the following conditions: 'No one must know why you were thrown out of school, I forbid you to talk to the other children!' Then he gave instructions to the teacher, Miss Lorentz, to put me in the back of the class room and to 'forget' me. This order became a terrible trial. Day after day the students made fun of me since for them there must have been a reason for my expulsion—either dishonesty or I was a dunce. I was without defense and kept silent, which made the hostility worse and the mockeries were coming fast and furious. In this school, every week we had to bring in a kilo of scrap metal, rags, or old papers for the military effort. Every child had a notebook to recording this, but I never participated in such a collection."

On June 2, 1943, Simone Arnold, not yet thirteen years old, refused to sign a statement before the Mulhouse tribunal denying her faith. In addition, she refused to hand over registration fees to take part in a Hitler youth camp.

"I had decided not to go because every day started and ended with the salute of the flag and the national anthem. Having determined to respect the flag and anthem by being physically present—standing and silent—and refusing any service, cult, or act of obedience, I knew that week would be hell."

Directed to rejoin her class at the train station or to report to the director's office, she chose the latter.

"I knocked on the director's door who obviously didn't expect to see me. He turned pale and then his neck reddened. He grabbed hold of me and made me sit in a classroom in the first row and shouted frenetic orders for the class to stand and sit. After an hour the class was breathless. He ordered each child up on the stage to get their notebooks, and once the child was standing in front of him, he used the notebook to hit them on both cheeks, and he threw the books across the classroom and pointed at me with his left hand—me the tall one sitting in the first row among a group of nine-year-old pupils—and he yelled:, 'It's all because of this vermin!' He was determined to set the pupils against me, but he wasn't able to. At the end of school, some came up to me and told me to hang on! He was also determined to make me pay for my insolence for foiling his plan, as he wanted me to sweat out the youth camp."

Simone then refused to collect salvage for the war effort. She also explained to the director that if she helped with the potato harvest for the soldiers, she "was not responsible for what the man who is fed does," but she is responsible for the vegetables she helped pick.

"His reaction was so violent that with the edge of his hand he gave me a punch on the back of the neck, a little bit as one would knock out a rabbit, and he threw me in a pile of rubbish full of noodles and worms, old papers, sardine cans, stinking bones, etcetera. I had to stay there until the end of classes. They other youngsters helped me home."

On the last day of school, she was treated like the plague. "The flag ceremony followed with the three salutes. Alone, planted in the middle of everyone with my arm at my side, I prayed God I wouldn't give in or tremble. I was awaiting severe punishment. But none came, if not for the enormous emptiness which opened up around me. Abandoned, pointed at and disapproved, I walked home wondering, 'What's the meaning of all this?' "

The next day, in the company of two social workers, she was forced to depart for a reformatory in Germany. Her mother accompanied her to Constance, advising, "Be honest, respectful, submissive, hard-working and polite as befits a Christian. Don't let anyone accuse you of being lazy, indolent, or disrespectful. Never pout and don't answer back." Simone continued, "She explained the need to understand the difference between a firm attitude and an attitude of revolt. I was to be submissive for all things as long as they didn't infringe on the Laws of God."

Simone, who would turn thirteen in two months, was soon to experience the Institute for Girl's Education, the Wessemberg House.

"A girl showed me my bed, an iron bed, and instead of a mattress a bag covered with a sheet. Wakeup call was 5:30 in the morning, and the washroom was one floor up with no hot water. For breakfast, at eight, a plate of soup was served, after which the whole house had to be cleaned by the pupils. School ran from eight thirty to one in the building. In the afternoon, all thirty-seven children, only ten of whom were over ten, divided up by work: laundry, hand washing, mending, and gardening. We produced all our vegetables and dairy products. The four adults just supervised the work: one the school, another the sewing, a third the kitchen, and the director, who was supposed to write a monthly report on each child. Those children were all delinquents. Also it was forbidden to talk to each other or to go to any place alone. Even to go to the toilet, a girl was designated to accompany us. I was given a smock dress and had my shoes taken away. From May until November we went around barefoot. I was given a number and new first name: Maria."

Simone was assigned mending, cleaning toilets, and taking care of a monitor's room. On Sunday, when the other children and the monitors were at Mass, she was assigned to stir porridge in an enormous pot. She became the cook for twenty-two months. She recalled the deplorable and ill-advised hygienic conditions: "We couldn't expose any part of our body except our backs for washing with cold water—the rest was taboo; a bath at Easter and another at Christmas. We had to wear our nightdress in the bathtub and wash underneath. Long hair and braids could only be washed then. The sheets were changed four times a year!"

After three months, she was called before the tribunal at Constance to "determine if my parent's indoctrination was still present." It was, and she persisted in the same choices she had made in Mulhouse. It was only after her second trial that she was able to receive visits from her maternal aunt, Eugenie Walter, who was able to take her out of the reformatory for a day's outing on about a dozen occasions. Her aunt provided news from her family and read biblical literature with her while she was supposed to be perfecting her "Germanic education" by visiting townships and the neighboring countryside.

These visits stopped after the Allied landings in Normandy. "The bombers were constantly flying over the town. I was being trained as a nurse. We spent the nights getting in and out of our beds." The trees in the park along the Swiss border were knocked down. "I was assigned, along with three other girls, to uproot stumps and plant potatoes. The wood which was no good for cabinetry had to be sawed up. Two of us sawed through trunks eighty centimeters in diameter in order to make firewood."

At the end of the war, while French troops were at the school's gate, the director, Miss Lederle, stated to Emma Arnold, who came to pick up her daughter, "I give you back your daughter in the same state of mind as you left her twenty-two months ago."

Emma Arnold had been summoned to the police station at Mulhouse-Dornach in early September 1943. She complied, having chosen not to flee. The Witnesses, it must be noted, seemed almost to accept their lot. Some *Bibelforscher* even returned to a prisoner convoy from which they had inadvertently strayed. For example, a Dutchman was sent by the Nazis from Germany to St. Malo, Brittany, via Holland. The Nazis had made him responsible for dividing up the rations, and when he found himself along the roadside in Holland, in his own country, having failed to get back on the train quickly enough, he rushed down the tracks and succeeded in catching up with his *Kommando*. This *Kommando* was headed to the Alderney (an island belonging to Great Britain) concentration camp and was one of the *Baubrigade* contingents from several concentration camps. Such *Kommandos* were virtually independent.

For her part, Emma Arnold was delivered to the Gestapo but suffered no interrogation or punishment and was immediately transferred to the camp at Schirmeck—two years after her husband—with five other female Witnesses. As her daughter Simone wrote, "She made herself a orthopedic corset with an air bladder designed to push up the stomach and had hidden a pocket Bible inside it which she divided up in six parts between her fellow inmates. They suggested that Mama repair a military jacket, a job she firmly rejected. She was locked up in a cell without food or drink. Since she still wasn't working, Buck, the camp commander told her, 'Why don't you do this jacket? Do you really think our soldiers wear patched-up jackets? Come on. These jackets are for prisoners in the Schirmeck camp.' " Emma Arnold agreed to mend the jacket, "all the while removing the epaulettes and the military tuck," for, as she told the furious commander, "My commandant, you told me yourself this jacket was for a prisoner, and I never saw a prisoner wearing stripes." This earned her more months of solitary confinement in the cell block, and finally she was placed in a barracks with prostitutes and antisocials.

During this time, her husband, Adolphe Arnold, interned at Dachau, became a guinea pig in a medical experiment and infected with malaria. A little cage was attached to the vein on his arm above his elbow joint in which were malaria carrying mosquitoes. "Every day tests for analysis were done." When the doctor decided that his experiment was finished, he did not put Arnold to death but had him transferred to the concentration camp at Mauthausen.

A TEN-YEAR-OLD IN THE CAMPS OF SILESIA

We live in a frothy whirlpool—all tumbled in the same mud.
—E. S. Discepolo

During an interview with the authors, Ruth Danner answered the following questions:

Authors: When were you deported?

Danner: At 3:30 in the morning of January 28, 1943, two SS came to my home and told us to get ready as our family was being deported to Upper Silesia. That same day the entire Jung family was deported, as well as Mr. and Mrs. Wurtz, who were interned at Strigau [near Breslau in Silesia]. Mr. Jung was a colleague of my father's and became a Witness, but his family did not. The SS didn't make a distinction and picked up the whole family, including a three-year-old child. On the deportation train I well remember a young woman's awful agonies; her husband was a Communist who fled. She had been caught with her young three-year-old child and eight-month-old twins who had whooping cough. [After a time] we arrived at our first camp: Kochlowitz (Upper Silesia), Lager #202. The other inmates were all political prisoners and Lorrains. SS in green uniforms put us through an interrogation.

Authors: What kind of interrogation?

Danner: They wanted to know who were the other Jehovah's Witnesses, their names, meeting sites, and where we obtained copies of *The Watch Tower.* Then they asked us to sign a renunciation of our faith. After our refusal, they said we had no hope of going back and that we would never see our house again. We were transferred to Gleiwitz (Upper Silesia), Lager #165. That was a former convent converted into a camp.

Authors: How would you characterize the camps at Strigau, Kocholwitz, and Gleiwitz?

Danner: They were internment camps, deportation camps, and not as harsh as concentration camps. Prisoners didn't have numbers, only the camps were numbered. We wore civilian clothes. We had no freedom, and the food was bad. They were small camps, guarded by the SS, with a hundred to 150 inmates. The deportees were all from Alsace and Lorraine, especially Lorraine. They were sentenced for criminal opinions. And then when Lorraine was annexed by Germany, many people left so as not to be recruited by the military. In reprisal, entire families were deported. In all the camps we were at, we were the only Jehovah's Witnesses. At Gleiwitz we went before the Racial Commission to [be inspected for] Semitic features.

Authors: Can you describe this Racial Commission?

Danner: There were four or five SS people. They examined us, my father, my mother, my sister, and I. They wanted to see, from their point of view, if we had Aryan features. They looked at our right profile and left profile. They were haunted by the Semitic type, and they saw it everywhere. Fortunately, we were lucky for we didn't have black hair or hooked noses.

Authors: Then what happened?

Danner: On 2 June 1943 we were transferred to Schwientochlowitz (Upper Silesia), Lager #13, and from there we went to Franckenstein (Silesia), Lager #91. Internees lived in the attic of a former convent. We were sixty-five men, women, and children mixed in, and there was only one water tap for everyone. There were no other Witnesses. In this camp there was no physical violence. I got some hard slaps a few times in punishment for refusing to say "Heil Hitler." My father got kicked because the camp commandant believed it was my father who forbade me to give the Hitler salute. For him, a child of that age (I was not quite ten years old) didn't have personal convictions. That same SS commandant told my father on the eve of his being shipped to the Russian front, "The Russian front is my punishment from your God for mistreating you all."

Authors: Do you have other memories of Franckenstein?

Danner: Well, in the beginning at Franckenstein we were not forced to make the Hitler salute. Then one day an SS *Obersturmführer* came to camp and the children didn't say "Heil Hitler." There were reprisals against the camp management. At first, all the children refused, and then little by little I became the only one who wouldn't do it.

Author: What happened when you refused?

Danner: I got slapped. In the end, the other children were happy because until then I hadn't been punished, and that vexed them. I was well behaved, people trusted me; I was a favorite and a little spoiled. I was sent from here to there, for example, to get white bread for the SS, which was worth a little bread for me from time to time. I was held up as an example, and that created some jealousy in the other children.

Authors: And then?

Danner: I remember that the camp commandant was pretty hard on the Lorrains, especially when the children of political deportees scoffed at him and sang *The Marseillaise* [the French anthem].Then they were punished and locked up. My father was separated from us. He was sent to another camp in Silesia and didn't rejoin us until January 1945.

Authors: What happened to the rest of the family?

Danner: My mother, sister, and I were transferred to Wolfsdorf in Silesia. This happened following the Racial Commission at Gleiwitz. Wolfsdorf was sort of a "light camp" with barracks. There, I had to go to the public school with the inhabitants of Wolfsdorf to get a Nazi education. But the next day I was expelled for refusing to salute. My mother was called in, and when the teacher told her I hadn't saluted, she turned to me and said, "Didn't you say Good morning?" Then the teacher said, "Yes. But not 'Heil Hitler.' " After this interview, my mother and sister were called to the police, which they had to clean up as punishment. Shortly after my father rejoined us, the area was surrounded by the Red Army. Everyone had left, the SS as well as the peasants, who let their animals go free. We were able to take advantage of that and ate well. But eight days later the SS returned. They evacuated the camp and forced us to walk 249 kilometers in three weeks in the freezing cold. They interned us at Steinfels in March 1945, which was our last camp. There, in addition to Lorrain inmates, there were French and Russian war prisoners. The camp was liberated on April 20, 1945, and we were repatriated on May 5, 1945.

Authors: What was the attitude of the inmates toward you in the camp and during that long march?

Danner: During the camp evacuation, when we were walking and pulling the carts, there was more solidarity among the inmates. The SS shot those who fell behind. Otherwise, the mood in these internment camps was everyone for himself; each defended his own interests. There was continuous mixing from one camp to another. Fellow inmates, the political deportees, couldn't understand our position of neutrality, but they respected it. The Nazis didn't blame us for anything except for being Jehovah's Witnesses. Ours was a crime of opinion, if the term is appropriate. Although the SS were furious with us for being so stubborn, they did have a respectful fear of us. By that I mean the SS were almost superstitious. On the one hand, we created problems for them and they didn't like that, but on the other, if they could do something for us . . . they had the impression of doing us a favor.

Authors: What are your worst memories?

Danner: My worst memories are the constant anxieties we experienced before the deportation, this continuous harassment without ever knowing where we would be the next day. During the deportation it was the cold and the hunger.

Authors: Can you describe the anguish?

Danner: Before the deportation I was upset from the first thing in the morning, at school with my personal problems, during recess, and in front of the teachers. I was only a kid, and all these worries had demolished my nerves. And then I thought of the searches. Would I see Father and Mother again? It was perpetual anguish. What would tomorrow hold? Once in the camp, we faced it a day at a time. But the threat that my parents would lose parental control constantly weighed on us, that the family would be split up. My parents were subjected to separate interrogations. And we knew of the existence of concentration camps. The worst was the cold and hunger. I remember at Wolfsdorf, the electricity was cut off for the night. There was one of those old cast-iron cook stoves. In the evening the water was boiling, and the stove was red-hot. In the morning it was a block of ice. At Franckenstein the food was deplorable. Even the pigs didn't want it. In spite of everything, we didn't feel like martyrs. It was a question of faith, and we suffered the consequences. If it's something you feel, you can put up with anything, you have the strength to do it. At first we didn't think we could succeed; later we got the strength, and we felt serenity effortlessly. Some inmates groused and complained and were full of hate. It was hard; you had to have a reason to resist. The SS were mere instruments, victims of Satan and his system. I have no resentment towards them, but I hope they change their conduct and come back to Jehovah. These tribulations convinced me of the of God's faithfulness. He wouldn't allow us these trials without given the strength to support them.

Authors: Can you talk about your return home?

Danner: For two and a half months during our march and until our arrival back in France, we hadn't been able to change or wash our clothes. We were full of lice and other vermin. When we got home in mid-May, we had nothing left. Not even clothes, for we had taken off our rags and borrowed clothes. I remember that my mother told us, "We all four came back, we have nothing, we are naked, but it's the happiest day of our life; were are all four here, and we made no compromises." My parents refused to file a complaint against those who informed on us. They didn't play martyrs. For them this period was closed. They didn't even file papers. It was only in 1978 that I took the necessary steps and, after many difficulties, my disability was recognized.

Authors: Do you have any news of other Jehovah's Witnesses?

Danner: The other Jehovah's Witnesses we knew came home except for Alain Relewicz. He was deported along with us in March 1943 to Straubing. It was a camp in Bavaria on the Danube between Nuremberg and Passau. He died following the maltreatment he was subjected to in January 1945, just before the liberation. The others came back from the deportation camps or concentration camps, for example, Joseph Hisiger, or even Paul Dossmann, who had been interned in the Struthof concentration camp and Dachau.

Authors: Have you been able to take up professional activity after all these trials and tribulations?

Danner: Not really. My health is always fragile, and the doctors have noted a premature aging of my organs. At twenty, I had the organs of a woman of sixty. That was due to constant stress in my youth.

38

HAFTLING LOUIS PIECHOTA

> Who knows if the new flowers I dream of—can find in the soil washed as a river bank—that mystical nourishment which furnishes their vigor?
>
> —Baudelaire

Despite enduring arrests and persecution, the Witnesses continued to distribute their publications. So it was that they secretly passed out a March 1943 *Mitteilungsblatt* (information flyer) on the subject of the escalating SS terror campaign: "The Nazis are powerless in the face of defeats suffered in Russia, which has provoked them to extraordinary fury. This explains their relentless pursuit of innocent men, adding new crimes to those already perpetrated."

"Cyranek's arrest on 3 July 1941, as well as others, did little to interrupt distribution of illegal literature for Engelhardt. After a brief stay at Essen, he found a hiding place at Oberhausen-Sterkrade where, from the beginning of 1924 until April 1943, he brought out twenty-seven issues of *The Watch Tower.*

During the first half of 1943, the concentration camp at Bergen-Belsen was set up, and the work camp for prisoners of war at Lublin was converted into the Maidanek concentration camp. Concurrently, an order from the German authorities instructed concentration camp commandants to simplify administrative procedures dealing with camp inmate deaths. SS authorities took over the diamond-cutting workshops attached to the Herzogenbusch camp, which became a concentration camp in January 1943. The authors cite a Dutch Red Cross study on the camp at Amersfoort that contained the following information: In December 1942, Amersfoort Transit Camp management received orders from the *Befehlshaber der Sichereitspolizei* (police and Criminal Investigation Division headquarters) to abolish the camp and to transfer all prisoners and staff to the new Herzogenbusch concentration camp at Vught, the Netherlands.

Nevertheless, in February 1943, camp management received orders from the *Hohere SS und Polizeifuhrer Nord West* (SS North West Police Chief) countermanding the camp's closure and stating that it would be reactivated after the transfer of the current prisoner population to Vught. The camp was designated a transit facility for nonpolitical prisoners, especially workers assigned to the Reich labor units, and other hostages, while the political prisoners were to be transferred to KL Herzogenbusch.

During a hearing at the Nuremberg War Crimes Tribunal on June 12, 1946, the question of the use of Jewish, Freemason, and Witness assets that Seyss-Inquart had confiscated was raised:

Prosecutor: When you say this money was confiscated during the first months, do you
mean 1940?

S-I: Yes, immediately after our entry into Holland.

Prosecutor: This liquidation—was it used for the needs of the Reich, yes or no?

S-I: No, if one does not consider the creation of the Vught camp for the Reich's benefit; but the money was used to this end, specifically because the Vught camp was ultimately destined to be an assembly camp for Jews.

Prosecutor: In summary, do you consider the construction of the Vught camp was in the interest of the Dutch?

S-I: Certainly. The costs of the Vught Camp to the extent I knew were covered by Jewish assets, and that is because it was an assembly camp for Jews. It was only later that Himmler turned it into a concentration camp.

A report dated June 21, 1945, prepared by the judge advocate's office of the Third American Army, described the Flossenburg camp and was cited at the Nuremberg tribunal on September 30, 1946: "The best description that can be given of the Flossenburg camp [is] that it was a death factory. Although the primary goal of this camp was the organization of forced labor; it served mainly as a means of doing away lives, thanks to methods used on the prisoners. Famine rations, sadistic maltreatment, insufficient clothing, lack of medical care, sickness, beatings, hangings, the cold, forced suicides, and executions all played a considerable role in achieving this result. Prisoners were murdered for no reason. Hateful murders of Jews were frequent, and poisonous injections and executions by bullet in the back of the neck were daily events. They employed typhoid and typhus epidemics, which spread freely, as a means of eliminating prisoners. Human life stood for nothing in this camp. Murder became an every day event."

In September 1943, the Principal SS Administrative and Economic Office prepared statistics on concentration camps and set the number of inmates at 224,000. On this subject, actions were initiated to ensure increased profitability of the labor force in the camps. Pohl issued orders to concentration camp commandants on October 26, 1943, directing that "inmates must be handled carefully because they must contribute through their labor to the great victory of the German people."

In a letter written to his wife, Franz Massors told her how he had converted Anton Rinker, a man sentenced to death, who had shared a cell with him since 1941.

Louis Piechota was sent to the camp at Vught after his fourth arrest at the Bethune jail in France. He described his itinerary from Belgium to the Netherlands:

> There, the Germans in turn came to arrest me because I had refused to work overtime on Sunday and, therefore, I had not supported the Nazi war effort. The Germans transferred me to the penitentiary at Loos, near Lille, and then a few weeks later to the St. Gilles prison near Brussels, where we were three Witnesses in a cell. The door opened, and another prisoner came in. With a defeated expression he said, "I am condemned to death." He was a Flemish resistant. He requested to be sent to the Russian front to fight alongside the Germans but was denied permission. Be-

> tween us, we admitted that many of us would compromise to save their lives, even if it meant renouncing their ideals or the struggle they were leading. Then I was locked up in the Citadel at Huy, near Liege, before being finally sent to the Vught concentration camp. There I became number 7045, and I was issued a uniform with a violet triangle identifying me as a Jehovah's Witness. They assigned me to block 17-A. It was painful for me to learn to walk barefoot in wooden shoes. The blisters turned my skin raw, and at the slightest misstep I risked a boot kick in the ankles. Fortunately the skin on my feet hardened, and I was able to walk as fast as the others. There were fifteen other Witnesses in the camp. All were Dutch except for three who came from France. One recollection really hit me from the first days of my arrival in camp. One evening the whole camp was assembled to be present at a beating of a prisoner accused of homosexuality. He was bent and stretched over a wooden horse. An inmate, a big strong guy, gave him twenty-five blows with a big baton. The guilty man had to count the strokes aloud. Once finished, he had to present himself before the camp commandant and say, "Prisoner such and such and giving his registration number admits to receiving twenty-five baton strokes for having committed a supposed homosexual act." That angered the commandant, who said, "For a supposed act? Go on, twenty-five more strokes." Again, he received twenty-five strokes without flinching and without complaint. This time he admitted the facts. Another event affected me. After the evening roll call, all the Witnesses were told to stay and to present themselves before the camp commander. There, they were asked if they wanted to be freed. Unanimously, everyone answered, "Yes." Then the commandant said, "Sign this statement recanting your membership in the Jehovah's Witnesses." All refused. The commandant told us, "You will stay in the camp." Such a proposition was presented frequently to the Jehovah's Witnesses but never to another religious or political group.

On orders from Himmler, the SS set up whorehouses in different concentration camps. A whorehouse for deportees was set up at the Flossenburg camp during the summer of 1943. The camouflage name was *Sonderbau* (special pavilion). Jehovah's Witnesses refused any visits to the whorehouse for reasons of conscience. These allegations were reported by Heinz Heger, a *Kapo* in a *Kommando* of twenty-five men.

39

VOYAGE IN THE NIGHT

> Light has an age. Night does not. But when was the instant of this entire source?
>
> —Rene Char

In Berlin in January 1944, the Gestapo arrested approximately one hundred Jehovah's Witnesses, of which seventy-three were later sentenced to lengthy prison terms. On January 7, Adolf Zanker, a thirty-three-year-old farmer from Gruibingen, was executed at Torgau prison. Charged as a Christian basing himself on the Holy Scriptures, he declined to participate in an armed military unit and don a uniform. His wife, Anna Zanker, later received formal notification of his execution.

That year, the situation at the front deteriorated so badly the Nazi government recruited even from within the ranks of concentration camp inmates, promising freedom to those who joined the *Dirlewanger* division. This offer was not made to the Jehovah's Witnesses. A number of Witnesses were assigned to care for Mme. Heydrich's estate in Czechoslovakia.

Victor Bruch, who had been locked up in Buchenwald since 1941, was "sent to Lublin, where they needed workers. There they tried to make us into good Germans; we weren't supposed to be Luxembourgers or even Jehovah's Witnesses." He refused to be a German and to renounce his faith. He was shipped off to a sawmill at the Pulawy camp, remained there for only a short time, and carried away awful memories of the place. The SS, harassed by partisans, lived in the same barracks with the prisoners. "Since the Russians were approaching, we were deported to Auschwitz. Brothers and Sisters who had been there for a time held positions of trust. Several Sisters were permitted to go to town, unescorted, to shop for their employers. There they copied whole articles from *The Watch Tower.*"

Rene Seglat was arrested as a Communist on November 11, 1943, at Grenoble, and the authors met up with him in Lyon on June 6, 1990. He narrated his departure from Compiegne on January 17, 1944, and his arrival at Buchenwald two days later. Assigned to block 51, he remembered seeing Jehovah's Witnesses for the first time. "The violet triangles were in a barracks near the crematorium. During my time there were about two hundred of them. What intrigued me about those violet triangles was their longer hair, whereas ours was shaved; we had been given the famous 'Strasse' treatment." During our discussions, he stated that he left Grenoble after the war and abandoned the Communist Party "because most of its members were atheists." He began to study Jehovah's Witness doctrine in 1954 and joined as a member.

Jacques-Christian Bailly, deported in May 1944 to Buchenwald, described his own experiences in concentration camps and especially his feelings for a particular inmate: "A small group of Frenchmen gathered around an old, white-haired German prisoner whose inmate number was only three digits. He told us about the camp's opening in 1937. At that time, he said, the Ettersberg Hill was covered with trees. We cut down the woods to set up the camp. Someone remarked, 'It stinks of burning flesh here.' The German turned around. 'You're looking at the only way out of camp,' he said. 'That's where you'll soon be leaving Buchenwald.' The old German's name was Erwin. Initially, I hadn't noticed his violet triangle. 'I am a Jehovah's Witness,' he explained. 'The Nazis have forbidden our movement since 1933. They didn't hunt us down then; it was only in 1937 that they interned us, when we refused to bear arms.' German inmates suffered a lot, especially at the beginning. Common criminals, called the greens, ran the camp at that time. The SS trusted them and gave them responsibility for internal administration. Things were hard; they only thought about getting the best deal for themselves from their positions."

Louis Piechota and other inmates were shunted to the camp at Vught in the spring of 1944. "Jammed in like cattle in little railway wagons, which carried eighty prisoners; we had to stand throughout three days and nights with no food or water and nowhere to relieve ourselves. Finally, the train reached Oranienburg about thirty kilometers north of Berlin. We had to run ten kilometers to the aircraft factory at Heinkel, guarded by SS dogs nipping at our heels if we slowed down." Transferred later to Sachsenhausen, he wore inmate number 98,827 inside his violet triangle. "When we approached the camp, we could smell burning. I wondered what it was. But, once in camp, I soon understood. This smell was coming from the crematorium ovens. It was the smell of human flesh. And to think, now some contend it was 'just a detail' and that others even deny its existence."

At the Sachsenhausen camp, Piechota met German Witnesses and benefited from their assistance. "As soon as a convoy arrived at the camp, the German Brothers wondered if there were any new Witnesses. If there were, they immediately came to their aid. Perhaps they gave them warm underwear, or a sweater, or leftovers from the guards' meals since some worked in the kitchen."

Louis Piechota continued his account: "The Nazis tried to break the Jehovah's Witnesses resistance, or they killed them. They killed many. Take the case of Brother Kurt Pape. He got orders to go out on a work party assigned to an armaments plant. He refused to go, which could have cost him his life. Surprisingly, the camp commandant allowed him to take another job. Another time, Brother Pape lectured me for having taken a little bread from the camp bakery where I worked. I did, so the Brothers could have a little more to eat, but he advised it was better to go hungry than to bring disgrace on Jehovah's name by passing for a thief. This reprimand made a big impression on me."

To the author's query as to whether he knew of examples of inmate conversions, he affirmed: "Yes, there were inmate conversions. Kurt Pape had a group of Russians and Ukrainians he preached to regularly on Sunday afternoons. I translated his German into Polish, which they understood. I remember a Ukrainian who was very well-disposed to the message of the Kingdom. His name was Fedor. Some got baptized. On Sunday afternoons we tried to contact other prisoners in the courtyard and engage them in conversations about the Bible. Copies of publications got into the camp such as *The Watch Tower.* Every evening we received our 'daily text' on a scrap of paper. It was a biblical verse with a commentary, and three or four of us would meet to discuss it. A Witness who worked at the reception office got me a Bible in French. What a joy and comfort! In the evenings I would read it."

Following an arrest during the autumn of 1943, Himmler ordered immediate searches of concentration camps named in documents and letters confiscated in Jehovah's Witnesses' homes. One day in 1944, the SS assembled all the Jehovah's Witnesses because "they learned that we corresponded secretly with the outside, and from camp to camp, and that we were meeting every day in groups of two or three on the parade ground to discuss a biblical text." All the inmates refused to stop their preaching and teaching activities.

Paul Grossmann, an inmate at the Berlin-Lichterfeld camp (a Sachsenhausen annex camp) related the following: "On April 26, 1944, two SS officers came to Lichterfeld to question me in detail about my activities as a liaison agent between Sachsenhausen and Lichterfeld. They showed me two illegal letters I wrote to Brothers in Berlin. So, the police knew all the details of our organization."

Several believers at Lichterfeld signed the following statement, and with no hesitation or regard for the consequences: "I, a Jehovah's Witness . . . swear to the theocratic unity which reigns in the Sachsenhausen concentration camp. I received daily texts and other printed materials which I read and passed to others." Eugen Kogon recalled a similar experience in May 1944 at Buchenwald. "All the Fundamentalists were assembled on the parade ground, and they were searched for tracts hostile to the regime (in a concentration camp!)." However, the Gestapo searched in vain. "The result: nothing."

On May 4, 1944, the police also intervened in Ravensbrück. Severe measures were taken against Witness "leaders," but they were soon restored to their regular jobs on work details.

Elisabeth Will, deported to Ravensbrück from February until July 1944 and who wore inmate number 27,856, reported the following event concerning the Witnesses: "Other martyrs, violet triangles, and conscientious objectors who had faith in a revelation refused to work." Citing the case of a neighboring block, where five or six women remained "deep in their prayers, neither the entreaties of the *Blockowa* or the prodding of the mice could budge them." The SS came in, booted them out, and beat them with rifle butts, taking them off by force to work. Elisabeth Will never learned of the outcome since barracks personnel were reassigned but concluded, "The only inmate registration numbers under 1,000 I ever saw alive were the violet triangles, and I remember an old man who wore number 66, sweeping rubbish at the inside infirmary courtyard. He had an infinitely luminous look about him."

Denise Dufournier, who left Compiegne in 1944, met Witnesses at Ravensbrück who "enjoyed a certain freedom. They could leave camp alone to go to their work housecleaning the SS barracks and gardening and were always assigned good jobs in the laundry, offices, and other places." She also recalled a convoy of those deemed "crazy" by the Nazis, which included about fifty other inmates. "Among them were three French women, some Jehovah's Witnesses, and several individuals judged undesirable. In that contingent there was no one suffering from the slightest mental alienation." In addition, Denise also recalled the grim fate of deportees who were victims of vivisection. A list of victims was drawn up by Nina Iwanska, who was a victim who helped organize resistance. The list cataloged seventy-four Poles; two Ukrainians (both whom died), one Russian (who died), a Belgian arrested in Germany (who died), and five German Witnesses (four of whom were dead). At Selters, Gertrud Potzinger had particularly poignant memories of Polish students who worked in the same *Kommando.* She knew several who were tortured to death or served as guinea pigs for barbaric medical experiments. "They were dragging themselves along and couldn't walk. I saw them in this lamentable condition, and they couldn't move and so faced execution."

On May 9, 1944, SS officer Glucks sent a memo to concentration camp commandants requesting that inmates from "eastern convoys" no longer be registered. The next day, Rachel Sacksini, a

Dutch Witness who was of Jewish extraction, was arrested in the Netherlands. She was first interned in the Dutch concentration camp at Westerbork (where many Jewish prisoners were being herded) and was scheduled to leave in a cattle car, but at the last moment her convoy was rerouted to Bergen-Belsen. Later evacuated to Beendorff and Malmö, Sweden, she returned to the Netherlands after the war, where she converted the wife and three daughters of a Nazi serving a prison term. The authors questioned the Dutch Bethel to learn which type of triangle Jewish Jehovah's Witnesses were assigned at the camps. After obtaining information from Jehovah's Witnesses of Jewish origin who were imprisoned for years, he responded, "A Jewish woman I questioned said, 'I was locked up with the Jews and wore a yellow triangle during my stay in the concentration camp.' The Germans called her *die jüdische Bibelforscherin* (the Jewish Bible Student). A Jewish Witness said he wore the violet triangle during his internment at Sachsenhausen camp. On the other hand, he noted that the Germans were unaware of his Jewish origins, as he was arrested for being a Jehovah's Witness."

Despite the Red Army's advance along the eastern front, which caused evacuation of the Lublin/Maidenek concentration camp on July 22, 1944, the executions continued. Julius Engelhardt, one of the Witnesses' leaders from Karlsruhe who was hunted down for years by the Gestapo, was finally arrested at Oberhausen-Sterkade, jailed, and subjected to terrible tortures at the Berlin-Potsdam prison with seven fellow Witnesses, whose numbers included many members of the Hetkamp family. All were sentenced to death for high treason and beheaded on June 2, 1944, by the Berlin *Volksgerichtshof*.

Julius Engelhardt was himself beheaded on August 14, 1944, leaving behind five children. His father, August, received a terse notice worded, "The death sentence of your son, Julius Engelhardt, was carried out on August 14, 1944. By order I am so informing you, and I expressly draw your attention to the effect that publication of an obituary is not authorized. Berlin, September 21, 1944. The Reich General Prosecutor of the *Volksgerichtshof*. To: Mr. August Engelhardt."

On September 18, 1944, the Hamm High Court sentenced dozens of Witnesses from Essen to long prison terms. The were guilty of organizing meetings and regularly distributing *The Watch Tower*. They would later be shipped off to concentration camps, where they died.

On August 24, 1944, the Allies bombed the armaments factory near the Buchenwald camp. Hundreds of bombs fell, resulting in a number of inmate victims (including two dead and twelve wounded among the Jehovah's Witnesses). Rene Seglat recalled, "The American B-17 bombings—hundreds of kilos of bombs fell on the factories. There were about five hundred SS and four hundred among us killed."

Josef Seitz described the Anglo-American planes that flew over the camp as all hell broke loose: "The bombs fell without interruption; our wooden barracks shook and tottered, but to the honor of the enemy aviators, it must be said they spared the camp. They didn't hold anything against us, and it was only the arms factories (DAW, Gusloff) that were bombed as well as SS lodgings, casernes, and other locations. Hundreds of comrades were killed and injured due to the guards' stupidity and the blindness of camp management. If they had left us in camp, nothing would have happened. The SS even fired at us because they thought we were trying to escape. Luckily, they shot at their own men."

Nighttime cremations were abolished in 1944 so that the camp would not be spotted by Allied aviation. By August 21, 1944, deportation of Jews to Auschwitz had practically ceased. On October 7, the Auschwitz *Sonderkommando* rioted, and on November 26, Himmler ordered the dismantling of the Auschwitz crematoria. Hermann Langbein retained positive recollections of the violet triangles: "There were only about two dozen men and women, but by August 1944 there were 122. Those that I knew there, and those I heard of, were very correct, helpful, friendly, and unequivocally rejected National Socialism. They didn't allow themselves to be corrupted by their privileged position. They were working for SS families, at the *Waffen SS* Club, and the Officers' Mess."

40

A GAULLIST RESISTER IN DACHAU

> The strength by which man perseveres in existence is limited—and infinitely surpassed—by the power of outside sources.
>
> —Baruch Spinoza

Francois-Fabien Lacombe (who died in December 1993) was jailed for Gaullist resistance activity at the Eysses Central Prison in southern France and on June 20, 1944, became inmate number 73.611 in Dachau. He sent the authors the following account: "I only met a few Jehovah's Witnesses during my say at the Dachau camp and in two other *Kommandos*. I remember three of them. Heineman and Dorfer in Dachau and another at Allach, whose name escapes me. I had heard in autumn 1936 and June 1937, from Protestant friends conversant with the matter, of Nazi persecutions against the International Association of Fundamentalists, better known as 'Jehovah's Witnesses' or '*Bibelforscher*.' Moreover, the Nazi newspaper *Völkische Beobachter* published an ordinance in the summer of 1937 from the Nazi Interior Ministry announcing 'the segregation' of foreign (American) Fundamentalists. But in Dachau, it was my own curiosity about the violet triangles that enabled me to make connections with them—they were few in number—those who were called Jehovah's Witnesses. One fellow did light carpentry, and the other was a tailor. At Allach, I knew a kitchen helper. Dissimulated and almost lost in the overall prison population, they spoke little and shared few confidences. Those I knew were attached to nonviolence, for which the SS despised them, and seemed resigned to their fates. They presented themselves as conscientious objectors, believing in the impending end of the world, and had a preference for the Apocalypse in the Bible. For all that, they seemed as indifferent to other prisoners as they were to the SS. Not one of them accepted the role of *Kapo.* I learned a bit about them, and because I spoke German and introduced myself as a student of philosophy, I noted their nostalgia for the period when their proselytizing flourished in Germany. They had their martyrs, especially the leaders of the sect arrested in Magdeburg in 1934. Some had wives who had been locked up in Ravensbrück since the beginning of the war. But none complained. Paradoxically, compared to other prisoners, they seemed devoted and conscientious in their work. Moreover, I knew of no SS brutality towards them. That contributed to their being set apart from the others."

On September 2, 1944, the Natzweiler-Struthof camp was evacuated in the teeth of Allied advances, and its inmates registered on arrival at Dachau. A few kilometers from there, at the approach of the French army, inmates at Schirmeck-Vorbruck were evacuated in the autumn of 1944. A first stage was spent at the Gaggenau transit camp in the Black Forest, and when they finally reached it after two hard weeks of transport travel, the camp was not finished, and the barracks were very basic.

It was there that Emma Arnold worked as a seamstress for an SS officer until coughing fits restricted her to the barracks. "In view of the frequent bombings, our departure for Ravensbrück was delayed. Then one day they decided to send us on foot to another rail line. . . . We were made to march for weeks in the twilight and were locked up during the daytime in farmhouse basements. It was March 1945, and not far from Rothau in the Black Forest. We were locked up in a basement again in the dark with no food. A couple of days later an inmate forced the door open to go out . . . to see . . . and he saw nothing. The SS had fled."

According to a letter from Himmler sent to Kaltenbrunner in September 1944, the SS chief expressed "admiration and recommend[ing], upon victory, that 'Witnesses' be settled on the vast

Russian plains, where, on the doorstep of the German Empire, they would serve as a barrier against Soviet ambitions. If they convert the local population . . . their pacifism would prevent them from taking up arms against the Nazis, and their hate of Catholics and Jews would keep them from collaboration with enemies of the Reich." This letter was sent to Kaltenbrunner, who, in turn, dispatched forty-two telegrams sent by RSHA services in Prague to Gestapo offices in Darmstadt.

"These internment orders were sent during the period from September 20, 1944, to February 2, 1945. Kaltenbrunner proceeded to intern targeted individuals in a number of camps, including Sachsenhausen, Ravensbrück, Buchenwald, Bergen-Belsen, Flossenburg, and Theresienstadt. . . . Grounds for these internments: refusal to work, religious propaganda, sexual relations with POWs, Communist sympathies, work slowdowns, anti-German activities, spread of demoralizing rumors, *Gitteraktion* [action against pacifictsts and people against the war], breaking work contracts, hostile and defeatist statements, thefts and escapes."

The authors quote from a October 19, 1944, telegram:

> Subject: Protective internment against a Reich German citizen, Thomas Bruecher, born 5.1.04 [January 5, 1904] at Darmstadt-Arheilgen.
>
> File: Report dated 7.9.44 [September 7, 1944]—IV 6 KLB 8066/44 BTZ/GR
>
> I order protective internment for the above-named individual until further notice.
>
> Detention examination expiration date: 17.1.45 [January 17, 1945].
>
> The inmate is informed that protective internment has been decreed on grounds he distributed sectarian religious literature detrimental to public order and for his relationship with the banned International Association of Bible Students (BIV); it is expected his continuing freedom would lead to the further spread of religious heresies.
>
> He is to be transferred to the Dachau Concentration Camp as a Category I prisoner.
>
> RSHA IV A/6KLB H NRB 36653—signed Dr. Kaltenbrunner.

Kaltenbrunner, who was chief of the Austrian police, chief of the Central Service of Reich Criminal Investigations, and head of security services, appeared before the Nuremberg War Crimes Tribunal and was questioned on April 12, 1946, by his lawyer, Dr. Kaufmann:

Dr. Kaufmann:
Concerning religious policies, the Public Ministry has charged you with the following: members of the *Bibelforscher* cult were condemned to death simply for deep religious convictions forbidding them to participate in the War. I ask you if you knew of these facts and in what way were you mixed up in this matter?

Kaltenbrunner (the accused): German legislation which was used against the *Bibelforscher* cult was based on the law for military protection of the German people. The law provides penalties such as denial of freedom, as well as the death penalty for individuals harmful to the military spirit of the German people and who refuse to submit to wartime service. On the basis of the law's provisions, the courts, both military and civil, have occasionally pronounced death sentences. The State's Secret Police did not, of course, proceed with capital executions. On this subject, the harshness which was unjustly manifested against cult members acting in accordance with their faith has often been described. On this subject I also personally intervened with the Party Chancellery as well as with the Justice Minister and Himmler and in my report to Hitler. I asked Thierack during many conversations that this procedure be modified. I obtained satisfaction on two levels; during our first meeting and after discussions initiated by Thierack with Bormann and Hitler, whom he did not see in person, the courts were given instructions to cancel sentences already handed down. During a second meeting I was able to obtain agreement that prosecutors be given orders to desist from requesting the death penalty. Finally, a third point, *Bibelforscher* were no longer brought before justice. I consider it is thanks to my personal intervention with Thierack, an intervention which was later discussed in Hitler's presence, that legal action against members of these cults definitively stopped.

Facts undermine Kaltenbrunner's thesis if we analyze the overall situation and corroborating historical evidence.

In April 1944, authorities ordered public hangings as punishment for acts of sabotage perpetrated in concentration camps. In November 1944, young Jonathan Stark, born on July 8, 1926, at Ulm, was hanged. In September 1943, he refused to take a loyalty oath to Hitler and was called before the *Arbeitsdienst*. He was then interned at Sachsenhausen, and in autumn 1944 the SS decided to murder him. Believing that he detected hesitation in one of the hangmen, Jonathan Stark declared, "Why are you hesitating? I am dying for Jehovah and Gideon." Jonathan Stark was only eighteen years old.

Jean Bezaut also mentioned this hanging, and to our question "Fifty years on what view do you have of the *Bibelforscher*?" he wrote, "One of the reasons for SS fury towards them was their refusal to bear arms, their conscientious objection. They belonged to a category of highly motivated inmates. The number of *Bibelforscher* in these camps was minimal from 1944 to 1945 during the time I was personally at Dachau and Sachsenhausen. Those who had survived were partly dispersed throughout the big camp and, in part, in the *Kommandos*. For this reason, they shared the same daily fate of the other inmates. The other inmates had no particular attitude towards them. They were part of the concentration camp universe alongside the Jews, the antisocials or the Gypsies. The inmates had negative feelings for only one category; the greens, that's to say common criminals whom the SS used in a parallel hierarchy they created. Even though I didn't share their religious beliefs, with the benefit of time passed I can only have a certain sense of respect for these men. Pages 67 to 69 of my study justify this sentiment. Even Rudolf Hess's testimony attested to the courage of these inmates. How many prisoners placed before the choice of assured death would have shown the same courage?

"Not every man can be as strong as Pierre Brossolette.[1] I think of all those who, for different reasons, made the same choice. I think of those lines from Malraux: 'Come in here, Jean Moulin[2] . . . with all those who died like you in caves without breaking silence, or even after talking which is more atrocious.'

"In Holland many Witnesses refused to perform work for military personnel and were arrested: Joan van der Berg was twenty when he refused to work on a military project. The camp commandant threatened to have him shot and made him dig his own grave next to which he was forced to stand half-naked. A volley of shots rang out, and the inmate was beaten and forced to do 'gymnastics' and all sorts of contortions. On October 11, 1944, three young Dutch Witnesses were machine-gunned in the garden of the house that served as Gestapo headquarters and buried there. On November 10, Bernard Polman was arrested at Zelhem and also refused to perform work of a military nature; he was beaten and subjected to all sorts of brutalities before being riddled with bullets and buried at the foot of a dike not far from Bubberich.

"By the end of December 1944, there were eighty-five Jehovah's Witnesses at Mauthausen, forty-six Germans or Austrians, thirty-six Poles, and three Czechs. During the year, six Germans or Austrians were freed, from which you could conclude that only this tiny number were willing to go in to the Wehrmacht. Marsalek described them in general as 'helpful,' while noting their relations with other inmates was not particularly open or demonstrative. They constituted 'a calm community: discrete, disciplined, patient, hard-working and faithful to their beliefs.' "

By the end of 1944, Joseph Hisiger was transferred from the Zweibrücken camp to the prison at Pirmasens and then to Siegburg, where he was assigned to a *Kommando* to work in metallurgy. One Sunday afternoon, while being marched around an enclosed courtyard surrounding the prison buildings, a Jehovah's Witness in another line dropped a paper for him: "I picked it up, but, unfortunately, one of the guards saw it and rushed at me. Seeing that, I slid the note underfoot and crushed it. We both got disciplinary sanctions—three weeks of solitary on bread and water. Afterwards, I was isolated in a cell where I couldn't communicate with anyone. I learned later that my spiritual brother was transferred to some unknown place and that he died, faithful to Jehovah. I was liberated from this prison on the arrival of the Allied troops around the end of April 1945 and taken to a hospital because I weighed only forty-five kilos and was sick with dropsy."

Milos Vitek described men who survived three weeks of forced marching: "Emaciated, in rags, barefooted, with arms and legs covered with incurable sores. A horrible procession of ghosts advanced towards the camp."

NOTES

1. A famous and important French resister who committed suicide on May 22, 1944, instead of talking when tortured by the Gestapo. He founded the Conseil National de la Résistance (CNR).
2. Another famous and important French resister who was a chief in the Resistence (president of the CNR). He died of torture, and he did not talk.

41

JANUARY 1945: THE RED ARMY ARRIVES AT AUSCHWITZ

In the plain
a noise is born
It is the breath
of night.
It wails
like a soul
that a flame
always follows.
—Victor Hugo

Gertrud Potzinger recalled, in one of her interviews with the authors, the housework and child care that she did for the Kiener family during the period 1944–1945:

Authors: What were you doing at the time for the Kiener family?

GP: I was sewing and altering the *Obersturmbannführer*'s pants for the children and cutting aviators' uniform cloth to make a coat for his wife. I had a little more freedom since Mme. Kiener worked. I took advantage of every moment to read Bible literature, which I hid in front of the mirror when I was doing my hair and my braid or when I was washing the dishes. On January 1, 1945, some SS personnel gathered at SS *Obersturmbannführer*'s place to celebrate the New Year. I brought and served them wine and beer. (The SS had access to these drinks.) After learning it was my birthday and having already taken in a lot of wine, they kept repeating, "*Wir wollen die Bibelbiene gratulieren*" (Our best wishes to the Bible bee). I got Mme. Kiener's permission to take refuge in my bedroom, and I heard them howling until the early hours of the morning. I am very grateful to the SS *Obersturmbannführer's* wife who protected me; she stood in front of my door and threatened all those who tried to come upstairs and threw them down the stairs.

On January 15, 1945, a WVHA census of concentration camp population established the number of male inmates at 511,537 and females at 202,674. By the time of the arrival of the Red Army at Auschwitz on January 27, 1945, the majority of deportees had been evacuated, and there were only a few thousand left in the camps.

Victor Bruch, who had been evacuated from Lublin and had recently arrived at Auschwitz, was once again transferred. "A mad pursuit across German had begun. Some of us were crammed into cattle wagons and taken on a three-day journey on a single slice of bread for food. On the eleventh day we arrived at Ravensbrück. More than 1,500 prisoners died of starvation." Albin Glowacz also spoke of the Auschwitz evacuees: "It was during the winter of 1944–1945 that I saw a transport of women coming from Poland, jammed into open wagons, disembarking from the Ravensbrück train. At that time the Germans were evacuating the camp. More than half had died, and those who were still alive walked like flies who had fallen on tar. The women had difficulty standing. It was a ghastly sight."

After being kept behind barbed wire at Ravensbrück for a while, they were again transferred, this time on foot. The "mad pursuit" continued as Victor Bruch walked with forty-eight Jehovah's Witnesses. Then one morning, he noticed that the German guards had disappeared, and he saw the American flag flying. They were free! "We then got together in a field on the edge of the village, and a Brother said a prayer of thanksgiving for the marvelous liberation. It was May 3, 1945, at Rubz." They continued on foot, and on June 18, 1945, Bruch finally reached his home at Esch-sur-Alzette.

Elsa Abt, Auschwitz inmate number 24402, was also shuttled

from one camp to another. Initially, she walked for two days and nights toward the Gross-Rosen camp, then one morning an SS doctor with whom Elsa had worked began shouting, "All Bible Students out of the ranks!"

They were assembled, and forty were taken to a station where they boarded a train. Some who were unable to reach the station proceeded of their own accord to the camp because, as they explained, "our Sisters would have been bothered if we had not rejoined them at the camp." After two weeks at Gross-Rosen, they were initially dispatched to Mauthausen, then to Bergen-Belsen (one of the violet triangles died en route). Conditions at Bergen-Belsen were so shocking that many did not survive. Some twenty-five women were moved to Dora-Nordhausen, where they were better fed since a Witness inmate worked in the kitchen. During their final transfer, which was to have taken them toward Hamburg, Elsa Abt and her fellow inmates were freed by American troops. "The SS dressed up in civilian clothes they had taken care to supply themselves and slipped away."

42

THE TRUTH WILL HAVE THE LAST WORD

The following account by Georges Wellers of his arrival at Buchenwald was provided to the authors on July 18, 1990. In January 1945, Wellers (who would die on May 2, 1991) was also evacuated from Auschwitz. "We had to do seventy-five kilometers in a day and a half on foot and in the snow. It was a hard trial. How to survive? Some said they were lucky; I saw it as a series of lucky things. Of necessity, I became fatalistic. Many times there were things which I thought were unfavorable, which later proved positive. It was unforeseeable. At Auschwitz we formed a little team. As a physiologist, I was miraculously assigned to the *Revier* (camp ambulance). I worked with Weiz, the head doctor, who was a professor of dermatology at the University of Strasbourg. I knew him before the war, and I was there for his departure to Drancy. We met up again there and got the idea to analyze the food we were given. Therefore, we sought the agreement of the SS doctors. We said we wanted to do blood analyses on different categories of prisoners (well-fed, relatively less well-fed, and those who were dying). One of the SS told us it was interesting, and he wanted to publish the results in his name. I did the work. Towards the end, when I learned the camp was to be evacuated, I made two copies of the results sheets—one for Weiz and one for me. When we arrived at Buchenwald, Weitz ran into some colleagues from the university and worked as a doctor. As for me, given conditions on my arrival at the concentration camp at Buchenwald, I lost the report. A few days later a director from an institute in Berlin came to Buchenwald, and the infirmary chief introduced Weiz. They asked him what he was doing at Auschwitz. He mentioned the study. That director was interested in the results and said he would welcome knowing the details. Weiz couldn't answer some of his questions, for although he had chosen the subjects, I had done the research. I got called. My block chief told me to get ready. The guy, very unpleasant, questioned me. Afterwards, he telephoned and I was assigned to the SS hospital. I only had to say *Jawohl*! That's how I remained at Buchenwald until the end."

Following an article that appeared in the review *Le Monde Juif* in which two former Jehovah's Witnesses were quoted concerning the "Leuchter Report" and the Auschwitz gas chambers, the authors wrote Georges Wellers asking him for a description of and for details on his knowledge of Jehovah's Witnesses. He responded, "I knew some Jehovah's Witnesses at Buchenwald. At Auschwitz, I don't recall having seen any. They had a pretty good reputation, in the sense that many people are very egotistical and some helped the more powerful people to the detriment of the less fortunate. It's my impression that they were people of good moral character. In any part of humanity, there are exceptions."

The authors also asked the following questions:

Authors: Why were former Jehovah's Witnesses quoted at a trial that took place in Canada?

GW: You mean the "Leuchter Report." It seems to me the Jehovah's Witnesses quoted were misinformed. For any discussion on the gas chambers, one needs to develop a line of argumentation, and that requires a certain reflection. So these two Witnesses didn't understand any of the arguments presented since they were ineptly presented, and the Witnesses didn't understand. They explained themselves in good faith, [but] in rather bizarre fashion.

Authors: What are your views on the Jehovah's Witnesses?

GW: I believe it's a rather widespread cult. And if two Jehovah's Witnesses were silly enough to testify at a trial when they understood nothing, they couldn't compromise the cult. One can't judge a cult by the silly things a couple of former members say, even in good faith.

Authors: What image do you have of the *Bibelforscher*?

GW: I remember people of conviction, honest people. In my mind, my memories, I had some consideration for them due to their attitude. They aren't people who could steal or lie.

Authors: Do you consider them resisters against the Nazis?

GW: Yes, especially since they weren't people who would prostrate themselves before their torturers.

Authors: Did you have much contact with them in the camp?

GW: No. In the camp I was assigned to another *Kommando*. We barely knew anyone other than the thirty people in the *Kommando*.

Authors: You said you met them at Buchenwald. What comes back to mind?

GW: There were some. I remember the color of the triangle with their country's letters in it. We spotted them very quickly because of the violet color.

Authors: Did you wonder why they had been interned?

GW: Because they were badly regarded by the Nazis. It was not a question one asked oneself.

Authors: When did you see them?

GW: In 1945, after the Auschwitz evacuation.

Authors: What recollections do you have of the Witnesses?

GW: I repeat, they are honest people, people who can't steal or lie.

43

EVACUATION OF THE CAMPS

> Act only according to principle, may that be an end for everyone and have the value of practical universal law. Act in a way to always treat humanity either in person or in the person of fellow man as and end in itself, and never as a means.
>
> —Immanuel Kant

By early 1945, Hitler had decided that no concentration camps inmate should survive the Reich's eventual collapse. Himmler dispatched a telegram to all camp commandants stating that "surrender [is] unthinkable. The camp must be immediately evacuated. No inmate must fall into enemy hands alive."

However, in the camps, the inmates resisted: After the bombing of the Mauthausen auxiliary camp at Amstetten on March 20, 1945, a women's *Kommando* declared its refusal to return to camp. A delegation of many Frenchwomen and an Englishwoman informed the *Lagerführer.* This was the first flagrant refusal to work, and it succeeded, in that no subsequent consequences were incurred.

Adolphe Arnold was assigned to the Ebensee annex camp beginning in January 1945. He was assigned to laundry duties in a swimming pool filled with hot water and detergent. The prisoners stomped dirty laundry in cadence, with dogs at their heels. With the approach of the Allies, it was decided to exterminate the inmates by herding them into a uncompleted tunnel that would then be dynamited. About twenty Jehovah's Witnesses were there. That took place in May 1945. However, the Allies advanced more rapidly than expected, and the guards took flight without dynamiting the tunnel. The inmates were taken out of the tunnel by American soldiers.

According to Evelyn Le Chene, on May 4, 1945, Mauthausen held the following inmate populations: 28,256 political prisoners, 96 Jehovah's Witnesses, 67 homosexuals, 9,822 Jews, 176 Gypsies, 4,502 prisoners of war, 15,020 young Russians, 1,253 criminals held under long sentences, 2,721 criminals with short-term sentences, 441 antisocials, and 2,457 others of undetermined affiliation.

Dr. Albert J. Rohmer, chief of the pediatric clinic at the Strasbourg medical faculty, was arrested in March 1944 and deported to Neuengamme, where he arrived on July 18, 1944. As inmate number 37087, he was shipped to an outside *Kommando* at Helmstedt in August. He served first as a doctor and then on a *Kommando* at the salt mines from October 1944 until the camp's evacuation in April 1945, at which time inmates were shunted off to Ludwigslust-Woebbelin.

The authors contacted Dr. Rohmer by telephone, and despite his advanced age and fatigue, he confirmed his earlier account in *Neuengamme Outside Kommando H: Helmstedt Salt Mine,* where he mentioned a Witness named Max, the bakery *Kapo* "didn't beat us. Max was a *Bibelforscher,* a Jehovah's Witness, and wore a violet triangle. Enslaved for four years inside the camp, he refused on four occasions to sign a retraction that would have freed him. Having become a *Kapo,* he took a liking to good food and women, but he still awaited the coming of Jehovah and the millennium. He cosigned a letter to Hitler comparing the chancellor to the beast of the Apocalypse, but the letter had no repercussions. For the SS, these men were mad. Yet when, at Woebbelin, our eight *Bibelforscher* whose food had run out got together for a reading of a prophetic text, these so-called madmen brought honor to humanity."

Dr. Rohmer went on: "Out of this herd of slaves some individuals subsisted, but the hierarchy was unlike that of civilian life. Pitiful collapse awaited all those whose social rank was based on exterior appearance or whose positions were owed to their good fortune or strictly to intelligence. We saw many in well-tailored suits completely shed their previous identity. Unfortunately, we saw people sink who should have remained upright. After a couple of weeks of concentration camp life, everyone showed what he had in his guts. The only ones who retained their dignity had character and a goal, those who cared for something other than themselves. When the body is a cadaver, one finds the spirit is all that counts." Rohmer paid the Witnesses further homage: "I would like to unify in the same thought our young Communists, our *Bibelforscher*, our Christian friends. Mad enough to believe in an ideal, they also had enough character to remain faithful to a principle. Most died—unbowed without consenting to sully themselves."

David Rousset provided a similar account: "Otto, the *Vorarbeiter*, was afraid of everything: the *Kapos*, the civilian work party chiefs, the guards. He was afraid of nighttime and even his dreams. Max, the baker, was a Roman powerhouse. He was a man of the Bible. He walked with an indifference, like a force of nature. He was a man of few words, but one evening he spent a lot of time with us (my friends Martin and Lorenz and me). He spoke in a most dignified fashion, glancing around, but with the slow assurance of someone conveying a message. Showing no emotion, he described Hitler as dedicated to destruction and the personification of the beast of the Apocalypse. Max, the *Kapo*, lived in the safety of the prophets. For ten years he calmly haunted the camps, never accepting SS propositions to go free. These men never renounced their God. Otto was one with his God. It was said also he was sleeping with the woman who was the boss of bakery."

The authors got the following description from a Count Bernadotte on his reaction to approaching the concentration camp at Neuengamme: "The gates opened and closed behind us. I was the first visitor from a neutral humanitarian organization authorized to visit a concentration camp. An extraordinary feeling came over me to see with my own eyes what was really happening inside these abominable creations of the Third Reich, of which the whole world spoke in horror. Neuengamme was a perfect example of this type of place."

Readers should bear in mind the tragedy of the evacuation of the Neuengamme camp and the thousands of inmates loaded on the ships *Cap Arcona, Thielbek*, and *Athen*. It is likely that the Germans intended sinking these boats on the high seas, but they were bombed by the British air force and sunk in the bay of Neustadt on May 3, 1945. A Polish prisoner, one of the few who escaped the sinking of the *Thielbeck*, also told of being with Karl Zietlow, whose violet triangle (inmate number 2969) was exhumed along with six other bodies from a mass grave at Haffkrug, near Scharbeutz, on November 1, 1950.

A Jewish detainee (wearing a yellow star in Auschwitz, number 69733) who became a Witness in the camp also remembered his evacuation to Buchenwald: "On January 10, when it was freezing cold and during a terrible blizzard, we had to walk sixty kilometers to Gleiwitz. All those who couldn't walk were shot. But thanks to my assignment at the Buna SS cafeteria, I had enough strength to keep up. We were on the station platform and were supposed to load up on flatcars. When the SS reappeared, the one who was from my home district insisted I distribute a bread ration and sausage to each SS guarding us. He gave me a ration. That helped me survive, for during the two weeks of the trip we only got bouillon every two days. The dead piled up so fast that every morning we gathered up the bodies and threw them onto the following wagon. The train was composed of a wagon of the living which visibly diminished every day and a wagon of the dead which piled up! Our destination was Buchenwald and its auxiliary camps."

Even though he wore the yellow star, this Jewish detainee became a Jehovah's Witness in 1940 during interments at Sachsenhausen and Neuengamme. Learning that the Witnesses worked in the kitchens, he got in touch with them. Otto Becker helped him get out of the auxiliary camp, which was raging with typhus. He was fortunate to be assigned to a barracks run by a Mr. Kinsinger, who was from his hometown and who "had been deported as a Communist. He helped me regain some strength by giving me extra food. He also allowed me to give my bread ration to Mr. Heikorn, another Jew whom I knew, and who had been contacted by the Jehovah's Witnesses. Upon the approach of the Russian troops, the camp chief decided on the extermination of all the Jews. Day after day the Jews were loaded like animals onto trains and taken out to the forest. There, they were told to dig mass graves. They were lined up and shot. The barracks chief was prepared to hide me for my protection, but when I asked him also to hide Mr. Heikorn, he brusquely refused."

Crouching behind a pile of wood while they were reading passages from the Apocalypse, they were went unnoticed on the train platform and, once again, escaped the hangman to later share the joy of Buchenwald's liberation with other Witnesses. "As far as I was concerned, I didn't want to leave the site without being baptized a Jehovah's Witness. Fritz Heikorn felt the same way. Mr. Leon Blum, the head of the former French government, was interned there and had a little house with a bathroom at his disposal. A Jehovah's Witness was assigned to him as a servant. It was in that bathtub we were baptized after our liberation from Buchenwald."

It was Leon Blum whom Witnesses from Nazi concentration camps petitioned seeking aid in having the ban on their association in France lifted. Blum, who was director of the Socialist Party newspaper *Le Populaire,* responded on April 21, 1947: "I received your letter of 31 March and I read it with great interest. In Germany, during my internment, I was able to experience the firmness and faith of your friends' convictions, and that is why I am willing to assist the Jehovah's Witnesses. Also I am intervening with the Prefect of Police to insure he grants you authorization to freely exercise your cult. Signed: Leon Blum." With Blum's help, the ban was lifted in France on September 1, 1947.

In his memoirs, drafted in April 1945, Joseph Seitz recalled the arrival at Buchenwald of Auschwitz evacuees of that year. They advised that the Russians were then in occupation at Auschwitz: "The Auschwitz survivors were in a terrible state. They had marched through deep snow for days on end, [after which they took] a train trip in open wagons at freezing temperatures with no warm clothes and nothing to eat. They were nothing more than skeletons who made it, and hundreds and hundreds who couldn't were executed en route. The number of dying climbed in January 1945 and reached nearly 2,000. By February it was 3,500, and in March there were even more than 5,000, and the number of deaths increased every day." The men perished from malnutrition: "Per day, we were down to three-quarters of a liter of soup, 250 grams of bread, and 25 grams of margarine. Cheese and sausage were given only every other day, and then without margarine." Hunger pushed some to theft: "Even friends took bread from each other, and that's how some died."

With the continued arrival of new convoys, the camp became overcrowded, with 60,000 prisoners occupying a camp built to hold one-third that number. "On February 9, enemy aviation bombed the Gustloff factories in Weimar. There were around 280 killed and 300 wounded and missing among us. One of our Brothers who had been jailed since 1934 also died." Infectious diseases were rampant—typhus, dysentery, and others—and an inmate security service was organized. "Some of our friends were always on the lookout at night to prevent any surprises by the SS, whom we didn't trust. And we learned later these measures were fully justified. One night the top *Lagerführer* and two armed *Scharführer* came around. When our infirmary guard was spotted, he was mistreated and threatened with death. This incident proved that we couldn't give them any credit. I told friends I was ready to die for my cause, but if those hordes wanted to blindly shoot us in the back, I would defend myself to the extreme limit."

On Friday, April 6, 1945, all the valuables in the *Effektenkammer* (warehouse) were packed up and assembly orders issued for the parade ground on Sunday, April 8, 1945, with the exception of prisoners in the infirmary, warehouse, and laundry blocks. Because the Allies were so close, the 60,000 prisoners resisted and refused to depart. Shots were fired, and several prisoners were struck by bullets. The first convoy of 4,000 inmates was formed and left for Weimar the same day, and another group of 4,800 inmates was shipped out in the evening. Over the next two days, other transports were organized, and thousands of inmates were forced to evacuate. "We can't be sure of the exact number because inmate registration numbers weren't recorded, which we took to mean the convoys were to be exterminated. They were supposed to go to Dachau, Flossenburg, and Leitmeritz. We are unsure if they reached their destinations. The only information we have on one of the convoys is, on arrival at Dachau, most of the inmates were dead. Others remained along the roadside, and those who couldn't continue and had to stop were just shot; few lived." Seitz concluded his grim recital with this observation: "There are many, many, many more things to say. I have only related the essentials. I can only hope that all the misery which we had to live through for all those years will breathe new life into humanity's well-being and that humanity will realize it won't be possible without faith in God and the love for one's fellow beings."

Nine convoys left Buchenwald carrying approximately 38,000 prisoners. On April 6, 1945, about 3,000 Jews were marched off to Flossenburg, which the survivors reached twelve days later. On April 7, three convoys were dispatched, one to Czechoslovakia with 1,500 inmates and another that left on foot for Dachau with 4,600 inmates. Only 300 survivors arrived on the evening of April 25. A convoy of 5,880 departed the Weimar train station, and 816 made it to Dachau by April 28. Other convoys of 4,000 or 5,000 inmates left later: one each on April 8 and 9 and three on April 10. The April 7 convoy left around 8:00 p.m. from Weimar and arrived in Nurschan on April 11 via Leipzig, Dresden, and Pilsen. From Nurschan, it departed on April 13 and arrived in Dachau on Saturday, April 28. It was on this convoy that Rene Seglat must have traveled, but it is also striking that his name was not included on the list of survivors drawn up by Francois Bertrand.

In his book describing the convoys, Simon Hochberg would report, "We arrived at the edge of the camp at Dachau at one o'clock in the morning and came along the tracks which are east of the main gate next to the road. We tumbled out of the rail wagons and rushed over to puddles, and, down on our knees, we lapped up the water."

Pierre Fourmentraux added, "The convoy of the living-dead stopped near Dachau around one o'clock in the morning. The last two wagons were half full of dead bodies mixed in with loose bones, whitening and sickening."

According to Jacques Chevignard, "Finally, apathetic and half-dead, we arrived at Dachau during the night of April 28, 1945. Once the wagon doors were opened, we fell out like heavy sacks of sand and crawled to the puddles of water and, like thirsty dogs, lapped water for a long time."

Rene Seglat confirms this story: "After a three-week journey, out of 5,000 who departed, we were only 800 on arrival at Dachau. [Of those] only 176 survived in the end. We fought like devils for a mouthful of bread."

The gates of Buchenwald swung open on April 11, 1945, and

inmate number 76667 described how Jehovah's Witnesses gathered together in prayer of thanks to Jehovah. Marcel Lorin, who had been a political prisoner at Schonebeck—a *Kommando* at Buchenwald—related the evacuation march lasting from the evening of April 11 until May 4, 1945: "Certain German staff attitudes also deserve reporting. A few German inmates were still with us after the evacuation. Without dressing them up as soldiers, the SS did arm them, and they acted as escorts. And we all well remember a fervent Jehovah's Witness who, upon arrival in a convoy of 20,000 on October 1943, refused to work at the factory. He was in line with his conscience. He was slapped around by the SS commandant and sent off to the *Lagerkommando*. Today that courageous and isolated man, who suffered at Buchenwald for years, and whose reason for being was to do no killing nor contribute to killings, was forced to take up a rifle with the ultimate mission of killing companions in suffering."

The detainees at the Sachsenhausen concentration camps were next to experience the horror of the death marches, episodes of which Witness Louis Piechota related: "We were going to have to leave Sachsenhausen for Lubeck, which meant a march of some two hundred kilometers. Departure was scheduled for the night of the 20th or 21st of April. First, all of the prisoners were grouped by nationality. All the Jehovah's Witnesses got orders to assemble in the tailor shop! We were 230 Brothers from six different countries (213 men and 17 women). By columns of six hundred inmates, the various national groups marched out of camp, first the Czechs, then the Poles, and so forth. In all, 26,000 prisoners began walking. The Jehovah's Witnesses were the last group to leave. The SS gave us a cart to pull, and I learned later it was part of the booty they had taken from prisoners."

Arthur Winker, the Witness who had been tortured by Klaus Barbie in Holland, was also part of this convoy and described an incident concerning the carts he was pulling, notably those with baggage and packages belonging to the camp guards and SS chiefs: "One of these two vehicles was transporting property—the fruits of the plundering of important persons in the camp—so precious, seemingly, they had taken the precaution of providing security." If he so chose, the column leader could modify the convoy's route. This column was a third the size of the others—only two hundred thirty people—and no one could interfere in the ranks. "Naturally, all this was not done out of concern for our well-being; it was more to preserve the treasure that these guys wanted to ensure. Nevertheless, as we would see later, our being separated from the great mass of prisoners was to our benefit." Arriving near Schwerin some fifty kilometers from Lubeck, they spent a final night in the Crivitz woods. "We had covered two hundred kilometers in twelve days. Of the twenty-six thousand prisoners who left Sachsenhausen, only a little more than fifteen thousand survived the death march. However, none of the two hundred and thirty Witnesses who left succumbed during the ordeal. They then drafted a resolution: '3 May 1945. Resolution adopted by two hundred and thirty Jehovah's Witnesses representing six nations and gathered in the forest near Schwerin in Mecklenburg: We, the Jehovah's Witnesses gathered here, send our warmest greetings to the faithful of Jehovah's alliance and his companions across the entire world. . . . The enemy's designs to force us to abandon our integrity have failed despite his use of innumerable violent and diabolical measures and thousands of acts worthy of a Middle Age Inquisition by torturing us, mentally and physically, or through flattering and entrapping us. A description of these various sufferings would fill volumes.' "

The Ravensbrück concentration camp was evacuated by the end of April 1945, and a few Jehovah's Witnesses were part the exodus. Margarete Buber-Neumann left Ravensbrück on April 21 and was put up by *Bibelforscher* in Gustrow (in the north of Mecklenburg), where she was able to pass along news of Klarchen Mau, who had been deported to Ravensbrück.

On April 29, the gates of Dachau also opened. Three days earlier, Paul Berben reported the number of inmates by categories: 43,344 political prisoners (*Schutzhaft*), 22,100 Jews (different categories according to the nature of the offense), 57 political prisoners serving second sentences, 128 military purged from the Wehrmacht (SAE, *Sonderaktion Wermacht*), 109 homosexuals and one homosexual serving a second sentence, 85 Bible Students (Bifo) (including 26 women), 16 émigrés and inmates without indication of offense, 1,106 antisocials (including 15 women), and 759 criminals (including one woman).

During our interview, Gertrud Potzinger recalled that she had been interned for almost seven years, four of which were spent at Ravensbrück:

Authors: What happened to you?

GP: I left with SS Kiener's family, for whom I worked. [She spoke with a permanent smile on her face and with an unswerving urge to share her faith.]

Authors: But what happened?

GP: Before the Russian advance, the SS packed their bags, and the families were evacuated by truck and headed for Munich and Bavaria. I asked the Kieners to take me. I was still caring for the two children during the evacuation, and I was sitting up front with them next to the truck driver, and, miraculously, we escaped the bombings.

Authors: And then?

GP: When we arrived at Nordlingen, the SS wives were billeted in different houses in the villages. I ended up with the Kieners in the presbyter at Monchdeggingen. Mme. Kiener didn't want to draw attention to herself or make them think she had anything to do with the Nazi organization. At Nordlingen I did a little sewing for the peasants.

Authors: Did you intend to await liberation with the Kieners?

GP: No. Shortly after our arrival in Nordlingen, I announced to Mme. Kiemer that I was going to leave them and go to Munich, the hometown of my husband, whom I hadn't heard from in two years. At that time, I was no longer wearing my inmate uniform. Mme. Kiener was quite sad, which was understandable since who could she trust now that the whole country was against the Nazis and the party members? Therefore, I left one nice morning at 4:00 a.m. with just a school bag and without money or ration card. After walking a while, it was then I finally felt free from anyone looking over my shoulder. The birds were singing. It was a marvelous morning. I was so happy to be free, I sang. A peasant driving a cart loaded with wood met me and asked me how I could be singing since we lost the war. I explained that I was free now and I was rejoicing in witnessing Jehovah.

44

FORGOTTEN ONES

> Fly your flags at half mast
> for today, and
> forever.
> Remembrance
> at half-mast
> for today and
> forever.
>
> —Paul Celan

The gates of the camps, prisons, and jails were thrown open and the inmates freed. Allied liberators were stupefied at the sight of mass graves, and a stunned world discovered that which had been wrought on the human spirit by a twisted system in a few short years. The Nazis' unspeakable barbarity, a specter burned into our collective consciousness, will endure in our memory—now and forever. It is time to render an accounting. As philosopher Vladimir Jankelevitch stated in *The Imprescriptible,* this is not the time to "forget" or even to allow one's conscience to entertain the question of forgiveness.

The unspeakable, coming straight from their Führer's lips, condemned men, women, and children to ashes and annihilation and the reality of life as *Untermensch* (subhuman) for the benefit of *Übermensch* (superhuman)—a man, a slave, a "subhuman" slaughtered in those awful days of 1945. Reason cannot dwell endlessly on its wounds, but lest we forget, may history's roll of horror record the price that humanity paid for liberty, freedom of religious expression, and being, whatever one's culture, beliefs, or skin color.

In concluding these fragments of history and to assess this horrendous darkness, we call forth the lessons of Hell (albeit some facts are not known or remain forgotten) from the tabulation of abominations so tragically recorded in the pages of this book.

Genevieve de Gaulle Anthonioz[1] wrote of the Witnesses on August 8, 1945, "I have real admiration for them." The authors interviewed her regarding her experiences with them:

Authors: Can you tell us about the *Bibelforscher*?

de G: At Ravensbrück, the *Bibelforscher* were arrested for their religious beliefs and their refusal to carry out wartime orders. They were pacifists. The women were dealt with very harshly and many executed. If they signed a statement and altered their attitude, they could have gotten out from one day to the next. I didn't personally know them well, for in some ways we were the subproletariat in camp. But while I was in jail, they were very helpful. One of them was a cleaning lady in this jail inside the camp, and she brought me a small package at Christmas; a package prepared by my friends who denied themselves meager rations.

Authors: Mme. Buber-Neumann recalled a comparable situation in her memoirs; however, she inferred somewhat negative connotations. What does that mean?

de G: She knew them well. They were interned at Ravensbrück from the very beginning. These men and women were arrested, deported, and killed for their profound, respectful religious faith. Those I knew at Ravensbrück did not betray their convictions. They managed to get themselves literature and were executed for that. They were women of trust who were housekeepers for the SS who knew they wouldn't attempt escape. For us, who had the urge for sabotage, their behavior was strange. For them, escape equated to giving up their faith. And that astonished us. Their constancy is admirable, even if I can't follow their reasoning. They refused to take part in Hitler's war. Hitler, who required complete obedience, was considered the master and overlord. They rejected this. None of them ever worked in the munitions factories and were assigned peacetime duties. The Jehovah's Witnesses were pacifists. They belonged to a group we don't talk about much, the Christian religious opposition. Along with Catholics and Protestants, some pastors and bishops were deported, notably to Dachau. But I must add other deportees were forgotten, too, especially those poor unfortunates belonging to what we call today a Fourth World. They were also inmates in the camps and held under frightful conditions. We should not forget that.

We should not forget the comment made at Klaus Barbie's trial in Lyon and reported by Alain Finkielkraut regarding the behavior of the Nazis: "So, you cannot affirm from this entire file that there is a single act which is not inhuman?" The victims of Nazi persecution suffered its terrible consequences.

In closing, the authors wish to cite to Diderot's visionary text, written in the eighteenth century, on the eminent, salutary, essential, and irrefutable role of the poet: "When will we see the poets born? After times of disaster, when harassed peoples begin to breathe. Imaginations shaken by terrible spectacles will depict unknown events, for those who failed to witness them. Have we not, under certain circumstances, experienced a kind of terror alien to us all? Why has that produced nothing?"

Finally, the authors would like to leave the reader (for the benefit of our conscience) with a verse from Primo Levi:

> If it is a man
> You who are living in all quietude
> Snug in your houses,
> You on returning home in the evening find
> The table set and friendly faces,
> Consider if this is a man
> He who labors in the mud,
> Who knows no rest
> Who must fight for every crust of bread,
> Who dies for an aye or a nay.
> Consider if this is a woman
> She who has lost her name and her locks

And with all her forces remembers,
With empty eyes and a cold breast
Like a frog in wintertime.
Do not forget what it was,
No, do not forget:
Engrave these words upon your heart.
Think of them in your home and on the street,
On going to sleep and upon awakening;
Repeat them to your children.
Lest your house crumbles,
Lest sickness strike at you
Lest your children turn away from you.

NOTE

1. General Charles de Gaulle's niece. She was resistant and went to Ravensbrück.

RENUNCIATION OF BELIEFS TRANSLATION

The Declaration Renouncing Beliefs
Concentration Camp. . . . . .
Department II

DECLARATION

I, ____________ born on ______________ in ______ here make the following declaration:

1. I have come to realize that the International Bible Students' Association is proclaiming erroneous teachings and under the guise of religion pursues purposes hostile to the State.

2. I have therefore left the organization entirely and made myself absolutely free from the teachings of this sect.

3. I therefore give assurances that I will never again take part in the activity of the International Bible Students' Association. Any persons approaching me with the teaching of the Bible Students, or who in any manner reveal their connection with them, I will denounce immediately. All literature from the Bible Students that is sent to my home will be delivered immediately to the nearest police station.

4. I will in the future honor the laws of the State, especially in the event of war. I will, with weapon in hand, defend the fatherland, and join in every way the community of the people.

5. I have been informed that I will at once be taken again into protective custody should I act against the solemn declaration I make here today.

Dated:
Signed:

GLOSSARY

Ahnenerbe—Literally, "ancestral heritage." SS society established in 1933.

"Alle Jugend dem Führer!"—"All youth for Hitler!"

Anschluss—Term used to describe Austrian annexation to the German Reich.

"Arbeit macht frei"—"Labor gives freedom." Inscription forged into the Dachau concentration camp's entry gate. Also inscribed over the entrance at Auschwitz concentration camp I.

Arbeitsappel—A call to work.

auf der Flucht (erschossen)—Shot during escape. This type of execution was also known as "woods fatigue duty."

Aufseher—An SS camp guard.

Ausenkommando—Inmate team that worked outside the camp.

Baubrigade, Baukommando—Work party charged with construction work.

Bekampfung vom Schmutz und Schund—The fight against dirt and rubbish. Name given by the Nazis to their "operations" against unbelievers.

Bethel—Headquarters of the Jehovah's Witness Association.

Bibelforscher (Ernste Bibelforscher or ***Bibelforscherin(-nen)***—Students of the Bible; also "scrutineers," "secties," "Bible zealots," "exegetes," "Fundamentalists," or "Jehovah's Witnesses."

Bibelvolk—Bible folk.

Bifo—Acronym for *Bibelforscher.*

Block:—Nazi concentration camp inmate barracks.

Blockalteste(r)—Barracks chief. Inmate responsible for keeping order in the barracks. Reported to the SS *Blockführer* and inmate *Lageralteste.*

Blockowa—Polish term commonly used in camp jargon to describe the female barracks chief. There was also a Czech variant: *blockova.*

Bock:—Sawhorse on which inmates were tortured.

Bund für Bibel und Bekenntis—Association for Bible Learning.

Bunker—"Prison" or "dungeon" in camp jargon.

Deutsche Arbeitsfront (DAF)—German Labor Front.

Deutsche Ausrustungswerke (DAW)—German machinery factories. Placed under the supervision of Oswald Pohl, who employed forced concentration camp labor.

Dirlewanger—Germany army unit composed of former inmates.

Dolmetscher (in)—Interpreter.

Eberfeld—Eberfeld rye bread: a Bible.

Effektenkammer—Goods warehouse. Repository or barracks where clothes and other confiscated prisoner personal effects were stored. Also a supply store where uniforms were provided prisoners (also called *Bekleidungskammer* or *Kleidungskammer*).

Endlosung—"Final solution" of the Jewish question, which provided for their transfer to the East, assignment to forced labor details, and final "disposition."

Erneste Bibelforscher—Students of the Bible (see *Bibelforscher*).

Friseur, Frisor—Inmate barber or hairdresser. They shaved a wide band down the middle of inmates' skulls called the Autobahn (highway or street).

Fruhschicht—Morning work detail.

Fünf und zwanzig—Twenty-five. A beating of twenty-five blows as punishment administered to the lower back of inmates by beef sinew, stick, cudgel, or blackjack. The inmate was required to count off the blows aloud.

Führer—Chief, guide, or leader.

Gartnerei—Gardening. Inmate work party assigned to flower and vegetable greenhouses.

Gaskammer—Gas chamber.

Geheime Reichssache—A Reich sate secret. Stamp on all correspondence dealing with the "final solution" and "special handling."

Gesonderte Unterbringung—Solitary confinement; deportees destined for the gas chamber.

Gestapa—Gestapo administrative services.

Gestapo *(Geheime Staatspolizei)*—State secret police created on April 26, 1933.

Gitteraktion—"Operation Iron Bars." Directed against Germans unwilling to serve in the army.

Gummi—Literally, "rubber." An SS bludgeon.

Haftling—Inmate.

Hangen!—To hang!

"Heil Hitler"—"Hail to Hitler" (*heil:* eternal, holy, sacred salute).

Hitlerjugend—Hitler Youth Organization.

Hundestaffel—SS-trained attack dogs.

Internationale Bibelforschervereingung (IBV)—International Association of Bible Students.

"Jedem das seine"—"To each his due."

Jugendlager—Youth camp, in fact, the Ravensbrück extermination camp.

Kanada/Canada—Name given to the work detail at the *Effektenkammer* (storehouse) at Auschwitz-Birkenau responsible for collecting and sorting baggage and personal effects confiscated from inmates on their arrival. Some French inmates referred to the operation as the "Galleries Lafayette."

Kaninchen—German word for "rabbit" as well as "guinea pig." In the camps, it referred to inmates subjected to pseudomedical experiments.

Kapo* or *Capo—Inmate responsible for good order of a *Kommando* work party; inmate in charge of a work party.

Kaputt—"Finished," "broken," "dead," or "busted."

Kommando—Detachment, column of inmates, unit or work party, or annex camp attached to a main camp.

Kommandoführer—Chief of a *Kommando.*

Konzentrationslager (KL)—Concentration camp.

Konzentrationslager (KZ)—Concentration camp.

Krematorium—Crematory oven, often attached to a gas chamber.

Kristallnacht—Crystal Night, an anti-Semitic pogrom during the night of November 9–10, 1938: the looting and destruction of 7,000 to 8,000 Jewish stores, mass destruction of synagogues and schools, and arrest of approximately 30,000 German Jews.

Lageratz—SS camp doctor.

Lagerkommando—Camp *Kommando.*

Lagerpolizei—Camp police or guard.

***Land* (pl. *Länder*)**—Weimar Republic state, province, and territorial division controlled after 1933 by the Reich leadership.

Lauskontrolle—Lice control. "Eine Laus dein Tod" (One louse—that's your death).

Lebensraum—Vital living space (Nazi expansionist doctrine).

Leichenkommando—Work party charged with stacking and removing dead bodies.

"Los!"—"Forward!," "Move!," or "Get along!"

Matricule—Registration number assigned to inmates (they had to recite it in German). This number was sown onto their jackets and in some cases tattooed on their forearm.

Mein Kampf—"My Struggle," the book that Hitler wrote after the failed *Putsch* of November 9, 1923.

Meister—Literally, "master" or "boss." Technician, specialized workman, foreman, or noninmate team leader.

Mischling—Mixed blood, half-Jewish.

Moor Express—Work party in the swamps; inmates who pulled truck trailers; a cart sinking into the muddy swamp.

Musulman—A dying inmate. There is no explanation why this term was used for an expiring inmate.

Mutze—Round cap, beret.

"Nacht und Nebel"—"Foggy night." A Wagnerian expression from "Gold on the Rhine" borrowed by the Nazis and applied to people officially targeted for disappearance without a trace; a December 7, 1941, decree by Marshal Keitel creating this new category of inmates.

Oberaufseher(in)—Chief SS guard.

Obermeister—Foreman.

Ogranisiere—To "organize" oneself, resourcefulness. In camp jargon, it signified getting a hold of something by dealing, theft, or pilferage.

Pieple—A young favored inmate of a *Kapo.*

Planierung—Site leveling and grading.

Politische, Abteilung—Camp political section. Camp administrative service where Gestapo files were maintained (registry of living and dead inmates). Inmate files contained details of their physical characteristics as well as their political opinions. For adverse opinions, inmates could be subjected to interrogation and torture.

Posten—Sentinel, watchtower, or concentration camp guard.

Prominent—Dignitary; a promoted inmate occupying a relatively comfortable position in the internal camp administration. Having somewhat broad responsibilities and a certain degree of power, he enjoyed special privileges; an aristocrat among camp inmates.

Rampendienst—Quayside service, the train unloading platform or inmate selection on convoy arrival.

Rapportführer—An SS officer responsible for controlling inmate population and discipline; SS inspector.

Rassenschande—Miscegenist.

Reichsarbeitsdienst (RAB)—Reich Labor Service.

Reichgesetzblatt—Official Reich newspaper.
Reichssicherheitshauptamt (RSHA)—Central office of Reich security; direction of Reich security services. The third bureau of this central SS organization was composed of the SD, the fourth was the SS, and the fifth was the criminal police.
Revier—German military term for "infirmary"; a camp "infirmary" in which sick and wounded prisoners were stacked.

Scheisbaracke—Latrine.
Scheiskommando—Latrine detail.
"Schnell!"—"Quick!" or "Move it!"
Schreiber—Secretary; inmate responsible for barracks and camp correspondence.
Schutzhaftling(e)—Protective detention; inmates in protective detention.
Schutzhaftgesetz—Law of protective incarceration.
Selektion, Selekcja—Selection; operation during which the SS sorted inmates; those "valid" for work parties, and others ticketed for extermination.
Sicherheitsdienst (SD)—Security service; a kind of Gestapo "police's police"; intelligence service.
Sonderkommando—Special inmate work detail assigned to the gas chambers and crematory ovens. This *Kommando* was billeted outside the camp near the crematorium. Members had no contact with other inmates and they, too, were periodically exterminated after some three months.
Sozialistische—German Socialist Party (SPD).
Sport—In the concentration camp, this term was used to describe corporal punishment.
Steintrager—Inmate stone carrier assigned to work in quarries.
Strafblock—Disciplinary barracks.
Strafkommando—Disciplinary *Kommando.*
Strarflager—Camp disciplinarian.
Strasse—Street (see also *Frisor, Friseur*).
Stube—Section, room, or hall. Blocks were divided into sections.
Stubendienst, Stubowa/Stubova—Cleaning person; inmate responsible for cleaning and maintaining the barracks. *Stubowa*

and *stubova* are Polish and Czech terms, respectively, designating the head cleaning person.

Stück—A lump, a piece. Term used by the Nazis when referring to inmates.

Sturmabeilung (SA)—Paramilitary NSDAP assault unit created in the early 1920s (the infamous (Brown Shirts).

"Toleranz bedeutet Schwache"—"Tolerance is weakness."

Totenkommando—Work party assigned to transporting corpses.

Totentrager—Cadaver collector.

Transport—Convoy; transport of inmates from one camp to another or within *Kommandos*. A "black convoy" was headed for an unknown destination and was, in effect, an extermination convoy.

Übermensch—Superman.

Vergasung—To be put to death by gas; gassed.

Vernichtung durch Arbeit—Extermination by hard labor.

Volkischer Beobachter—Literally, "people's observer." The name of the official press organ of the Nazi Party.

Volkgerichtshof—People's tribunal. Nazi exceptional jurisdiction for which there was no appeal.

Wachtturm—Name of an illegal tract distributed by the *Bibelforscher* in Dortmund.

Wachtturmgesellschaft—The Watch Tower Society.

Waffen SS—SS armed unit comprised of German and foreign volunteers (notably the SS Death's Head Unit). The "Charlemagne Division" included, among others, French volunteers (originating mainly from the LVF/Legion of French Volunteers Against Bolshevism). After 1940, this formation became auxiliary troops in the Wehrmacht.

Washraum—Washroom.

Wehrmacht—German army that replaced the Reichswehr in 1935.

Wilde Lager—Unofficial camps.

BIBLIOGRAPHY

Alcan, Louise. *Le temps écartelé* [Time torn apart]. Paris, 1942.

Allach "Kommando" de Dachau [Commando of Dachau], under the direction of Dr. Henri Laffitte, Association of the Veterans of Dachau, Paris, 1985.

Alleg, Henri. *Les Chemins de l'Espérance* [The paths of hope]. 2nd ed. Paris: FNDIRP (National Federation of Deported and Imprisoned Resistance Fighters and Patriots), 1979.

Améry, Jean. *Par Delà le Crime et le Châtiment* [Beyond crime and punishment], *Actes Sud.* Paris, 1995.

Annuaire des Témoins de Jéhovah , 1974, 1976, 1977, 1980, 1982, 1984, 1986, 1989 [Directory of Jehovah's Witnesses]. New York: Watchtower Society.

Anthologie bilingue de le poésie allemande [Bilingual anthology of German poetry], *La Pléiade* (collection). Paris: NRF/Gallimard, 1993.

Antoni, Ernst. *KZ-Von Dachau bis Auschwitz* [Concentration camps from Dachau on]. Frankfurt: Röderberg Verlag, 1979.

Arendt, Hannah. *Eichmann à Jérusalem* [Eichmann at Jerusalem]. History Folio 32. Paris: Gallimard, 1991.

Arnould, Roger. *Les témoins de la nuit* [Witnesses of the night]. 2nd ed. Paris: FNDIRP, 1979.

Attali, Jacques. *Verbatim II 1986–1988.* Paris: Fayard, 1995.

Auschwitz, *Camp hitlérien d'extermination* [Auschwitz, Hitler's extermination camp]. Interpress, 1978.

Auschwitz vu par les SS [Auschwitz as seen by the S.S.], Hoess, Broad, Kremer. Editions of the State Museum at Oswiecim, 1974.

Axelrad, Edouard, *Le Jaune* [Yellow], J. C. Lattès, 1988.

Badia, Gilbert. *Historie de l'Allemagne contemporaine* [History of contemporary Germany]. Paris: Éditions sociales, 1962.

Bailly, Jacques-Christian. *Un lycéen à Buchenwald* [A lycée student at Buchenwald]. Ramsay, 1979.

Les Barbelés de l'Exil [Barbed-wire exiles]. Grenoble: PU Grenoble, 1979.

Berben, Paul. *L'Histoire du camp de concentration de Dachau (1933–1945)* [The history of the Dachau concentration camp (1933–1945)]. Brussels: Comité international de Dachau, 1976.

Bernadac, Christian. *Les mannequins nus* [The naked mannequins]. Paris: France-Empire, 1971.

Bernadotte, Comte F. *La Fin* [The end]. Marguerat, 1945.

Bertrand, François. *Notre devoir de mémoire. Convoi de Buchenwald à Dachau du 7 au 28 avril 1945* [Our duty of remembering. Convoy from Buchenwald to Dachau, April 7–28, 1945], *Héraclès, Pau*, 1997.

Bettelheim, Bruno. *Le Cœur Conscient* [The sentient heart]. Robert Laffont, 1972.

———. *Survivre* [To Survive]. Robert Laffont, 1979.

Bezaut, Jean. *Oranienburg 1933–1935, Sachsenhausen 1936–1945*. Hérault-Éditions, 1989.

Bible [The Holy Bible]. Translated into French under the direction of the Bible School of Jersualem (The Jerusalem Bible). Paris: Cerf, 1955.

Billig, Joseph. "Alfred Rosenberg dans l'action idéologique, politique et administrative du Reich hitlérien, Inventaire commenté de la collection des documents conservés au CDJC" (Alfred Rosenberg in the ideological, political and administrative action of Hitler's Reich: Annotated study of the collection of documents conserved at the CDJC [Center for Contemporary Jewish Documentation]). Paris, 1963.

———. *Les camps de concentration dans l'économie du Reich hitlérien* [The concentration camps in the economy of Hitler's Reich]. PUF, 1973.

Blandre, Bernard. *Les Témoins de Jéhovah. Un siécle d'histoire* [The Jehovah's Witnesses: A century of history]. Paris: Desclée de Brouwer, 1987.

Bonifas, Aimé. "Les déportés et le christianisme dans les camps de concentration nazis" (The interned and christianity in the nazi concentration camps). Paper presented at the National Conference on Churches and Christians in the Second World War, Lyon, 1978. Published as postscript in Bonifas, Aimé, *Détenu 20 801 dans les bagnes nazis*. 4th ed. (Paris: FNDIRP, October 1985).

Bouaziz, Gérard. *La France torturée* [France tortured]. 2nd ed. Paris: FNDIRP, 1979.

Brecht, Bertold. *Die Gedichte von Bertold Brecht in einem Band* [The poems of Bertold Brecht in one volume]. Suhrkamp, 1981.

Brille, Ady. *Les techniciens de la mort* [Technicians of death]. 2nd ed. Paris: FNDIRP, 1979.

Broszat, Martin. *L'État hitlérien. L'origine et l'évolution des structures du troisième Reich* [Hitler's state: Origin and development of the structures of the Third Reich]. Paris: Fayard, 1985.

———. "Nationalsozialistische Konzentrationslager 1933–1945" (Nazi concentration camps 1933–1945). In Martin Broszat, Hans Buchheim, Hans-Adolf Jakobsen, and Helmut Krausnick, eds., *Anatomie des SS-Staates*. Freiburg, 1965; 6th ed., Munich, 1994.

Brüdigam, Heinz. *Faschismus an der Macht. Berichte. Bilder. Dokumente über das Jahr 1933 50 Jahre danach* [Fascism in power. Accounts, pictures, documents on the year 1933 fifty years later]. Frankfurt: Röderberg, 1982.

Buber-Neumann, Margarete. *Als Gefangene bei Stalin und Hitler. Eine Welt im Dunkel* [As prisoner to Stalin and Hitler: A world in darkness]. Stuttgart-Herford: Seewald Verlag, 1985.

———. *Milena.* Paris: Seuil, 1986.

Buchenwald, Dokumente und Berichte [Buchenwald, documents and reports]. Frankfurt: Röderberg, 1960.

Buchheim, Hans. "Die SS: das Herrschaftsinstrument" (The S.S.: The Instrument of Power.) In Martin Broszat, Hans Buchheim, Hans-Adolf Jakobsen, and Helmut Krausnick, eds., *Anatomie des SS-Staates*. Freiburg, 1965; 6th ed., Munich, 1994.

Cahiers Internationaux de la Résistance [International cahiers of the resistance], no. 3 (July 1960).

Camp de Concentration Natzwiller Struthof [Natzwiller Struthof concentration camp]. Nancy: Impr. Humblot et Cie, 1982.

Casamayor. *Nuremberg 1945. La guerre en procès* [Nuremberg 1945: War on trial]. Paris: Stock, 1985.

Cerna, Jana.*Vie de Milena* [Life of Milena]. Paris: Maren Sell & Cie, 1988.

Char, René. *La nuit talismanique* [The talismanic night]. Skira, 1978.

Consolation, no. 144, 13th year, Berne, October 1945; no. 150, 14th year, Berne, April 1946; and no. 505, October 1, 1943.

Conway, J. S. *La persécution nazie des églises* [Nazi persecution of the churches]. Paris: France-Empire, 1969.

Dachau 1939–1945 (Le camp de concentration de) [Dachau (concentration camp) 1939–1945]. Brussels: Comité International de Dachau, 1979.

Dagerman, Stig. *Automne allemand* [German autumn]. Actes Sud, 1989.

Dante, *La divine comédie. L'Enfer* [The divine comedy, hell]. Translated by Jacqueline Risset. Flammarion, 1985.

Datner, Szymon, Janusz Gumkowski, and Kazimierz Leszczynski. *Le génocide nazi 1939–1945* [The nazi genocide 1939–1945]. Varsovie-Poznan, 1962.

Dauchauscopies paradoxales 44–45: Récit concentrationnaire [Paradoxical Dachau-scopies 44–45: Concentration tale]. Helldayheir: Auto-Éditions, 1985.

Dawidowicz, Lucy S. *La guerre contre les Juifs 1933–1945* [The war against the Jews 1933–1945]. Paris: Hachette, 1977.

Deceze, Dominique. *Esclavage concentrationnaire* [Concentration camp slavery]. 2nd. ed. Paris: FNDIRP, 1979.

Denzler, Georg, and Volker Fabricius. *Die Kirchen im Dritten Reich* [The churches in the Third Reich]. Fischer, 1988.

La Déportation [Deportation and internment]. FNDIRP, Paris, 1967.

Desroche, Alain. *La Gestapo* [The Gestapo]. de Vecchi, 1972.

Dessarre, Ève. *Les Sacrifiés* [Those sacrificed]. Olivier Orban, 1978.

De Toulouse-Lautrec, Béatrix. *La Victoire en pleurant* [The victory through the tears]. Rouen: La Préfecture, 1967.

Dinslaken in der NS-Zeit. Vergessene Geschichte 1933–1945 [Dinslaken at the time of the Nazis: Forgotten history 1933–1945]. Publication of the Municipal Archives of Dinslaken. Kleve: Boss-Verlag, 1983.

"Documentation über Jehovas Zeugen-Beriech Karlsruhe" (Documentation on the Jehovah's Witness area Karlsruhe) (gathered by Harald Nagel, December 8, 1983).

"Documents concernant les traitements infligés en Allemangne à des nationaux allemands" (Documents concerning the Treatment Inflicted on German Nationals in Germany), Presented to Parliament by Order of His Majesty by the Secretary of State for Foreign Affairs. English White Paper No. 2. Official and authorized translation of the document published by His Majesty's Stationery Office, Paris, 1939.

Documents inédits sur les camps d'extermination nazis [Unpublished documents on the nazi extermination camps]. Paris: Éditions Réalité, 1945.

Dufournier, Denise. *La maison des mortes: Ravensbrück* [The house of the dead: Ravensbrück]. Paris: Hachette, 1945.

Durand, Pierre. *La Chienne de Buchenwald* [The bitch of Buchenwald]. Paris: Messidor/Temps Actuels, 1982.

———. *Les arbres de l'espoir. Les Français à Buchenwald* [The trees of hope: The French at Buchenwald]. Paris: Éditions sociales, 1982.

Dutillieux, Max. *Le camp des armes secrétes. Dora-Mittelbau* [The secret weapons camp: Dora-Mittelbau], Ouest-France, 1993.

Erasmus. *L'éloge de la folie* [In praise of folly]. Paris: Flammarion, 1989.

Erwachet! [Awake!] Periodical published by the Watchtower Bible and Tract Society, Vienna-Selters/Taunus (RFA). German editions from February 8, 1985; March 8, 1985; June 8, 1985; and April 8, 1989.

Fascime ou Liberté [Fascism or freedom]. Brooklyn, N.Y.: Watchtower Editions, 1939.

Figaro-Magazine, October 28, 1989 (articles on the notebooks of Pastor Boegner presented by his son Philippe Boegner).

Finkielkraut, Alain, *La mémoire vaine. Du crime contre l'humanité* [The vain memory: Crime against humanity]. Paris: Gallimard, 1989.

FNDIR/UNADIF (National Federation of Deported and Interned of the Resistance/National Union of Deported, Interned and Families). *Leçcons de ténébres, Résistants et déportés* [Lessons of Darkness, Resisters and Interned]. Plon, 1995.

Fraenkel, Ernst. *Der Doppelstaat, Recht und Justiz im Dritten Reich* [Law and justice in the third reich]. Frankfurt am Main: Fischer, 1974. (The book was edited for the first time in 1941 under the title *The Dual State* [New York: Oxford University Press]).

Les Françaises à Ravensbrück [French women at Ravensbrück]. Association of Ravensbrück and Association of the Deported and Interned of the Resistance. Paris: Gallimard, 1965.

"Frauen, die nicht vergessen" (Women, those not forgotten). Television program directed by Fritz Poppenberg for Freies Berlin in 1989.

Frauen in Konzentrationslagern. Berger-Belsen. Ravensbrück [Women in concentration camps: Bergen-Belsen, Ravensbrück]. Temmen, Bremen, 1994.

Garbe, Detlev. *Zwischen Widerstand und Martyrium. Die Zeugen Jehovas im Dritten Reich* [Between resistance and martyrdom: The Jehovah's Witnesses in the Third Reich]. Munich: Oldenburg Verlag, 1994.

———. "Neuzeitliche Christenverfolgung im nationalsozialistichen Hamburg" (Modern Christian persecutions in nazi Hamburg). In *Verachtet-Verfolgt-Vernichtet*. Hamburg, 1986.

Gouri, Haïm. *Face à la cage de verre. Le procès Eichmann, Jérusalem, 1961* [Facing the glass cage: The Eichmann trial, Jerusalem, 1961]. Tirésias, 1995.

Heger, Heinz. *Les hommes au triangle rose. Journal d'un déporté homosexuel 1939–1945* [The men of the pink triangle: Journal of an interned homosexual 1939–1945]. Persona, 1981.

Heigl, Peter. *Konzentrationslager Flossenbürg* [Flossenburg Concentration Camp]. Regensburg, 1989.

Hilberg, Raul. *La destruction des Juifs d'Europe* [The destruction of European Jews]. Paris: Fayard, 1988.

Historiens-Géographes [Historian-geographers], no. 299 (May 1984) (interviews with Michel Lejoyeux and Hubert Tison, by Vladimir Jankélévitch, May 20, 1983).

Histoire pour tous [History for everyone], no. 87 (July 1987).

Hoess, Rudolf. *Kommandant in Auschwitz: Autobiographische Aufzeichnungen* [Commanding officer in Auschwitz: Autobiographical notes]. Stuttgart: Institute for Contemporary History, Deutsche Verlag-Anstalt, 1958.

Hollweg, Max. *Est ist unmöglich von dem zu schweigen, was ich erlebt habe. Zivilcourage im Dritten Reich* [Impossible to keep silent about what I have experienced: Standing up for one's beliefs in the Third Reich]. 2nd ed. Bielfeld: Mindt, 1998.

Intolleranza religiosa alle soglie del duemila [Religious Intolerance at the Threshold of the Year 2000]. FUSA, 1990.

Jacob, Max. *Le laboratoire central* [The central laboratory]. Paris: Gallimard, 1921.

Jankélévitch, Vladimir. *L'Imprescriptible—Pardonner? Dans l'honneur et la dignité* [The indefeasible—Forgive? In honor and dignity]. Paris: Seuil, 1986.

Jesenska, Milena. *Vivre* [To live]. Lieu Commun, 1985.

Kaminski, Andrzej Jozef. "Les camps de concentration nazis, phénomène social et économique" [The nazi concentration camps, a social and economic phenomenon]. *Cahiers internationaux de la Résistance* [International cahiers of the resistance], no. 3 (July 1960).

Karlsruhe 1945: Unter Hakenkreuz. Trikolore und Sternenbanner [Karlsruhe 1945: Under swastika. Tricolor and stars and stripes]. Documentation set up by Josef Werner. G. Braun, 1985.

Kater, Michael H. "Die Ernsten Bibelforscher im Dritten Reich" (The serious Jehovah's Witnesses in the Third Reich.) In *Vierteljahreshefte für Zeitgeschichte*. Munich, 1969.

Kiedrzynska, Wanda. "Ravensbrück, le camp de concentration des femmes" (Ravensbrück, the women's concentration camp). *Cahiers Internationaux de la Résistance*, no. 3 (July 1960).

King, Christine Elizabeth. *The Nazi State and the New Religions.* The Edwin Mellen Press, 1962.

Klönne, Arno. *Jugend im Dritten Reich* [Youth in the Third Reich]. 1990.

Klotzbach, Kurt. *Gegen den Nationalsozialismus: Widerstand und Verfolgung in Dortmund 1930–1945* [Against national socialism: Resistance and persecution in Dortmund 1930–1945]. Hanover, 1969.

Kogon, Eugen. *L'Enfer organisé: Le systéme des camps de concentration* [Organized hell: The system of the concentration camps]. Paris: La Jeune Parque, 1947.

———. *L'état SS* [The S.S. state]. Paris: Points, Seuil, 1970.

Laffitte, Jean. *La pendaison* [The hanging]. Paris: Julliard, 1983.

———. *Ceux qui vivent* [Those alive]. Paris: Editions Hier et Aujourd'hui, 1947.

Laks, Simon. *Mélodies d'Auschwitz* [Melodies of Auschwitz]. Paris: Cerf, 1991.

Langbein, Hermann. *La Résistance dans les camps de concentration nationauxsocialistes 1938/1945* [The resistance in the nazi concentration camps 1938/1945]. Les Nouvelles Études Historiques. Translated from the German. Paris: Fayard, 1981.

Langhoff, Wolfgang. *Les soldats du marais* [The soldiers of the bog]. Paris: Trad. A. Pierhal, Plon et Nourut, 1935.

Le Chêne, Evelyn. *Mauthausen ou la comptabilité de l'horreur* [Mauthausen or the accountancy of horror]. Translated by Paul Alexandre. Belfond, 1974.

Lechner, Silvester. *Das KZ Oberer Kuhberg und die NS-Zeit in der Region Ulm/Neu-Ulm* [The Oberer Kuhberg concentration camp and the nazi era in the Ulm/Neu-Ulm region.] Stuttgart: Simberburg Verlag, 1988.

Le Choc—1945, la presse révèle l'enfer des camps nazis [The Shoc—1945, the press reveals the hell of the nazi camps]. Paris: FNDIRP, 1985.

Le Monde [The world] (January 1, 1994; January 30, 1998; and May 15, 1998).

Le Monde Juif [The Jewish world], April–June 1989, Paris.

Le Nouvel Observateur, no. 801 (March 17–23, 1980) (article by Michel Bosquet on Gérard Sandoz's book *Ces Allemands qui ont défié Hitler* titled "Réhabilitation du peuple allemand").

Les Livres [Books], no. 364, Paris: National Pedagogical Documentation Center, National Ministry of Education, May 1992.

Levi, Primo. *Si c'est un homme* [If it's a man]. Paris: Julliard, 1987.

———. *Les naugragés et les rescapés: Quarante ans aprés Auschwitz* [The shipwrecked and the rescued: Forty years after Auschwitz]. Paris: Arcades, 1989.

———. *La Trêve* [The truce]. Paris: Grasset, 1966.

Lévinas, Emmanuel. *Essai sur le penser—à—l'autre* [Essay on thinking of others]. Paris: Grasset, 1991.

Levy, Guenter. *L'église catholique et l'Allemange nazie* [The catholic church and nazi Germany]. Paris: Stock, 1965.

Lewinska, Pelagia. *Vingt mois à Auschwitz* [Twenty months in Auschwitz]. Nagel, 1945.

Livres Hebdo [Books weekly], no. 280 (February 13, 1998), and no. 293 (May 15, 1998).

L'ordre nazi: Les enfants aussi [The nazi order: Children too]. Association de Ravensbrück, 1979.

Lorin, Marcel. *Schönebeck, un kommando de Buchenwald* [Schönebeck, commando of Buchenwald]. Association of the Interned of Schönebeck-Mülhausen-Buchenwald, 1989.

Luzi, Mario. *L'avènement nocturne* [Nighttime coming]. Milan, 1940.

Mann, Erika. *Zehn Millionen Kinder. Die Erziehung der Jugend im Dritten Reich* [Ten million children: The upbringing of children in the Third Reich]. 1989.

Mann, Thomas. *Deutsche Hörer! Radiosendungen nach Deutschland aus den Jahren 1940 bis 1945* [German listeners! Radio broadcasts to Germany from 1940 to 1945]. Fischer Verlag, 1987.

Manvell, Roger, and Heinrich Fraenkel. *Le crime absolu, Témoins de notre temps* [Absolute crime, witnesses from our time]. Paris: Stock, 1968.

Mark, Ber. *Des voix dans la nuit. La résistance juive à Auschwitz-*

Birkenau [Voices in the night: The Jewish resistance at Auschwitz-Birkenau]. Plon, 1982.

Marsalek, Hans. *Konzentrationslager Gusen. Ein Nebenlager des KZ*-Mauthausen [Gusen concentration camp: An annex camp of the Mauthausen concentration camp]. 2nd ed. Vienna, 1987.

———. *Die Geschichte des Konzentrationslagers Mauthausen: Dokumentation* [The History of the Mauthausen Concentration Camp—Documentation]. 2nd ed. Vienna, 1980; 3rd ed., Vienna: Linz, 1995.

Marshall, Bruce. *Le lapin blanc* [White rabbit]. L'Air du Temps (collection). Paris: Gallimard, 1953.

Match, Paris (January 11, 1940).

Michelet, Edmond. *Rue de la Liberté* [Freedom street]. Paris: Seuil, 1955.

Noguères Henri. *La vérité aura le dernier mot* [The truth will have the last word]. Paris, 1985.

Parker, Daniel. *Le Choix décisif* [Decisive choice]. Paris: Labor et Fides, Geneva/Librairie Protestante.

Les Patriotes Résistants à l'Occupation [The patriot resisters to the occupation]. Paris: FNDIRP, 1986.

Plötzensee: Lieux de persécution et de résistance à Berlin 1933–1945 [Plötzensee: (Memorial to) Places of persecution and of resistance in Berlin 1933–1945]. Berlin.

Polenberg, R. "Les libertés civiles aux États-Unis" (Civil liberties in the United States). In *Revu d'histoire de la deuxième guerre mondiale*. Paris: PUF.

Poliakov, Léon. *Bréviaire de la Haine. Le III*e *Reich et les Juifs* [Breviary of hate: The Third Reich and the Jews]. Calmann-Lévy, 1951.

Portail, Pierre. "Deux aspects de la criminalité systématique dans les camps de concentration allemands" [Two aspects of systematized crime in the German concentration camps]. Thesis for the Criminal Law section, Chambéry, 1947.

La Résistance dans les camps de concentrations nationaux-socialistes 1938/1945 [The Resistance in the nazi concentration camps 1938/1945. Les Nouvelles Études Historiques. Paris: Fayard, 1979.

Reynaud, Michel. *La Foire à l'Homme Écritis-Dits dans les camps du systéme nazi de 1933 à 1945* [Expo: Horrors on humanity. Written and oral accounts in the camps of the nazi system 1933–1945]. Tirésias, 1996–1998.

Ritter, Gerhard. *Échec au dictateur. Histoire de la Résistance Allemande* [Defeating the dictato: History of the German resistance]. Plon, 1956.

Röhm, Eberhard, *Sterben für den Frieden* [Death for peace]. Stuttgart: Calwer Verlag, 1985.

Röhmer, Albert J. "Aussenkommando H de Neuengamme : Helmstedt, mine de sel" (External foreign work group H from Neuengamme: Helmstedt salt mines). In *De l'Univerité aux Camps de Concentration: Témoignages Strasbourgeois.* 3rd ed.: PUF, 1989.

Rousset, David. *Le pitre ne rit pas* [The clown laughs not]. Paris, 1948.

———. *Les jours de notre mort 10/18* [Days of our death, 10/18]. Paris, 1974.

———. *L'Univers concentrationnaire* [The universe of the concentration camp]. Minuit, 1965.

Rovan, Joseph. *Le catholicisme politique en Allemagne* [Political catholicism in Germany]. Paris: Seuil, 1956.

Sachs, Nelly. *Eli-Lettres-Énigmes en feu* [Eli-Letters-Enigmas on fire]. Paris: Belin, 1989.

Sachsenhausen (Damals in) [Sachsenhausen in that time]. Berlin: Kongress Verlag.

Sachso: Au cœur du système concentrationnaire nazi [Sachso: At the core of the nazi concentration camp system], Association of Oranienburg-Sachsenhausen. Terre Humaine, Plon, 1982.

Saint-Clair, Simone. *Ravensbrück: L'enfer des femmes* [Ravensbrück: Women's hell]. Tallandier, 1945.

Sandoz, Gérard. *Ces Allemands qui ont défié Hitler 1933–1945* [These Germans who defied Hitler 1933–1945]. Pygmalion/Gérard Watelet, 1980.

Sartre Jean-Paul. *L'existentialisme est un humanisme* [Existentialism: A humanism]. Paris: Nagel, 1970.

Schaeper-Wimmer, Sylva. *Das Unbegreifliche berichten: Zeugenb-*

erichte ehemaliger Häftlinge des Konzentrationslagers Dachau [Reporting the unimaginable: Testimonials of the ex-interned from the Dachau concentration camp]. Munich: MPZ, 1997.

Schätzle, Julius. *Stationen zur Hölle: Konzentrationslager in Baden und Württemberg 1933–1945* [Stations toward hell: The concentration camps in the Bade-Württemberg 1933–1945]. Frankfurt: Röderberg, 1974.

Schramm, Hanna, and Barbara Vormeier. *Vivre à Gurs. Un camp de concentration français 1940–1941* [To live at Gurs: A French concentration camp 1940–1941] (translated from the German). Paris: Maspéro, 1979.

Sedel, Fred. *Habiter les ténèbres* [To live in the darkness]. Paris: A. M. Métailié, 1990.

Seger, Gerhart. *Oranienburg 1933, la Pensée sauvage* [Oranienburg 1933: The savage thought.] 1984.

Sehn, Jean. *Le camp de concentration d'Oswiecim-Brzezinka (Auschwitz-Birkenau)* [The Oswiecim-Brzezinka (Auschwitz-Birkenau) concentration camp]. Warsaw: General Research Commission on Hitler's Crimes in Poland, 1957.

SIR (International Research Service). "Le nombre des victimes de la persécution nationale-socialiste" (The number of victims of the nazi persecution), Statement issued by A. de Cocatrix, SIR Director, at the International Conference of the International Committee on the Camps, Vienna, April 22–25, 1977.

Sommet, Jacques. *L'honneur de la liberté. Entretiens avec Charles Ehlinger* [The honor of freedom: Interviews with Charles Ehlinger]. Le Centurion, 1987.

SS im Einsatz. Eine Dokumentation über die Verbrechen der SS [S.S. in deployment: A documentation on the crimes of the S.S.] Berlin: Kongress-Verlag, 1957.

Stroumsa, Jacques. Tu choisiras la vie. Violoniste à Auschwitz [You will choose life: Violinist at Auschwitz]. Paris: Cerf, 1998.

"Täter und Opfer" (Perpetrators and Victims). Dachau Booklets No. 10. Dachau, 1994.

Témoignages Strasbourgeois: De l'Université aux Camps de Concentration [Strasbourg testimonials: From the university to the concentration camps]. 3rd ed. Strasbourg: PUF, 1989.

Tichauer, Eva. *J'étais le numéro 20832 à Auschwitz* [I was number 20832 at Auschwitz]. L'Harmattan, 1988.

Tillion, Germaine. *Ravensbrück* (1), Les Cahiers du Rhône XX [Cahiers from Rhône XX] (65). Neuchâtel: La Baconière, December 1946.

———. *Ravensbrück. L'Histoire immédiate* [Ravensbrück: The immediate history] (2). Paris: Seuil, 1973.

———. *Ravensbrück* (3), Paris: Seuil, May 1988.

La Tour de Gaurde [The watchtower] (July 15, 1980; November 15, 1980; June 15, 1981; September 15, 1981; September 1, 1985; September 1, 1986; and March 15, 1986; bimonthly published by the Association of Jehovah's Witnesses, Boulogne-Billancourt).

Tribunal Militaire International de Nuremburg [International military tribunal of Nuremberg]. 42-volume publication of the Trial of Nuremberg (November 14, 1945–October 1, 1946), Nuremberg, 1947.

Vaillant-Couturier, Marie-Claude. *Elles, la résistance* [The women, the resistance]. Messidor, 1985.

Verachtet-Verfolgt-Vernichtet. Zu den vergessenen Opfern des NS-Regimes [Hated-Persecuted-Annihilated: For the forgotten victims of the nazi regime]. Published by the Group for the Forgotten Nazi Regime Victims of Hamburg. Hamburg: VSA Verlag, 1986.

Verfolgung, Widerstand, Neubeginn in Freiburg. [Persecution, Resistance, New Beginnings in Freiburg] Documentation of the VVN (Vereinigung der Verfolgten des Naziregimes) (Organization of Nazi Regime Persecution Victims) of Freiburg.

Vidal-Naquet Pierre. *Les assassins de la mémoire* [The assassins of memory]. La découverte, 1987.

Vie et mort des Français 1939–1945 [Life and death of the French 1939–1945]. Paris: Hachette, 1971.

Vierteljahreshefte für Zeitgeschichte [Quarterly issues for contemporary history], no. 17 (Year's Issue, 1969).

Voutey Maurice. *Évolution et rôle du système concentrationnaire nazi* [Development and role of the nazi concentration camp system]. Dijon: CNDP, CRDP, 1984.

Der Wachtturm [The watchtower]. Published by the Watchtower Bible and Tract Society. Vienna: Selters/Taunus (RFA).

Watchtower Bible and Tract Society. *Geschte der Zeugen Jehovas in Österreich* [History of the Jehovah's Witnesses in Austria]. Vienna: Selters/Taunus (RFA), 1989.

Watchtower Society. *Les Témoins de Jéhovah dans les desseins divins* [The Jehovah's Witnesses in the divine plan]. New York: Watchtower Society, 1971. (in French)

Wellers, Georges. *Les chambres à gaz ont existé* [The gas chambers existed]. Paris: Témoins, Gallimard, 1981.

———. *Un Juif sous Vichy* [A Jew under Vichy]. Paris: Tirésias, 1991.

Widerstand aus christlicher Überzeugung: Jehovas Zeugen im Natioalsozialismus. Dokumentation einer Tagung [Resistance through Christian conviction: Jehovah's Witnesses in Nazism. Documentation of a conference], Historical Writings of the Kreismuseum Wewelsburg, Klartext, Essen, 1998.

Widerstand aus Glauben [Resistance through faith]. Berlin: Union Verlag, 1985.

Wiechert, Ernst. *Der Totenwald* [The death forest]. Ullstein 24 038. Frankfurt am Main and Berlin, 1996. (This account was published for the first time in Munich in 1946.)

Wiesel, Elie. *Le testament d'un poète juif assasiné* [Testament of a Jewish poet assassinated]. Sevil, 1980

Wilde, Oscar. *La Ballade de la geôle de Reading* [The ballad of Reading Gaol]. Paris: Stock, 1989.

Will, Elisabeth. *De l'Université aux Camps de Concentration: Témoignages Strasbourgeois* [From the university to the concentration camps: Strasbourg testimonials]. 3rd ed. Strasbourg: PUF, 1989.

Der Wind weht weinend über die Ebene. Ravensbrücker Gedichte [The wind blows weeping across the plain: Ravensbrück histories]. Collected by Christa Schulz, Brandenburg Memorial Foundation/ avensbrück Memorial and Rememberance. Paris: Tirésias, 1995.

Wormser-Migot, Olga. "Le systéme concnetrationnaire nazi

(1933–1945)" (The nazi concentration camp system [1933–1945]). *Recherches* series, vol. 39. Paris-Sorbonne: PUF, 1968.

Wormser-Migot, Olga, and Henri Michel. *Tragédie de la déportation/1940–1945, témoignages de survivants des camps de concentration allemands* [Tragedy of deportation and internment/1940–1945, accounts of survivors of the German concentration camps.] Paris: Hachette, 1955.

Zeugen Jehovas. Vergessene Opfer des Nationalsozialismus? [Jehovah's Witnesses: Forgotten victims of national socialism]. Documentation Archive of the Austrian Resistance/DÖW. Wien, 1998.

Zürcher, Franz. *Croisade contre le christianisme: Persécution moderne des chrétiens, une documentation* [Crusade against christianity: Modern persecution of Christians, a documentation]. Paris: Rieder, 1939.

INDEX

To come

OTHER COOPER SQUARE PRESS TITLES OF INTEREST

MENGELE
The Complete Story
Gerald L. Posner and John Ware
New introduction by Michael Berenbaum
400 pp., 41 b/w photos
0-8154-1006-9
$18.95

THE WEEK FRANCE FELL
June 10–June 16, 1940
Noel Barber
336 pp., 18 b/w photos
0-8154-1091-3
$18.95

CORREGIDOR
The American Alamo of World War II
Eric Morris
560 pp., 23 b/w photos
0-8154-1085-9
$19.95

DEFEAT INTO VICTORY
Battling Japan in Burma and India, 1942–1945
Field-Marshal Viscount William Slim
New introduction David Hogan
576 pp., 21 maps
0-8154-1022-0
$22.95

HITLER'S COMMANDERS
Officers of the *Wehrmacht*, the *Luftwaffe*, the *Kriegsmarine*, and the *Waffen-SS*
Samuel W. Mitcham Jr. and Gene Mueller
384 pp., 52 b/w photos, 8 maps
0-8154-1131-6
$18.95

KASSERINE PASS
Rommel's Bloody, Climactic Battle for Tunisia
Martin Blumenson
358 pp., 18 b/w photos
0-8154-1099-9
$19.95

JAPAN'S WAR
Edwin P. Hoyt
With a new preface
568 pp., 57 b/w photos, 6 maps
0-8154-1118-9
$19.95

THE TRAGIC FATE OF THE *U.S.S. INDIANAPOLIS*
The U.S. Navy's Worst Disaster at Sea
Raymond B. Lech
336 pp., 52 b/w photos, 2 maps
0-8154-1120-0
$18.95

HUNTERS FROM THE SKY
The German Parachute Corps, 1940–1945
Charles Whiting
240 pp., 12 b/w photos, 8 maps
0-8154-1145-6
$17.95

HITLER'S FIELD MARSHALS
And Their Battles
Samuel W. Mitcham, Jr.
456 pp., 27 b/w photos, 22 maps, 9 tables
0-8154-1130-8
$18.95